McGraw-Hill Education

6 IELTS™

Practice Tests

McGraw-Hill Education

6 IELTS™
Practice Tests

Monica Sorrenson

New York | Chicago | San Francisco | Athens | London | Madrid
Mexico City | Milan | New Delhi | Singapore | Sydney | Toronto

1 2 3 4 5 6 7 8 9 0   RHR/RHR   1 2 1 0 9 8 7 6 5

ISBN   978-0-07-184515-1
MHID   0-07-184515-1

e-ISBN   978-0-07-184517-5
e-MHID   0-07-184517-8

IELTS is a trademark of IELTS Partners, defined as the British Council, IELTS Australia Pty Ltd (solely owned by IDP Education Pty Ltd), and the University of Cambridge: Cambridge English Language Assessment. These organizations were not involved in the production of, and do not endorse, this product.

McGraw-Hill Education books are available at special quantity discounts to use as premiums and sales promotions or for use in corporate training programs. To contact a representative, please visit the Contact Us pages at www.mhprofessional.com.

CONTENTS

To access the online audio tracks that accompany the tests in this book, go to:

www.mhelELTS6practicetests.com

INTRODUCTION

Welcome to this book.

The number of people around the world who now take the IELTS exam is astounding. By working through this book, you'll be closer to your IELTS goal and your post-IELTS dream.

McGraw-Hill Education 6 IELTS Practice Tests contains around 25 hours of material. Its six practice tests develop exam technique, and its advice focuses on the Listening and the Academic Reading tests. You'll do best in IELTS if you use this book together with other materials, like *McGraw-Hill Education IELTS*, or with classes that improve your vocabulary, grammar, spoken fluency, pronunciation, academic writing style, and knowledge of the world.

Like many things in life, attitude counts with IELTS. By that I don't mean preparing for a week, then imagining that if you try your best, think positive thoughts, or compliment your Speaking examiner, you'll receive a high score. I mean *realistically* assessing where you are now, in relation to where you need to be, and putting in the effort to get there.

For those of you yet to sit IELTS, the exam is not easy, and the tests in this book are *at the level* of real exams.

For those of you who've already sat IELTS, it takes months and even years to go up IELTS bands. Teachers, tutors, classmates, people who comment on websites, friends, parents, loved ones, and writers of books like this will all offer you advice, but the responsibility for your IELTS score lies with you and you alone.

There are three parts to this book: (1) **Introduction** (pp vii-21): This appraises your general knowledge of IELTS with a **Quiz** (pp 1-9). It includes information on the four individual tests and the nine band scores. It gives an overall impression of **what makes a strong candidate** in speaking and writing (pp 6-8). It describes the different **question types** (pp 11-15) you'll encounter, and has specific advice on the **Listening and Reading tests** (pp 18-21).

(2) **Tests 1 and 2** (pp 22-114): are mainly printed on right-hand pages, while tips, called 'How to get a Seven', are on the left. By following these tips, you'll be able to predict answers, find cues or signposts, listen or look for paraphrases, understand inference, avoid common errors, and, hopefully, get a Seven.

(3) **Tests 3 to 6** (pp 115-227): have no tips. Questions for Tests 3 and 4 are at the level of real IELTS exams, but those for Tests 5 and 6 are slightly higher. This is to help people who have already scored a Six aim for a Seven.

For easy access, answers to activities and tests appear throughout the book. Pay particular attention to the highlighted answers in the recording scripts and reading passages. Go through all the writing and speaking models carefully, so you understand what examiners really expect.

The IELTS Quiz

The Listening Test and the Academic Reading Test

What do you know about IELTS? For each question, circle the letter of your choice.

1	In total, how long is an IELTS exam?						
	a	2 hours 15 minutes	**b**	2 hours 45 minutes	**c**	3 hours 15 minutes	
2	How many questions are there in the Listening or Reading test?						
	a	40	**b**	50	**c**	100	
3	How much is each question worth in the Listening or Reading test?						
	a	½ a mark	**b**	1 mark	**c**	It varies from test to test.	
4	Which mark approximately represents a band Seven in Listening?						
	a	27/40	**b**	30/40	**c**	33/40	
5	Is this the same for Reading?						
	a	No. Reading is lower.	**b**	No. Reading is higher.	**c**	Yes	
6	In Listening or Reading, if a candidate doesn't answer a question, or writes a wrong answer, what happens?						
	a	He or she gets zero for that question.	**b**	He or she loses one mark.	**c**	He or she loses half a mark.	
7	What is the maximum number of words (or words and numbers) candidates can write for a Listening or Reading answer?						
	a	There is no maximum.	**b**	Five	**c**	Three	
8	Must all answers for a Listening or Reading test come from the recordings or passages, or can candidates write down any answers they can think of that are correct?						
	a	As long as answers are right, it doesn't matter where they come from.	**b**	Answers must come from the recordings or the passages, but candidates can change them slightly, for example, into plurals or participles.	**c**	Answers must come from the recordings or the passages, and they must not be changed in any way.	
9	How important is spelling in the Listening or Reading test?						
	a	Extremely important. To get a mark in Listening, an answer must be correctly spelt, conforming to standard UK, US, or Australian spelling. In Reading, if a correct answer is *copied* wrongly, it is marked wrong.	**b**	Very important. Usually, to get a mark in Listening, an answer must be correctly spelt, but if there's just one letter wrong, then the mark is still awarded. In Reading, if a word is copied wrongly, but is recognisable, the mark is given.	**c**	Not so important. As long as a person marking the Listening answer sheet can work out what the word is, incorrect spelling doesn't matter. In Reading, if a word is copied wrongly, but is recognisable, the mark is given.	
10	When do candidates have an extra ten minutes to transfer their answers to answer sheets?						
	a	In Listening only	**b**	In Reading only	**c**	In both Listening and Reading	

11	What is the best use of the ten-minute transfer time at the end of the Listening test?						
	a	Making sure most answers are correct, and guessing the others	**b**	Making sure all answers are correct, and leaving the others	**c**	Checking uncertain answers; checking spelling; guessing difficult questions	
12	What is played twice in the Listening test?						
	a	Nothing	**b**	A single example at the beginning of Section 1	**c**	Each of the four sections	
13	Do candidates hear the answers in the Listening test, or see them in the Reading test, in order, from #1 to #40?						
	a	Yes	**b**	Mostly	**c**	No. They are all mixed up.	
14	Should candidates write anything down while a person or people are speaking during a Listening section, or should they wait until there is a pause?						
	a	Find correct answers as you go, and circle or write them down. Take notes throughout, but especially in Section 4. The pauses should be used to read the questions *ahead*. Use the transfer time to go back over uncertain answers.	**b**	Find correct answers as you go, and circle or write them down. *Making* notes is a better idea than *taking* notes. Then, check the answers during the pauses. After all, a narrator says, 'You now have 30 seconds to check your answers.'	**c**	Concentrating *without* writing anything down is a good idea. You'll be able to remember the answers, and do them in the pauses. There are so many pauses that you can relax during some of them.	
15	In which section of the Listening test do candidates *below* IELTS Six guess most answers or leave them blank?						
	a	2	**b**	3	**c**	4	
16	In which section of the Listening test does one person give a short talk about an everyday situation?						
	a	1	**b**	2	**c**	3	
17	In which section of the Listening test could there be three people talking?						
	a	1	**b**	2	**c**	3	
18	What kind of environment would those three be in?						
	a	A domestic one	**b**	An academic one	**c**	A work one	
19	Which section of the Listening test has two people discussing a familiar transaction?						
	a	1	**b**	2	**c**	3	
20	In which section of the Listening test is there *no* 30-second pause partway through?						
	a	2	**b**	3	**c**	4	
21	When there are MCQs (Multi-Choice Questions: Options A, B, or C) in Listening, and there are twelve letters in total in a test's answers, what is the likely distribution of the letters?						
	a	It is entirely random.	**b**	The letters will usually be evenly distributed: 4 As, 4 Bs, 4 Cs.	**c**	The letters will usually be slightly unevenly distributed: 3 As, 4 Bs, 5 Cs; or 4 As, 5 Bs, 3 Cs etc.	

22	Which factors make the Listening test difficult?					
	a	It has nine sets of questions; it has around 20 word answers; the topic of Section 4 may be conceptually difficult.	**b**	It has speakers with all kinds of accents; many of its word answers are hard to spell; Section 4 is very long.	**c**	Although it doesn't have many word answers, its MCQs have a lot of words in their stems and options to read; Section 3 has three speakers; Section 4 is on a scientific topic.
23	*Excluding* the questions, about how many words are there to read in the three passages of the Reading test?					
	a	1700	**b**	2200	**c**	2700
24	Do the three Reading passages have a roughly equal number of words?					
	a	Yes	**b**	No. While Passage 3 almost always has the most, Passage 1 or 2 could have the second-most.	**c**	No. Passage 3 has more than Passage 2; and, Passage 2 has more than Passage 1.
25	What level of difficulty are the Reading passages?					
	a	They range from the level of an 18-19-year-old student in an English-speaking high school to a university graduate.*	**b**	They are all the level of a first-year university student in an English-speaking country.	**c**	They are all the level of an 18-19-year-old student in an English-speaking high school.
26	Why is Passage 3 usually harder than the other two?					
	a	Because it is the longest	**b**	Because the writer discusses his or her views	**c**	Because it has the most questions
27	To what extent is this sound advice? Read all the questions (stems and options) before answering anything in the Reading test.					
	a	It is a good idea.	**b**	It is poor advice – there isn't time. Read the passages themselves first.	**c**	It is advisable to read all the questions *before* starting the reading passages, but, for MCQs, *only* their stems not their options – there won't be time for these. Read the options as you answer later.
28	Is the Reading test more difficult for some nationalities?					
	a	No. It doesn't matter what your background is, it is still hard.	**b**	Yes. Reading is a transferrable skill, so if people in your culture rarely read much that is long or complex in any language, you're going to struggle to get a Seven.	**c**	Yes. The Reading test is designed to trick certain nationalities.

---

*If you're interested in reading levels, look up 'Readability' or 'Flesch-Kincaid'.

29	What strategies should candidates adopt in the Reading test?					
	a	Read the questions first so you can identify where to skim or scan in a passage, or where to read slowly and carefully; look for inference as well as detail answers.	**b**	Read every single word as fast as you can; the questions are all about detail, so finding where items are in a passage is really important – most answers rely on synonyms.	**c**	Do Passage 3 first because it is the hardest; read everything as fast as you can; guess often because you can still get a Seven by guessing.
30	How can candidates dramatically improve their Reading scores?					
	a	By reading academic texts in English for about 30 minutes a day.	**b**	By reading in English as well as in their own language for a total of 60 minutes a day.	**c**	By doing as many IELTS practice tests as possible.

Answers: **1.** b; **2.** a; **3.** b; **4.** b; **5.** c; **6.** a; **7.** c; **8.** c; **9.** a; **10.** a; **11.** c; **12.** b; **13.** b; **14.** a; **15.** c; **16.** b; **17.** c; **18.** b; **19.** a; **20.** c; **21.** c; **22.** a; **23.** c; **24.** b; **25** a; **26.** b; **27.** c; **28.** b; **29.** a; **30.** b

The Academic Writing Test and the Speaking Test

1	How many words must candidates write in the Writing test?		
	a	150 in Task 1; 250 in Task 2	**b**	250 in both tasks
2	What happens if candidates do not write enough words?		
	a	Nothing happens. Examiners are more interested in quality than quantity.	**b**	They lose marks.
3	What is each task worth?		
	a	Both tasks are worth the same.	**b**	Task 2 is worth twice as much as Task 1.
4	In Task 1, which is more difficult: charts and tables; or, maps, plans, and diagrams?		
	a	Maps, plans, and diagrams are more difficult.	**b**	Candidates may believe maps, plans, and diagrams are more difficult, but they are as difficult as charts and tables.
5	How can candidates score a Six in Task 1 if the task is a chart or a table?		
	a	By including an overall statement; by describing the main features (not all); and, by including key data.	**b**	By noting all the features, and all the data associated with them.
6	How can candidates score a Six in Task 1 if it is a diagram?		
	a	By outlining the process from start to finish in one sentence (similar to the overall statement above); describing the key steps; and, using the passive voice.	**b**	By describing all the steps in the process from start to finish; by using the active voice and personal pronouns, like 'you'.
7	How can candidates score a Six in Task 1 if it is two plans or two maps?		
	a	By stating the major differences in one sentence (similar to the overall statement above), then describing the key similarities and differences. It is not necessary to describe them all.	**b**	By listing all the similarities and all the differences.
8	Aside from lacking the vocabulary or grammar, why do many candidates not score a Six in Task 2?		
	a	Their essay is long enough but simplistic.	**b**	Their essay is interesting but a little short.

9	Which better describes a Task 2 essay that is awarded a Seven?		
	a	A piece of writing that is highly academic in style. It may not be so pleasurable for an examiner to read.	**b**	A piece of writing that is academic in style and pleasurable for an examiner to read.

10	What criteria are used to mark the Writing test?		
	a	The criteria are: Task Achievement; Coherence and Cohesion; Vocabulary Range and Accuracy; Grammatical Range and Accuracy.	**b**	The criteria vary from country to country and IELTS centre to centre. The most important things are that the essay is long enough, and the grammar is perfect.

11	Do some nationalities do poorly in the Writing test?		
	a	No. It's equally difficult for everyone.	**b**	Yes. In some countries, the high-school and university education systems do not encourage students to write at length, and what is written follows formulas. Moreover, if these students do not read widely in their own language or in English, they lack sophisticated ideas necessary to get a Seven. You can go to www.ielts.org for a list of countries and languages to see how different ones score.

12	How long is a Speaking test?		
	a	Between 11-14 minutes	**b**	It must be 14 minutes.

13	What criteria are used to mark the Speaking test?		
	a	Criteria vary from country to country and IELTS centre to centre. The most important things are that candidates speak at length, and their grammar and pronunciation are very good.	**b**	Criteria are: Fluency and Coherence; Vocabulary Range and Accuracy; Grammatical Range and Accuracy; Pronunciation.

14	What is the basic difference in the Speaking test between Parts 1-2 and Part 3?		
	a	Parts 1-2 deal with familiar situations – things in and around a candidate's own life. Part 3 deals with abstract ideas – things beyond a candidate's own life.	**b**	Parts 1-2 require short answers, whereas in Part 3, a candidate needs to speak at length. More complex vocabulary is usually needed for Part 3.

15	Is it important for candidates to speak for the entire two minutes in Part 2? How many words should a candidate say?		
	a	Yes. These days, they have to speak for two minutes, which is around 350 words.	**b**	It doesn't really matter if candidates don't reach the two-minute mark. Quality is more important than quantity. The number of words could be between 150-250.

16	Do some nationalities do better in the Speaking test?		
	a	No. It is equally difficult for everyone.	**b**	Yes. In Part 3, some people lack sophisticated ideas, and can only talk about their own experience rather than the world beyond. There are other people for whom English pronunciation is very difficult, and these people may need private tuition or to live in an English-speaking country to improve.

Here are the answers for pp 4-6: **1**. a; **2**. b; **3**. b; **4**. b; **5**. a; **6**. a; **7**. a; **8**. a; **9**. b; **10**. a; **11**. b; **12**. a; **13**. b; **14**. a; **15**. a; **16**. b

What Do Strong Academic Writing and Speaking Candidates Do?

Here are some adjectives to describe candidates or the answers they give in the Writing and Speaking tests.

In the Writing test, what do examiners like?

Tick the positive attributes, and cross the negative ones as in the examples.

Examiners like candidates' scripts that are:
x   x   √   √
biased   bogus   edited   elegant   exemplified   facile   formal   formulaic
grammatically complex   grammatically inaccurate   legible   lexically narrow
logical   persuasive   pertinent   rambling   succinct   tangential   tempered   under-length

What do the adjectives above mean?*

Complete each sentence on the left about a candidate with the best item on the right.

1	His writing is clear, logical, and well-supported. He uses less common items of vocabulary, and his cohesion is unobtrusive. His writing is	**A** persuasive.
2	Her writing has appropriate vocabulary, much sourced from Latin. She avoids slang, personal pronouns, 'get', phrasal verbs, or texting. Her language is	**B** grammatically complex.
3	His sentences are varied, and include subordination. His word choices for number, tense, aspect, and voice are sophisticated. His writing is	**C** succinct.
4	Her arguments are convincing or believable. Her writing is	**D** tempered.
5	His examples are completely relevant or	**E** elegant.
6	Although she uses complex grammar, she does not include unnecessary words. Her vocabulary is so precise that she can use one word where a lesser writer would use four or five. Her writing is	**F** edited.

---

*An IELTS Seven knows many of these words; a Six knows five or six; and, a Five knows just two or three.

| 7 | His arguments and examples are never extreme. They are moderate or | **G** | formal. |
| 8 | On her test paper, some words have been crossed out and replaced; others have had minor changes made for spelling. Her writing is | **H** | pertinent. |

In the Speaking test, what do examiners like? Tick or cross again.

Examiners like candidates or their answers that are:
amenable   articulate   boastful   coherent   contemplative   courteous   decontracted
expansive   hesitant   idiomatic   insincere   memorised   natural   obsequious
opinionated   over-confident   scruffy   self-correcting   shallow   unruffled

What do the adjectives above mean?

Complete each sentence on the left about a candidate with the best item on the right.

1	She speaks clearly with fluent, sophisticated ideas. She's	**A**	coherent.
2	He organises his ideas logically. He's	**B**	idiomatic.
3	She gives thoughtful, considered answers. She's	**C**	unruffled.
4	He's friendly, or he gives extended answers. He's	**D**	self-correcting.
5	She uses phrasal verbs and less common items of vocabulary in everyday speech. Her language is	**E**	expansive.
6	He's relaxed, and he freely gives his genuine opinions. He's	**F**	contemplative.
7	Although the questions become a little difficult, she doesn't show any anxiety, and she answers as well as she can. She's	**G**	natural.
8	Aware of his mistakes, he reformulates his answers. He's	**H**	articulate.

What Are Some Differences Between the IELTS Bands?

Many examiners can judge a writer or a speaker in one or two sentences.

Read the items, below, from Writing tests, and rank them from most to least competent: A-E. There is an example.

	The popularity of the fast food may be attributed to it's cost and convenience.
	In a nutshell, peoples nowaday's love fast food because it is cheep and convinent.
	In a nuts hell, pepol now a day liking the fast food. Is chip and convient.
C	It is well known around the world that fast food is getting more popular due to prize and convenient.
	Fast food is gaining popularity since it is cost-efficient and convenient.

An A from above would probably score an Eight; a B a Seven; a C a Six; a D a Five; and, an E a Four. (*The order is: ADECB.*) There isn't space here to explain why these bands would be awarded, but you might like to compare the items, and discuss them with another candidate or a teacher.

Read the utterances below from Speaking tests, and rank them from most to least competent (8-4), bearing in mind that you can't hear the candidates' pronunciation although some words are written as they've been said. There is an example.

6	Yes, I would love to lorn more about photo-graphy. However, I will have to wait until my children are at school. Furthermore, I think taking a course is a good ide-ea.
	I'd like to learn more about photography, but, um, I'd have to wait till my kids were in the school, and I'd need to take a course.
	I'd like to learn more about taking photos, but I would have to wait until my children are at school. And I think it is necessary for me to take the course.
	Yes. I like to lorn to... to teck photo. But... but no time. Children at the home.
	Yes, I love to learn new stuff. Why not the photography? But, um, my son, he's, like, at home. When he's gonna school, then I learn the stuff.

Here are the answers for pp 6-8.

Adjectives to describe strong writing candidates: edited, elegant, exemplified, formal, grammatically complex, legible, logical, persuasive, pertinent, succinct, tempered. **Weak ones:** biased, bogus, facile, formulaic, grammatically inaccurate, lexically narrow, rambling, tangential, under-length.

Sentence completion: Writing: **1.** E; **2.** G; **3.** B; **4.** A; **5.** H; **6.** C; **7.** D; **8.** F.

Adjectives to describe strong speaking candidates: amenable, articulate, coherent, contemplative, courteous, expansive, idiomatic, natural, self-correcting, unruffled. **Weak ones:** boastful, decontracted (*Eg: 'I am' instead of 'I'm'; 'it is' or 'it has' instead of 'it's'; 'they will' instead of 'they'll' etc*), hesitant, insincere, memorised, obsequious, opinionated, overconfident, scruffy, shallow.

Sentence completion: Speaking: **1.** H; **2.** A; **3.** F; **4.** E; **5.** B; **6.** G; **7.** C. **8.** D.
Speaking utterances: 68745.

Description of the IELTS Bands

There are ten IELTS bands, and the creators of the IELTS exam describe them thus:

Band 9	Expert user	Has fully operational command of the language: appropriate, accurate and fluent with complete understanding.
8	Very good user	Has fully operational command of the language with only occasional unsystematic inaccuracies and inappropriacies. Misunderstandings may occur in unfamiliar situations. Handles complex detailed argumentation well.
7	Good user	Has operational command of the language, though with occasional inaccuracies and misunderstandings in some situations. Generally handles complex language well and understands detailed reasoning.

6	*Competent user*	Has generally effective command of the language despite some inaccuracies, inappropriacies and misunderstandings. Can use fairly complex language, particularly in familiar situations.
5	*Modest user*	Has partial command of the language, coping with overall meaning in most situations, though is likely to make many mistakes. Should be able to handle basic communication in own field.
4	*Limited user*	Basic competence is limited to familiar situations. Has frequent problems in understanding and expression. Is not able to use complex language.
3	*Extremely limited user*	Conveys and understands only general meaning in very familiar situations. Frequent breakdowns in communication occur.
2	*Intermittent user*	No real communication is possible except for the most basic information using isolated words or short formulae in familiar situations and to meet immediate needs. Has great difficulty understanding spoken and written English.
1	*Non user*	Essentially has no ability to use the language beyond possibly a few isolated words.
0	*Did not attempt the test*	No assessable information provided.*

Go to www.ielts.org for more information on the bands, and on the public-access criteria examiners use to mark the Writing and Speaking tests.

Raw-Score Conversion Table for the Listening and Academic Reading Tests

Here is a table of *approximate* marks out of 40 needed to achieve certain bands. Bear in mind that the makers of the IELTS exam do not release this information, and that from time to time, marks needed may be one higher or one lower, depending on the ease or difficulty of a real IELTS Listening or Reading test.

Use this table to work out which bands you would score for the tests in this book.

Band	4	4.5	5	5.5	6	6.5	7	7.5	8	8.5
Marks out of 40	9-11	12-15	16-18	19-22	23-26	27-29	30-32	33-34	35-36	37-38

My scores from this book	Listening /40	Reading /40	My band
Test 1			
Test 2			
Test 3			
Test 4			
Test 5			
Test 6			

LISTENING AND READING QUESTION TYPES

Question Types Used in the Listening Test Only

Multi-Choice Question (MCQ):

<u>Choosing one answer from **three** options</u>

Eg: What is the purpose of the lecture?

- **A**   To get students to recycle smartphones
- **B**   To let students know more about e-waste
- **C**   To encourage students to develop an app

Eg: The lecturer talks about her family's behaviour because it is

- **A**   typical.
- **B**   exceptional.
- **C**   ideal.

In the first example, the stem is a question; in the second, the stem is the first part of a sentence, which one option will complete, so the options end with full stops (periods).

Question Types Used in Both the Listening and Reading Tests

THOSE WITH ANSWERS THAT ARE LETTERS: A-L

MCQ

<u>Choosing two answers from five options</u>

*Eg: Choose **TWO** letters, **A-E**.*

Which **TWO** of the following happen at Zoe's day care?

- **A**   Parents must provide diapers and food for their children.
- **B**   Children's birthdays are celebrated with songs and games.
- **C**   Children are divided by age into rooms named after animals.
- **D**   Parents who collect their children fifteen minutes late are fined.
- **E**   The centre reserves the right to send home children who are ill.

Multi-Matching

Remember, in the Listening test, the information (**11** and **12** below) goes in order of the recording, but the options (in a box or a list) are almost always out of order.

Eg: *Choose* **FOUR** *answers from the box, below, and write the correct letter,* **A-F***, next to questions 11-14 below.*

A	Eliezer Montefiore
B	Grace Cossington-Smith
C	Paul Cézanne
D	Arthur Boyd
E	Wendy McEwen
F	A voluntary guide

11   He / She trains guides.   ....

12   He / She was the gallery's first director.   ....

In the Reading test, where there is a list (mostly of people), it almost always goes in order of the information in the passage, but the questions are out of order. Be careful.

In questions where the answers are out of the recording or passage order, you'll notice in the answers, after the correct letters, the phrase '*in any order*' is written.

Labelling

There are three possible items to label – a diagram, a plan, or a map – by choosing an option (A-?) from a list. See questions 26-28 in Test 6 Listening for an example. Labelling a plan or a map is similar. See questions 17-20 in Test 5 Listening, or 17-20 in Test 3.

THOSE WITH ANSWERS THAT ARE WORDS OR NUMBERS

Gap-fill

There are several types of these, described in many books as: Sentence completion, Table completion, Note completion, or Flowchart completion.

Essentially all types are the same. You must fill a gap, and write the word, words, number, or word and number on your answer sheet. The maximum number of words to write is three.

Note: if you're asked: *Write UP TO THREE WORDS* for an answer, then make sure in that group of answers, there's at least one three-word answer. Likewise, if you're asked: *Write ONE WORD AND / OR NUMBER*, then one answer will be a word + a number. Where you have to fill gaps in a table, note the direction of the answers: across or down. Mostly, they're across.

Table completion

Eg: *Complete the table below.*

Write **ONE WORD OR A NUMBER** *for each answer.*

Teacher	Class	Days	Location	Other information
Sally Burton	Working with (**5**)		In her studio	Number of students per class: (**6**) ....

Form completion

There's no difference between table and form completion, except the forms are similar to ones from real life, so this type of question usually appears in Listening Section 1.

Note completion

There's no difference between table and note completion other than layout: notes tend to be in one box, whereas tables have cells and columns within a box.

Sentence completion

Eg: *Complete the sentences below.*

Write **NO MORE THAN THREE WORDS OR A NUMBER** *for each answer.*

16   Since living in Mozambique, Charlotte has not used a fridge or a................. .

17   Charlotte believes children who live in small houses tend to.................. more.

Short-answer

Eg: *Write* **NO MORE THAN THREE WORDS AND/OR A NUMBER** *for each answer.*

15   What is the process of giving the same information about the same artworks?

    ....

16   How long is each guided tour?

    ....

Question Types Used in the Reading Test Only

THOSE WITH ANSWERS THAT ARE LETTERS: A-L

MCQ

Choosing one answer from four options

Eg: According to the writer, how much night lighting should there be in relation to what there is now?

    A   Much more
    B   A little more
    C   A little less
    D   Much less

MCQ

Choosing **two** answers from five options **for a single mark**

Eg: **13** The list below includes associations Russians make with the colour red. Which **TWO** are mentioned by the writer of the passage?

- **A** danger
- **B** wealth
- **C** intelligence
- **D** faith
- **E** energy

Classification

Usually, there are three items (A, B, or C) in classification, but occasionally, four.

Eg: Classify the following things that relate to:

- **A** Report 1.
- **B** Report 2.
- **C** Report 3.
- **D** Report 4.

*Write the correct letter, **A**, **B**, **C**, or **D**, in boxes 21-27 on your answer sheet.*

21 This is unique because it contains interviews with both parents.

22 This looks at how children might be at risk.

Summary completion

These questions test grammar and vocabulary as well as comprehension of the passage. Typically, there are answers you can predict before reading the passage.

Eg: *Complete the summary using the dates or words, **A-L**, below.*

*Write the correct letter, **A-L**, in boxes 8-13 on your answer sheet.*

A	accept	B	adapting	C	adopting
D	believes	E	fantasy	F	non-linear
G	novel	H	rational	I	supernatural
J	Use	K	1925	L	1927

The genre of Márquez's fiction is known as Magical Realism, a term first applied to painting in (**8**).................. . Magical Realism is often described in negative terms, as not being Realism, Surrealism, Science Fiction, or (**9**).................. .

Which paragraph / section contains the following information?

You can usually skim these questions, although close reading is sometimes required.

The list of statements includes functions, eg: description, example, explanation, prediction, theory etc.

> Eg: *Reading Passage 2 has seven sections, **A-F**.*
>
> *Which section contains the following information?*
>
> *Write the correct letter, **A-F**, in boxes 14-18 on your answer sheet.*

14   a comparison of football clubs

15   a hope for the future

16   a brief history of Egyptian football

17   a description of the manipulation of football for political ends

18   hypotheses on the allure of football for spectators

Sentence completion

This is not a gap-fill question as in the Listening test. It requires matching the beginning and ending of each statement. It tests grammar as well as comprehension.

> Eg: *Complete each sentence with the correct ending, **A-G**, below.*
>
> *Write the correct letter, **A-G**, in boxes 36-40 on your answer sheet.*

36   The Convention for the Safeguarding of Intangible Cultural Heritage is designed to

37   The World Heritage Committee worries about

38   The US refused to sign the 2003 convention due to concerns about

A	changes to or disappearance of traditions.
B	price rises due to world-heritage listing.
C	over-regulation connected to world-heritage listing.
D	protect traditions.
E	protect built environments.

THOSE WITH ANSWERS THAT ARE ROMAN NUMERALS: I-X

Matching headings

These questions require skimming. Don't spend long on them. If there are two headings that seem possible, choose the one that the paragraph or section contains more information about. Measure this amount with your finger.

Always cross out the answers you've chosen as well as distractors as you go. If you have time at the end, check you've got the right numerals on your answer sheet as it's easy to write down the wrong one accidentally.

See questions 15-19 in Test 2 Reading.

FACT OR CLAIM QUESTIONS

True/False/Not Given

These concern **facts** mentioned in the passage.

A false answer is one that is the opposite of what is true or only partially true.

> Eg: Do the following statements agree with the information given in Reading Passage 1?
>
> *In boxes 5-10 on your answer sheet, write:*

> **TRUE**   *if the statement agrees with the information.*
>
> **FALSE**   *if the statement contradicts the information.*
>
> **NOT GIVEN**   *if there is no information on this.*

5   Stainless steel does not stain.

6   Carbon steel rusts as its surface molecules are smaller than those of iron oxide.

Some candidates think the most difficult questions in IELTS are choosing between False and Not Given, or between No (below) and Not Given. In general, without specific evidence in the passage, an answer is Not Given.

Note: the answers for these kinds of questions are evenly distributed in IELTS, so if there are three T/F/NG questions in a group, it's likely there's one of each. Likewise, if there are six questions in a group, it's likely there are two of each.

Yes/No/Not Given

These concern **the claims or views of the writer** or of other people mentioned. They are laid out like T/F/NG questions. See questions 25-27 in Test 3 Reading.

You can write the letters T/Y, F/N, or NG as your answers.

THOSE WITH ANSWERS THAT ARE WORDS OR NUMBERS

Gap-Fill

Flowchart completion

See questions 32-35 in Test 2 Reading.

Labelling a diagram

Choosing letters from a box of options is one way to label a diagram; another way is to fill in the gaps.

Note: there are usually three labels to fill in, and the information for these almost always occurs close together in a single paragraph. See questions 12-14 in Test 2 Reading.

GLOSSARY

Familiarise yourself with the items below used in 'How to get a Seven' for Tests 1 and 2.

Cue = Information that *prepares* a listener for an answer. (Called a **signpost** word, in reading, and usually an adverb or adverbial phrase.)

> Eg: Let's imagine the question is: 'When was the woman in the UK?'
>
> In the recording, a woman says: 'I was in London in 2012.' The cues are: 'London', the capital, and the preposition 'in', which comes before a year.

Eg: Let's imagine the question is: 'How many children does Ben have?'

In the recording, a woman asks: 'You've got kids, haven't you, Ben?' Ben replies: 'Actually, I don't have any.' 'Actually' means some information is about to be contradicted, and what follows is correct, so 'actually' is the cue.

Identifying cues is the best way to guarantee correct answers in IELTS. It means you must concentrate hard throughout each recording because if you miss a cue, you may also miss an answer.

Distractor = An answer that has some common elements with the correct answer, but is wrong. A distractor may be a false or a partial answer, or it may be information that relates to someone or something else.

Eg: Let's imagine the question is: 'What does the woman want?'

The options are: **A** A holiday; **B** A new vehicle; **C** A promotion.

In the recording, a man says: 'I'd like to go to Bali.' Later, a woman says, 'It's time to replace my car.' **A** is a distractor as someone else does mention it.

False answer = An answer that is not true.

Eg: 'blue shirt' instead of 'red pants'

Eg: 'Japanese teacher' instead of 'Chinese teacher'

Partial answer = An answer that does not have all the correct information.

Eg: 'Mondays' instead of 'Mondays and Fridays'

Inference = Reaching a conclusion. Putting two or more pieces of information together to find an answer.

Eg: In the recording in Test 1 Listening, a receptionist tells a teacher: 'You'll start the term with 15 students, but end up with five' + 'The high dropout rate is no reflection on your teaching.'

The question: 'What do many students do?'

The answer is: 'Not finish the course'

With inference, the focus might change between the recording and the question (here, from the teacher to the students), and few or no words in the recording are the same as those in the question or answer.

Most answers in IELTS Listening or Reading tests involve detail (a transfer of a single piece of direct information). However, there are inference questions in each test. One difference between an IELTS Six and a Seven is that a Seven answers most inference questions correctly.

Paraphrase = Words that convey the same meaning as others. Often, a paraphrase is an easier way of saying something complex or formal.

Eg: <u>Original</u>: 'Goods are produced locally and inexpensively.'

<u>Paraphrase</u>: 'Nearby, people make things cheaply.'

Eg: <u>Original</u>: 'Simultaneously, lighting is dimmed.'

<u>Paraphrase</u>: 'At the same time, the lights are turned down.'

Many questions and answers in IELTS Listening or Reading tests contain paraphrases of information in the recordings or passages.

Parts of speech = Within a word family, there are different parts of speech.

Eg: noun, verb, adjective, adverb, gerund (-ing form). The 'Beauty' family contains: the nouns = 'beauty' and 'beautification'; the verb = 'beautify'; the adjective = 'beautiful'; the adverb = 'beautifully'; and, the gerund = 'beautifying'.

An IELTS Listening or Reading question often uses one part of speech (eg, an adjective), while in the recording or passage there is another (eg, a noun).

Eg: The question has 'voluntary (adj) guides', while the woman in the recording talks about 'volunteers (plural noun)'.

Pronunciation: Intonation = The rise or fall of the voice to convey meaning. A rising voice may mean a speaker has a question or a doubt.

Pitch = A high or low voice. High pitch may show enthusiasm.

Sentence stress = A word or words said more strongly or loudly in a sentence to convey meaning. Sentence stress may show a contrast between one idea and another, or let the listener know something is important.

Eg: 'I'll have a **black** coffee' (*not* coffee with milk).

Eg: 'Won't it be **noisy**, so close to the **motorway**?'

In IELTS Listening one speaker may contradict another or clarify a point, so you'll hear sentence stress. Often answers are stressed.

Word stress = One syllable is said more strongly or loudly than the others.

Eg: 'fourTEEN' but 'FORty'.

Stem and Option = In IELTS Listening or Reading tests, a stem is the question line, which may be a question or the first part of a sentence. An option is a possible answer to the stem. (There may also be a box of options. Eg: A-H.)

Eg: What does the woman teach? (The stem = a question)

A Arabic (option)
B Spanish (option)
C Korean (option)

Eg: The woman would like to study (The stem = the first part of a sentence)

A History. (option)
B Development. (option)
C Tourism. (option)

Synonym = A word that means almost the same as another.

Eg: 'expensive' = 'costly'.

Antonym = A word that means almost the opposite of another.

Eg: 'expensive' = 'affordable'.

ADVICE FOR THE LISTENING TEST

Read through the advice below that uses vocabulary from the glossary. These items are used again in 'How to get a Seven' for Test 1 and Test 2.

You need to do all these things to answer IELTS Listening questions correctly. Many of them also apply to the Reading test.

In general:

- Familiarise yourself with all the question types.
- **Take notes throughout**, but *especially* in Section 4; if you have to guess, you'll have words to choose from. By the time the 10-minute transfer comes, you'll probably have forgotten details from Sections 1-2.
- **Use the pauses to read *ahead*** rather than back over your answers, as is recommended in the recording.
- Think logically. Use your general knowledge.
- Predict before you listen. Confirm your prediction.
- Notice the titles for the four sections.
- Listen for cues in the recording (before, but sometimes after the answer you write).
- Don't rush to answer. Wait for clarification.
- Know your numbers. Know your dates. Write numerals not words.
- Know your alphabet.
- Spell correctly, especially plurals.
- Know your grammar.
- Listen carefully for any answers that are close together.
- Where there are two possible answers, choose the one that's easier to spell.
- Remember, most answers follow in order, but a list of options (five or more) is not usually in the same order as in the recording.
- Don't worry if an answer seems easy – lots of them are.
- Answer every question, even if it means guessing.

Specifically:

Listen for detail

- Listen for the same word (in the question / stem / option as in the recording).
- Listen for a different part of speech.
- Listen for a synonym, or occasionally an antonym with a negative question.
- Listen for a paraphrase.
- Match an example in the question / stem / option with a concept in the recording.
- Match a concept in the question / stem / option with an example in the recording.
- Match a definition in the question / stem / option with a word in the recording.

Understand inference

- Put two or more pieces of information together for the answer.
- Identify a function: apology, clarification, digression, example, or explanation.

Listen for pronunciation

- Listen for intonation, pitch, sentence or word stress.

Beware of distractors

- Ignore false or a partial information.
- Ignore information that relates to someone else.
- Ignore a number that refers to something else.
- Ignore an option that isn't mentioned at all.
- Avoid answering from your own beliefs. Ignore anything you think is true, but which a speaker doesn't say.

ADVICE FOR THE ACADEMIC READING TEST

Read the advice for the Listening test on the previous pages as most of it pertains to the Reading test.

For many people, the Academic Reading test is difficult because it has more question types than the Listening test, and the questions themselves contain more words. Since readers can reread material, the test is much longer – at least 3700 words (instructions + questions + passages). Its language and concepts are also more sophisticated than those in the Listening test.

Usually, an IELTS Six finishes the Reading test in around 58 minutes, and has two minutes to check. He or she will guess about seven questions. A Seven or an Eight has seven minutes left to check, with only two or three guesses.

Topics in the Academic Reading test are mostly scientific. While much information is factual, at least one passage (usually Passage 3) contains the views of the writer or of other people.

The majority of Reading answers require a transfer of detail, but there are always inference questions too. Just as there are cues to listen for in the Listening test, there are signposts to look for in the Reading (usually adverbs like 'however' or 'unfortunately'). Skimming, scanning, and reading closely are all tested. Despite what some people believe, there are no tricks in IELTS – no questions aimed deliberately at tripping you up. Once you understand the system, you will see that everything is straightforward.

It may seem unlikely, but the reading passages in real IELTS exams are both interesting and pleasurable to read.

Familiarise yourself with all the question types: those that apply to both Listening and Reading (pp 10-12) *and* those for Reading alone (pp 12-15).

Before **reading a passage, skim the questions for that passage,** but don't read any stems.

- Circle any key words.

- Predict any answers.

When reading a passage:

- **Use the titles** (set in grey in this book) to activate your knowledge of the topic.

- **Read with your eyes,** not your finger, but *do* circle key words or underline evidence. (If you can't underline evidence, an answer is probably Not Given.)

- As there won't be time to read an entire test slowly and carefully, **choose when to skim** (read quickly), **to scan** (look mainly for names or dates), **or to read closely** (slowly and carefully). All gap-fill questions need close reading.

- **Keep an eye on the time.** If you have trouble finding an answer, move on. Return to it at the very end, or guess it.

- Stick to the advice about spending 20 minutes per passage, or spend less time on Passage 1 and more on Passage 3.

When answering:

- **Confirm your predictions.**

- **Think logically.**

- **Look for synonyms or paraphrases.**

- **Check reference.** Reference means one word refers back (or sometimes forward) to a longer idea. Most of these words, called **referents**, are pronouns.

Here are two sentences containing two referents: 'Most people believe spending time with family is important. It strengthens bonds, and helps them relax.'

'It' refers back to 'spending time with family'; 'them' refers to 'most people'.

- **Understand connotation** – whether a concept or a writer's opinion is positive or negative.

- **Understand inference.**

- **Note a shift in focus.** Often a question focuses on one idea first with another second, while the information in the passage puts the second idea first.

- **Beware of exaggeration.** If there is the word 'always' or 'never' in a question (particularly T/F/NG), make 100% sure you can find evidence for it in the passage, and *vice versa*.

- **Beware of distractors.**

- Follow all the rest of the advice for the Listening test on page 18-19.

- **Don't panic.**

When writing on your answer sheet:

- **Copy all answers correctly** from the passages.

- **Answer every question,** even if you have to guess.

Before You Do Test 1

- Prepare some snacks and drinks.
- Find a reliable stopwatch or clock.
- Use an electronic device to access the audio at www.mheIELTS6practicetests.com.
- Find a place you can work with no interruptions for two to seven hours.
- You'll need two hours if you read 'How to get a Seven', do Test 1, and go through the highlighted answers in the recording scripts.
- You'll need four hours if you go through the Reading answers too.
- You'll need seven hours if you also do Writing Test 1, listen to Speaking Test 1, and read through the model answers and scripts.

HOW TO GET A SEVEN

Section 1 Question 1	**Listen for the same word in the recording as in the question**, here: 'retiring'.
	Listen for a cue (the words that let you know when the answer is coming). Here, the cue is: 'at the end of the term'.
	Don't rush to answer. Amal *does* ask if the principal has 'found another job', but the receptionist says: 'No, he's *retiring*'. There are contradictions and clarifications in IELTS Listening.
Q2	**Don't rush to answer.** The principal gives feedback by observing new teachers' lessons, but 'student feedback', mentioned next, 'is taken more seriously'.
	Listen for a cue, here: 'actually', before 'student feedback'. ('Actually' means 'the previous information was wrong; what comes next is important.')
Q3	**Understand inference.** This answer is *not* stated directly; you have to work it out from two separate pieces of information. These are: 'You'll start the term with 15 students, but end up with 5' + 'The high dropout rate…'.
	Avoid answering from your own belief. Here, some options are true in life, but are not mentioned by any speaker.
Q4	**Listen for a paraphrase of the question in the recording.** The receptionist says: 'take one class' which means 'enroll in'.
	Listen for the same words, here: '10%'.
	Beware of a distractor. Option A (100%) is true for 'a few courses, like Life Drawing [and] Cooking with Seafood', but 'a few courses' is not 'most'.
	Note: '10%', is said twice. Sometimes, numbers or dates are said twice in IELTS Listening.

TEST 1

Listening

Firstly, tear out the Test 1 Listening / Reading Answer Sheet at the back of this book.

The recordings of the Listening test last for about 20 minutes. There are four separate recordings, called sections. There are ten questions to answer in each section, totalling 40. Except for an example at the beginning of Section 1, everything is played <u>once</u> only.

Write your answers on the pages below as you listen. After Section 4 has finished, you have ten minutes to transfer your answers to your Listening Answer Sheet. You will need to time yourself for this transfer, but in an IELTS exam, a recorded voice gives you the time.

Each question in the Listening test is worth one mark, and a band from 1-9 is calculated from the mark out of 40.

After checking your answers on pp 57-61, go to page 9 for the raw-score conversion table.

Play Audio **PLAY RECORDING #1.**

SECTION 1   Questions 1-10

COMMUNITY COLLEGE CLASSES

Questions 1-4

*Choose the correct letter, **A**, **B**, or **C**.*

Example What does the woman, Amal Nouri, teach?

    A   Arabic

    B   Spanish √

    C   Korean

1   What is the principal doing at the end of the term?

    A   Starting another job

    B   Going to Spain

    C   Retiring

2   According to the receptionist, from whom is feedback most important for new teachers?

    A   Their students

    B   The principal

    C   Other teachers

3   What do a lot of people do who take an evening class?

    A   Make new friends there

    B   Not finish the course

    C   Find better jobs afterwards

4   What percentage of students' fees do teachers pay for most classes they enroll in at the college?

    A   70

    B   50

    C   10

HOW TO GET A SEVEN

Q5	Although 'wool' is a common word, you might expect to hear it in the context of a knitting or sewing class, but here it relates to a sculpture class. 'Wool' is repeated later. **Listen for cues**, here: 'Sally Burton' and 'Working with...'.
Q6	**Think logically.** The class is held in Sally's studio. It's likely a studio can't hold many people, so the number of students will be small.
Q7	**Notice the grammar around the answer. Follow the pattern.** Here, 'Tuesdays' and 'Fridays' are plural. You will not get a mark if you write 'Tuesday' without its final 's'. There are *between 1-4* plural answers in an average IELTS Listening test. In your ten-minute transfer, check you have some plurals.
Q8-9	**Listen carefully for answers that are close together.** You have seen in the table that answers to #8 and #9 occur close together. **Listen for cues.** Here, 'the river' is mentioned twice, with the 'excursions' as the first cue. 'End-of-term' is the cue for 'exhibition' (Some words can be predicted correctly in IELTS Listening, and a Seven will predict 'exhibition'.) **Spell correctly**: 'exhibition' has an 'h'.
Q10	**Know your numbers.** Section 1 often has a phone number. **Listen for confirmation**: the final three digits are repeated.
Section 2 Q11-14	**Remember, the list of people in the box is not usually in the order of the speech.** The statements (Q11-14) *are* in the order of the speech. You can guess Q13, Paul Cézanne, if you know about modern art.
Q11	**Match an example in the statement with a concept in the recording.** The statement mentions 'voluntary guides'; Wendy says she trains 'volunteers'.
Q12	Looking at the box, the answer could be almost anyone from A-F. **Listen for a cue**, here: '1882'. This could be the year when the first director started work. (This gallery is in Australia, part of which became a British colony in 1788.)
Q13	**Predict before you listen – in the 30-second pause. Listen for confirmation** in the recording. **Listen for a cue**, here: 'the single most expensive purchase this gallery has ever made was...'.
Q14	The information in the recording about this answer is inferred, but you can **predict before you listen.** (See the highlighted evidence in the recording script.) **Listen for confirmation.** The answer is most likely to be 'a voluntary guide', since a voluntary guide probably doesn't train other guides (Q11), couldn't be the gallery's first director (Q12), or someone from whom the gallery bought expensive work (Q13). Although Q14 could be Wendy McEwen, you've used her in Q11, and there's no instruction, here, to say you can use a letter more than once.

| LISTENING | SECTION 1 | SECTION 2 | SECTION 3 | SECTION 4 |
| READING |
| WRITING |
| SPEAKING |

Questions 5-10

Complete the table below.

Write **ONE WORD OR A NUMBER** *for each answer.*

Teacher	Class	Days	Location	Other information
Sally Burton	Working with (5)		In her studio	Number of students per class: (6) ....
Kostia Lebedev	Watercolour Painting	(7) .... and Fridays	At college in Room 14	Class includes excursions to the (8) .... and an end-of-term (9) ....
Amal Nouri	Spanish	Wednesdays		Her phone number: (10) ....

 PLAY RECORDING #2.

SECTION 2   Questions 11-20

VOLUNTARY GUIDING

Questions 11-14

Choose **FOUR** *answers from the box, below, and write the correct letter,* **A-F**, *next to questions 11-14 below.*

> A   Eliezer Montefiore
> B   Grace Cossington-Smith
> C   Paul Cézanne
> D   Arthur Boyd
> E   Wendy McEwen
> F   A voluntary guide

11   He / She trains guides.   ....

12   He / She was the gallery's first director.   ....

13   The gallery paid a lot for his / her work.   ....

14   He / She must not be diverted by trivial questions.   ....

HOW TO GET A SEVEN

Q15	**Match an example in the statement with its concept in the recording.** Wendy says 'guiding is systematic', which is a concept. Your answer is a process that is 'standardised', which Wendy mentions twice. **Listen for a cue (the same words as in the statement)** *after* **the answer you write.** Note: grammar is tested in IELTS Listening. Although you may not clearly have heard Wendy say the '-ed' in 'standardised', it's a participial adjective before 'delivery'. If you write 'standard' or 'standardise', you will not get a mark.
Q16	**Don't worry if an answer is easy.**
Q17	**Listen for word stress:** 'fourTEEN' or 'FORty'? Logically, how many artworks could a guide talk about in an hour?
Q18	**Listen for cues** *after* **the answer you write,** here: 'school curriculum' and 'international visitors'. 'Works by Australian painters' is a possible answer, but it's four words, so you will not get a mark. Also, you can't write 'Australian paintings', because Wendy doesn't say these exact words. All answers must come from the recording. **Is this answer singular or plural?**
Q19	Occasionally, there's more than one correct answer in IELTS, so **don't rush to answer**: the first possibility is hard to spell; choose the second one. **Know your grammar.** From the question, you can see that you'll need an infinitive as an answer: 'A guide might intervene **to …**'. You must write three words as your answer. 'To move' means something different from 'to move on', and you will not get a mark. The phrase 'To let others speak' fits, but with four words, you won't get a mark. If an instruction says *WRITE NO MORE THAN THREE WORDS*, then there *must* be at least one three-word answer. Also, if an instruction says, *AND / OR A NUMBER*, then there *must* be a number alone as an answer, or a phrase containing a number.
Q20	**Don't worry if an answer is easy.**

Questions 15-20

Answer the questions below.

Write **NO MORE THAN THREE WORDS AND/OR A NUMBER** *for each answer.*

15   What is the process of giving the same information about the same artworks?

.............................……………………..

16   How long is each guided tour?

.............................……………………..

17   About how many artworks do guides discuss in a tour?

.............................……………………..

18   What do schoolchildren and international visitors expect to see at the gallery?

.............................……………………..

19   When a member of the public is talking about an artwork, why might a guide intervene?

.............................……………………..

20   Which language do two of the new volunteers speak?

.............................……………………..

LISTENING   SECTION 1   SECTION 2   SECTION 3   SECTION 4
READING
WRITING
SPEAKING

HOW TO GET A SEVEN

Below are tips for some but not all questions (#26-27).

Section 3; Q21	**Listen for a cue**. The man asks: 'What course do you want to do?'
Q22	**Don't rush to answer.** Sovy says she quit her regular job, 'working in the university library'. **Listen for a cue**, here, Vibol asks: 'What are you doing now?' **Ignore false information.** What kind of teacher is Sovy?
Q23	**Ignore a partial answer.** A BA is part of what Sovy has.
Q24	**Listen for a cue**, here: 'I do worry about my background.'
Q25	**Listen for the same word in the question and the recording.** Often sentence completion answers are played twice, as is the case here. **Notice the grammar around the answer.** The adjective is preceded by the verb 'feels' and followed by the preposition 'of'.
Q28-30	**When choosing two or more letters, remember the options in the answers are usually *not* in the same order as the information in the recording.** Some options will not be mentioned; others will be contradicted by the speaker, or be partially true; and, yet others will relate to someone else. **Ignore information that relates to someone else.** Who is single: Sovy or Vibol? **Ignore a partial answer.** Vibol only says he's travelled to Melbourne. **Ignore false information.** Vibol did a Master's in International Taxation.

Play Audio PLAY RECORDING #3.

SECTION 3   Questions 21-30

PREPARING FOR A SCHOLARSHIP INTERVIEW

Questions 21-24

Choose the correct letter, A, B, or C.

21   The woman, Sovy, would like to study

    A   History.

    B   Development.

    C   Tourism.

22   Sovy works as

    A   a volunteer.

    B   a librarian.

    C   a Russian teacher.

23   Sovy has

    A   a BA only.

    B   a BA and part of an MA.

    C   a BA and an MA.

24   Sovy thinks the scholarship selectors

    A   favour people from big cities.

    B   favour people from the provinces.

    C   award scholarships all around the country.

Questions 25-27

Complete the sentences below.

*Write **ONE WORD ONLY** for each answer.*

25   Sovy feels……………..of her background.

26   Sovy doubts the selectors would be interested in her……………... .

27   Sovy thinks showing her passion for……………..might help during her interview.

Questions 28-30

*Choose **THREE** letters: A-F.*

Which **THREE** relate to Vibol?

    A   He is single.

    B   He opened a restaurant.

    C   He travelled around Australia.

    D   He studied in Adelaide.

    E   He did a Master's in International Law.

    F   He wants an easy life.

HOW TO GET A SEVEN

Section 4 Q31	**Understand purpose**, which is often required in Section 4. **Listen for intonation**, as well as what a speaker says. **Ignore answers that are too specific.** Here, the lecturer does do two out of the three options, but these are *not* the overall purpose of her lecture.
Q33	**Listen for a word in the recording that one option defines.**
Q34	**Listen for a cue**, here: 'The EPA believes that only…' **Ignore numbers that refer to other things.** Here, one option refers to the million metric tons of e-waste; another refers to the age of the speaker's daughters.
Q35	**Avoid answering from your own belief.** It's probably true that European countries have reduced their e-waste, but the speaker doesn't say so. One option is mentioned, but not in relation to the Basel Convention. The correct option is inferred. (See the highlighted evidence in the recording script.)
Q37	**Remember, phrasal verbs have Latinate equivalents**, here: 'find their way into' = 'contaminate'.
Q38	**Where two answers are correct, choose the one that's easier to spell.** 'Guangdong' has three 'g's, and you will not get a mark if it is wrongly spelt.
Q40	**Predict before you listen. Wait for confirmation.** This word is an adjective because it precedes 'products'.

LISTENING   **SECTION 1**   **SECTION 2**   **SECTION 3**   SECTION 4
READING
WRITING
SPEAKING

Play
Audio   **PLAY RECORDING #4.**

SECTION 4   Questions 31-40

E-WASTE DISPOSAL

Questions 31-35

Choose the correct letter, A, B, or C.

31   What is the purpose of the lecture?

   A   To get students to recycle smartphones

   B   To let students know more about e-waste

   C   To encourage students to develop an app

32   The lecturer talks about her family's behaviour because it is

   A   typical.

   B   exceptional.

   C   ideal.

33   According to the lecturer, an e-waste recycler in the US receives a......amount of cash.

   A   very small

   B   small

   C   moderate

34   According to the EPA, only...... of e-waste sent for recycling is actually recycled.

   A   8%

   B   13%

   C   20%

35   European countries signed the Basel Convention,

   A   and greatly reduced their e-waste.

   B   but still send e-waste abroad illegally.

   C   so local recyclers have enough e-waste to process.

Questions 36-40

Complete the sentences below.

Write **NO MORE THAN TWO WORDS OR A NUMBER** *for each answer.*

36   An average smartphone has about...................different chemical elements inside.

37   Toxins from burnt electronic devices find their way into the.................. .

38   Currently, the city of Guiyu, in.................., deals with the most e-waste.

39   The EPA predicts that by.................., global e-waste will reach 100 million metric tons a year.

40   Only a tiny amount of recycled e-waste is used to make more..................products.

HOW TO GET A SEVEN

Passage 1 Question 1	**Understand inference.** If Tammy Chou feels disheartened when she receives a scrawled handwritten message, and she judges the sender negatively, then…
Q2	**Find examples and a paraphrase** in the passage of a 'more active brain'. **Beware of a distractor.** It is inferred that handwriting *contributes* to academic performance, but whether it *raises* performance is not mentioned.
Q3	**Think logically.** If 'dysgraphia' is a problem with writing (and you know 'dis' is a negative prefix, as in 'dislike'), then 'dyslexia' is a disorder of some kind. ('Lexis' means 'language' or 'vocabulary'.) **Beware of a distractor.** Just because the word 'dysgraphia' appears in both the list of headings and the passage, it doesn't mean you should choose it. There is no mention of the 'disgrace' of dysgraphia in the passage. ('Disgrace' means 'shame'.)
Q4	**Match two ideas in a heading with two paragraphs in one section.** Find an example of a social advantage of handwriting, related to personal behaviour. Find an example of a cultural advantage of handwriting.
Q5	**Know your idioms.** What does 'to have had its day' mean? Find a paraphrase for it in the passage.

LISTENING
READING
WRITING
SPEAKING

PASSAGE 1 PASSAGE 2 PASSAGE 3

Reading

Firstly, turn over the Test 1 Listening Answer Sheet that you used earlier.

The Reading test lasts exactly 60 minutes. There are three passages to read, and 40 questions to answer in total. There are no examples.

Certainly, make any marks on the pages below, but transfer your answers to the answer sheet as you read since there is no extra time at the end to do so.

Each question in the Reading test is worth one mark, and a band from 1-9 is calculated from the mark out of 40.

After checking your answers on pp 64-66, go to page 9 for the raw-score conversion table.

PASSAGE 1

*Spend about 20 minutes on **Questions 1-14**, based on Passage 1.*

Questions 1-5

Passage 1 on the following page has six sections: **A-F**.

*Choose the correct heading for sections **B-F** from the list of headings below.*

*Write the correct number, **i-ix**, in boxes 1-5 on your answer sheet.*

List of Headings
i Handwriting and a more active brain
ii The disgrace of dysgraphia
iii A school subject
iv Handwriting has had its day
v Handwriting raises academic performance
vi Handwriting reduces typing ability
vii The medium is the message?
viii Cursive may treat a reading disorder
ix The social and cultural advantages of handwriting

Example	Answer
Section A	iii

1   Section **B**
2   Section **C**
3   Section **D**
4   Section **E**
5   Section **F**

LISTENING   PASSAGE 1   PASSAGE 2   PASSAGE 3
READING
WRITING
SPEAKING

LISTENING
READING
WRITING
SPEAKING

PASSAGE 1   PASSAGE 2   PASSAGE 3

THE VALUE OF HANDWRITING

A 'When I was in school in the 1970s,' says Tammy Chou, 'my end-of-term report included Handwriting as a subject alongside Mathematics and Physical Education, yet, by the time my brother started, a decade later, it had been subsumed into English. I learnt two scripts: printing and cursive,* while Chris can only print.'

The 2013 Common Core, a curriculum used throughout most of the US, requires the tuition of legible writing (generally printing) only in the first two years of school; thereafter, teaching keyboard skills is a priority.

B 'I work in recruitment,' continues Chou. 'Sure, these days, applicants submit a digital CV and cover letter, but there's still information interviewees need to fill out by hand, and I still judge them by the neatness of their writing when they do so. Plus there's nothing more disheartening than receiving a birthday greeting or a condolence card with a scrawled message.'

C Psychologists and neuroscientists may concur with Chou for different reasons. They believe children learn to read faster when they start to write by hand, and they generate new ideas and retain information better. Karin James conducted an experiment at Indiana University in the US in which children who had not learnt to read were shown a letter on a card and asked to reproduce it by tracing, by drawing it on another piece of paper, or by typing it on a keyboard. Then, their brains were scanned while viewing the original image again. Children who had produced the freehand letter showed increased neural activity in the left fusiform gyrus, the inferior frontal gyrus, and the posterior parietal cortex – areas activated when adults read or write, whereas all other children displayed significantly weaker activation of the same areas.

James speculates that in handwriting there is variation in the production of any letter, so the brain has to learn each personal font – each variant of 'F', for example, that is still 'F'. Recognition of variation may establish the eventual representation more permanently than recognising a uniform letter printed by computer.

Victoria Berninger at the University of Washington studied children in the first two grades of school to demonstrate that printing, cursive, and keyboarding are associated with separate brain patterns. Furthermore, children who wrote by hand did so much faster than the typists, who had not been taught to touch type. Not only did the typists produce fewer words but also the quality of their ideas was consistently lower. Scans from the older children's brains exhibited enhanced neural activity when their handwriting was neater than average, and, importantly, the parts of their brains activated are those crucial to working memory.

Pam Mueller and Daniel Oppenheimer have shown in laboratories and live classrooms that tertiary students learn better when they take notes by hand rather than inputting via keyboard. As a result, some institutions ban laptops and tablets in lectures, and prohibit smartphone photography of lecture notes. Mueller and Oppenheimer also believe handwriting aids contemplation as well as memory storage.

D Some learners of English whose native script is not the Roman alphabet have difficulty in forming several English letters: the lower case 'b' and 'd', 'p' and 'q', 'n' and 'u', 'm' and 'w' may be confused. This condition affects a tiny minority of first-language learners and sufferers of brain damage. Called dysgraphia, it appears less frequently when writers use cursive instead of printing, which is why cursive has been posited as a cure for dyslexia.

---

*A style of writing in which letters are joined, and the pen is lifted off the paper at the end of a word.

LISTENING
READING
WRITING
SPEAKING

PASSAGE 1   PASSAGE 2   PASSAGE 3

HOW TO GET A SEVEN

Q6-9	Where there is a box containing a list of people, in the passage A is mentioned first, B second, C third, and D last, but the statements (#6-9) are out of order. **Scan to find the people in the passage, circle them, and *then* see which statements they match.**
Q6	**Understand connotation.** 'Unimportant' in the statement matches a negative idea in the passage.
Q7	Match the *positive* phrase in the statement about *handwriting*, which 'generated more ideas', with a *negative* idea in the passage related to *typing*.
Q8	**Note the shift in focus.** In the statement, the focus is on 'universities'; in the passage, it is on the researchers.
Q9	**Look for a synonym** in the passage for 'assess' in the statement.

LISTENING
READING
WRITING
SPEAKING

PASSAGE 1   PASSAGE 2   PASSAGE 3

E Berninger is of the opinion that cursive, endangered in American schools, promotes self-control, which printing may not, and which typing – especially with the 'delete' function – unequivocally does not. In a world saturated with texting, where many have observed that people are losing the ability to filter their thoughts, a little more restraint would be a good thing.

A rare-book and manuscript librarian, Valerie Hotchkiss, worries about the cost to our heritage as knowledge of cursive fades. Her library contains archives from the literary giants Mark Twain, Marcel Proust, HG Wells, and others. If the young generation does not learn cursive, its ability to decipher older documents may be compromised, and culture lost.

F Paul Bloom, from Yale University, is less convinced about the long-term benefits of handwriting. In the 1950s – indeed in Tammy Chou's idyllic 1970s – when children spent hours practising their copperplate, what were they doing with it? Mainly copying mindlessly. For Bloom, education, in the complex digital age, has moved on.

Questions 6-9

Look at the following statements and list of people below.

*Match each statement with the correct person: **A**, **B**, **C**, or **D**.*

*Write the correct letter, **A**, **B**, **C**, or **D**, in boxes 6-9 on your answer sheet.*

6   According to him / her / them, education is now very sophisticated, so handwriting is unimportant.

7   He / She / They found children who wrote by hand generated more ideas.

8   Universities have stopped students using electronic devices in class due to his / her / their research.

9   He / She / They may assess character by handwriting.

List of people
A   Tammy Chou
B   Victoria Berninger
C   Paul Mueller and Daniel Oppenheimer
D   Paul Bloom

LISTENING
READING
WRITING
SPEAKING

PASSAGE 1   **PASSAGE 2**   **PASSAGE 3**

HOW TO GET A SEVEN

Q10-14	Summary questions test grammar and vocabulary as well as comprehension. There's often at least one question you can correctly predict, based on your knowledge of grammar or vocabulary. In this case, there's only one answer to Q11 – a verb; only one answer to Q12 – a singular noun followed by the preposition 'between'; and only one answer to Q14 – an adjective. Logically, Q13 must be a plural noun, and there's one answer much better than another. This means, only Q10 needs confirmation in the passage.
Q10	**Find the same word** in the passage as in the list.

LISTENING
READING
WRITING
SPEAKING

PASSAGE 1 PASSAGE 2 PASSAGE 3

Questions 10-14

Complete the summary using the list of words, A-H, below.

Write the correct letter, A-H, in boxes 10-14 on your answer sheet.

A	correlation	B	dispute	C	essentially	D	evidence
E	inevitable	F	proponents	G	psychologists	H	teachers

The value of handwriting

Educators in the US have decided that handwriting is no longer worth much curriculum time. Printing, not cursive, is usually taught. Some (**10**)……………….. and neuroscientists (**11**)……………….. this decision as there seems to be a(n) (**12**)……………….. between early reading and handwriting. Children with the best handwriting produce the most neural activity and the most interesting schoolwork. (**13**)……………….. of cursive consider it more useful than printing. However, not all academics believe in the necessity of handwriting. In the digital world, perhaps keyboarding is (**14**)……………….. .

PASSAGE 2

*Spend about 20 minutes on **Questions 15-27**, based on Passage 2 below.*

Growing up in New Zealand

It has long been known that the first one thousand days of life are the most critical in ensuring a person's healthy future; precisely what happens during this period to any individual has been less well documented. To allocate resources appropriately, public health and education policies need to be based upon quantifiable data, so the New Zealand Ministry of Social Development began a longitudinal study of these early days, with the view to extending it for two decades. Born between March 2009 and May 2010, the 6,846 babies recruited came from a densely populated area of New Zealand, and it is hoped they will be followed until they reach the age of 21.

By 2014, four reports, collectively known as *Growing Up in New Zealand* (GUiNZ), had been published, showing New Zealand to be a complex, changing country, with the participants and their families' being markedly different from those of previous generations.

Of the 6,846 babies, the majority were identified as European New Zealanders, but one quarter were Maori (indigenous New Zealanders), 20% were Pacific (originating in islands in the Pacific), and one in six were Asian. Almost 50% of the children had more than one ethnicity.

The first three reports of *GUiNZ* are descriptive, portraying the cohort before birth, at nine months, and at two years of age. Already, the first report, *Before we are born*, has made history as it contains interviews with the children's mothers *and* fathers. The fourth report, which is more analytical, explores the definition of vulnerability for children in their first one thousand days.

LISTENING
READING
WRITING
SPEAKING

PASSAGE 1 | PASSAGE 2 | PASSAGE 3

Before we are born, published in 2010, describes the hopes, dreams, and realities that prospective parents have. It shows that the average age of both parents having a child was 30, and around two-thirds of parents were in legally binding relationships. However, one third of the children were born to either a mother or a father who did not grow up in New Zealand – a significant difference from previous longitudinal studies in which a vast majority of parents were New Zealanders born and bred. Around 60% of the births in the cohort were planned, and most families hoped to have two or three children. During pregnancy, some women changed their behaviour, with regard to smoking, alcohol, and exercise, but many did not. Such information will be useful for public health campaigns.

Now we are born is the second report. Fifty-two percent of its babies were male and 48% female, with nearly a quarter delivered by caesarean section. The World Health Organisation and New Zealand guidelines recommend babies be breastfed exclusively for six months, but the median age for this in the *GUiNZ* cohort was four months, since almost one third of mothers had returned to full-time work. By nine months, the babies were all eating solid food. While 54% of them were living in accommodation their families owned, their parents had almost all experienced a drop in income, sometimes a steep one, mostly due to mothers' not working. Over 90% of the babies were immunised, and almost all were in very good health. Of the mothers, however, 11% had experienced post-natal depression – an alarming statistic, perhaps, but, once again, useful for mental health campaigns. Many of the babies were put in childcare while their mothers worked or studied, and the providers varied by ethnicity: children who were Maori or Pacific were more likely to be looked after by grandparents; European New Zealanders tended to be sent to day care.

Now we are two, the third report, provides more insights into the children's development – physically, emotionally, behaviourally, and cognitively. Major changes in home environments are documented, like the socio-economic situation, and childcare arrangements. Information was collected both from direct observations of the children and from parental interviews. Once again, a high proportion of New Zealand two-year-olds were in very good health. Two thirds of the children knew their gender, and used their own name or expressed independence in some way. The most common first word was a variation on 'Mum', and the most common favourite first food was a banana. Bilingual or multi-lingual children were in a large minority of 40%. Digital exposure was high: one in seven two-year-olds had used a laptop or a children's computer, and 80% watched TV or DVDs daily; by contrast, 66% had books read to them each day.

The fourth report evaluates twelve environmental risk factors that increase the likelihood of poor developmental outcomes for children, and draws on experiences in Western Europe, where the specific factors were collated. This, however, was the first time for their use in a New Zealand context. The factors include: being born to an adolescent mother; having one or both parents on income-tested benefits; and, living in cramped conditions.

In addition to descriptive ones, future reports will focus on children who move in and out of vulnerability to see how these transitions affect their later life.

To date, *GUiNZ* has been highly successful with only a very small dropout rate for participants – even those living abroad, predominantly in Australia, have continued to provide information. The portrait *GUiNZ* paints of a country and its people is indeed revealing.

LISTENING
READING
WRITING
SPEAKING

PASSAGE 1   PASSAGE 2   PASSAGE 3

HOW TO GET A SEVEN

Passage 2 Q15	**Note the shift in focus.** The focus of the statement is on 'findings', but the focus of the passage is on '[allocating] resources'. However, both say the same thing.
Q16	**Scan for a number.** Is it the same in both the statement and the passage?
Q19	**Find an antonym** in the passage for a key word in the statement.
Q20	**Avoid answering from your own belief.** While you may personally believe this to be true, there's no information about it in the passage.
Q21-27	These questions need scanning, skimming, *and* close reading. The answers are easy, but you might accidentally write down the wrong letter (A-D).
	While the reports are mentioned in order in the body of the passage, there are two references to reports in the introduction. Therefore, skim the whole passage to make sure you don't miss anything.
	A classification question shows why you should always read the questions before the passages. Without doing so, you can't circle the report titles as you read. Once you've circled them, or written the numbers, 1-4, in the margin, it's easy to go back to find what you need.
Q21	On the question, write the first word of each report title next to each letter before you answer, to make your search easier.
	Eg: *A Report 1. = Before…*
	In the passage, look for a reason why a report might be 'unique'. Look for examples of 'parents'.
Q22	**Find a paraphrase** of 'at risk'.
Q23	**Look for the language of suggestion** in the passage that uses modal verbs. Find an example of 'financial hardship'.
Q25	**Match the phrase** 'electronic devices' **in the statement with some examples in the passage.**

LISTENING
READING
WRITING
SPEAKING

PASSAGE 1   PASSAGE 2   PASSAGE 3

Questions 15-20

Do the following statements agree with the information given in Passage 2?

In boxes 15-20 on your answer sheet, write:

> **TRUE**   *if the statement agrees with the information.*
> **FALSE**   *if the statement contradicts the information.*
> **NOT GIVEN**   *if there is no information on this.*

15   Findings from studies like *GUiNZ* will inform public policy.

16   Exactly 6,846 babies formed the *GUiNZ* cohort.

17   *GUiNZ* will probably end when the children reach ten.

18   Eventually, there will be 21 reports in *GUiNZ*.

19   So far, *GUiNZ* has shown New Zealanders today to be rather similar to those of 25 years ago.

20   Parents who took part in *GUiNZ* believe New Zealand is a good place to raise children.

Questions 21-27

Classify the following things that relate to:

> **A**   *Report 1.*
> **B**   *Report 2.*
> **C**   *Report 3.*
> **D**   *Report 4.*

*Write the correct letter, **A**, **B**, **C**, or **D**, in boxes 21-27 on your answer sheet.*

21   This is unique because it contains interviews with both parents.

22   This looks at how children might be at risk.

23   This suggests having a child may lead to financial hardship.

24   Information for this came from direct observations of children.

25   This shows many children use electronic devices.

26   This was modelled on criteria used in Western Europe.

27   This suggests having a teenage mother could negatively affect a child.

LISTENING   PASSAGE 1   PASSAGE 2   PASSAGE 3
READING
WRITING
SPEAKING

LISTENING
READING
WRITING
SPEAKING

PASSAGE 1   PASSAGE 2   PASSAGE 3

PASSAGE 3

*Spend about 20 minutes on **Questions 28-40**, based on Passage 3 below.*

• •

LET THERE BE LIGHT?

<u>A</u> 'Incandescent light bulbs lit the 20th century; the 21st will be lit by LED lamps.' So stated the Nobel Prize Committee on awarding the 2014 prize for physics to the inventors of light-emitting diodes (LEDs).

Around the world, LED systems are replacing most kinds of conventional lighting since they use about half the electricity, and the US Department of Energy expects LEDs to account for 74% of US lighting sales by 2030.

However, with lower running costs, LEDs may be left on longer, or installed in places that were previously unlit. Historically, when there has been an improvement in lighting technology, far more outdoor illumination has occurred. Furthermore, many LEDs are brighter than other lights, and they produce a blue-wavelength light that animals misinterpret as dawn.

According to the American Medical Association, there has been a noticeable rise in obesity, diabetes, cancer, and cardio-vascular disease in people like shift workers exposed to too much artificial light of any kind. It is likely more pervasive LEDs will contribute to a further rise.

<u>B</u> In some cities, a brown haze of industrial pollution prevents enjoyment of the night sky; in others, a yellow haze from lighting has the same effect, and it is thought that almost 70% of people can no longer see the Milky Way.

When a small earthquake disabled power plants in Los Angeles a few years ago, the director of the Griffith Observatory was bombarded with phone calls by locals who reported an unusual phenomenon they thought was caused by the quake – a brilliantly illuminated night sky, in which around 7,000 stars were visible. In fact, this was just an ordinary starry night, seldom seen in LA due to light pollution!

Certainly, light pollution makes professional astronomy difficult, but it also endangers humans' age-old connection to the stars. It is conceivable that children who do not experience a true starry night may not speculate about the universe, nor may they learn about nocturnal creatures.

<u>C</u> Excessive illumination impacts upon the nocturnal world. Around 30% of vertebrates and over 60% of invertebrates are nocturnal; many of the remainder are crepuscular – most active at dawn and dusk. Night lighting, hundreds of thousands of times greater than its natural level, has drastically reduced insect, bird, bat, lizard, frog, turtle, and fish life, with even dairy cows producing less milk in brightly-lit sheds.

Night lighting has a vacuum-cleaner effect on insects, particularly moths, drawing them from as far away as 122 metres. As insects play an important role in pollination, and in providing food for birds, their destruction is a grave concern. Using low-pressure sodium-vapour lamps or UV-filtered bulbs would reduce insect mortality, but an alternative light source does not help amphibians: frogs exposed to any night light experience altered feeding and mating behaviour, making them easy prey.

Furthermore, birds and insects use the sun, the moon, and the stars to navigate. It is estimated that around 500 million migratory birds are killed each year by collisions with brightly-lit structures, like skyscrapers or radio towers. In Toronto, Canada, the Fatal Light Awareness Program educates building owners about reducing such deaths by darkening their buildings at the peak of the migratory season. Still, over 1,500 birds may be killed within one night when this does not happen.

Non-migratory birds are also adversely affected by light pollution – sleep is difficult, and waking up only occurs when the sun has overpowered artificial lighting, resulting in the birds' being too late to catch insects.

LISTENING   PASSAGE 1   PASSAGE 2   PASSAGE 3
READING
WRITING
SPEAKING

Test 1 47

LISTENING
READING
WRITING
SPEAKING

PASSAGE 1   PASSAGE 2   PASSAGE 3

Leatherback turtles, which have lived on Earth for over 150 million years, are now endangered as their hatchlings are meant to follow light reflected from the moon and stars to go from their sandy nests to the sea. Instead, they follow street lamps or hotel lights, resulting in death by dehydration, predation, or accidents, since they wander onto the road in the opposite direction from the sea.

D Currently, eight percent of all energy generated in the US is dedicated to public outdoor lighting, and much evidence shows that lighting and energy use are growing at around four percent a year, exceeding population growth. In some newly-industrialised countries, lighting use is rising by 20%. Unfortunately, as the developing world urbanises, it also lights up brightly, rather than opting for sustainability.

E There are several organisations devoted to restoring the night sky: one is the International Dark-Sky Association (IDA), based in Arizona, US. The IDA draws attention to the hazards of light pollution, and works with manufacturers, planners, legislators, and citizens to encourage lighting only what is necessary when necessary.

With 58 chapters in sixteen countries, the IDA has been the driving force behind the establishment of nine world reserves, most recently the 1,720-square-kilometre Rhon Biosphere Reserve in Germany. IDA campaigns have also reduced street lighting in several US states, and changed national legislation in Italy.

F Except in some parks and observatory zones, the IDA does not defend complete darkness, acknowledging that urban areas operate around the clock. For transport, lighting is particularly important. Nonetheless, there is an appreciable difference between harsh, glaring lights and those that illuminate the ground without streaming into the sky. The US Department of Transportation recently conducted research into highway safety, and found that a highway lit well only at interchanges was as safe as one lit along its entire length. In addition, reflective signage and strategic white paint improved safety more than adding lights.

Research by the US Department of Justice showed that outdoor lighting may not deter crime. Its only real benefit is in citizens' perceptions: lighting reduces the fear of crime, not crime itself. Indeed, bright lights may compromise safety, as they make victims and property more visible.

The IDA recommends that where streetlights stay on all night, they have a lower lumen rating, or are controlled with dimmers; and, that they point downwards, or are fitted with directional metal shields. For private dwellings, low-lumen nightlights should be activated only when motion is detected.

G It is not merely the firefly, the fruit bat, or the frog that suffers from light pollution – many human beings no longer experience falling stars or any but the brightest stars, nor consequently ponder their own place in the universe. Hopefully, prize-winning LED lights will be modified and used circumspectly to return to us all the splendour of the night sky.

LISTENING
READING
WRITING
SPEAKING

PASSAGE 1   PASSAGE 2   PASSAGE 3

HOW TO GET A SEVEN

Passage 3 Q28	**Note the connotation.** 'Light-hearted' means 'amusing'. The adverb 'just' and the exclamation mark (!) show that this story is funny.
Q31	**Think logically.** You may not know the word for 'baby animals' used in the passage, but logically these animals have just left their nests, heading for the sea, so they're babies. **Beware of distractors.** Animals are mentioned in another section, but not *baby* animals.
Q32	**Read the question carefully.** Many drawbacks of lighting are mentioned, but you're only looking for '*new* lighting technology'.
Q33	**Note the shift in focus.** In the question, 'light' comes first; in the passage, examples of the illnesses come first. Occasionally, there are two correct answers in IELTS, as is the case here.
Q34	**Scan for a percentage**: look for the symbol.
Q35	**Scan for a number.** 'Million' appears twice in the passage. Make sure the one you want is connected to the death of birds.

Questions 28-32

Reading Passage 3 has seven sections, **A-G**.

Which section contains the following information?

*Write the correct letter, **A-G**, in boxes 28-32 on your answer sheet.*

28   A light-hearted example of ignorance about the night sky

29   An explanation of how lighting may not equate with safety

30   A description of the activities of the International Dark-sky Association

31   An example of baby animals affected by too much night light

32   A list of the possible drawbacks of new lighting technology

Questions 33-35

Complete the sentences below.

*Choose **ONE WORD OR A NUMBER** from the passage for each answer.*

Write your answers in boxes 33-35 on your answer sheet.

33   Too much ……………….. light has led to a rise in serious illness.

34   Approximately ……………….% of humans are unable to see the Milky Way.

35   About ……………... million migratory birds die crashing into lit-up tall buildings each year.

HOW TO GET A SEVEN

Q36-39	Yes/No/Not Given questions ask about a writer's opinions or views. Often, you need to find vocabulary that has positive or negative connotations.
Q36	**Look for connotation.** The word 'alarming' in the statement is negative. Match this with two negative words (one adverb; one adjective) in the passage.
Q37	**Look for connotation.** The word 'good' in the statement is positive, but the writer starts to mention lighting in the developing world by saying, 'Unfortunately'.
Q38	**Read closely.** Reduced street lighting in Italy appears in Section E, paragraph 2, but is the writer's view of this mentioned?
Q39	**Look for connotation.** The words 'necessary' and 'safe' in the statement are positive. When the writer mentions lighting for transport, he or she starts by saying it is 'important', but continues with 'Nonetheless', a word that introduces a contrast. The words 'harsh' and 'glaring' are both negative.
Q40	**Identify an overall view.** Q40 often asks about a writer's overall view or position. There are many clues in this passage.

Test 1 51

LISTENING
READING
WRITING
SPEAKING

PASSAGE 1   PASSAGE 2   PASSAGE 3

Questions 36–39

Do the following statements agree with the claims of the writer in Passage 3?

In boxes 36–39 on your answer sheet, write:

YES	*if the statement agrees with the claims of the writer.*
NO	*if the statement contradicts the claims of the writer.*
NOT GIVEN	*if it is impossible to say what the writer thinks about this.*

36 It is alarming that so many animals are killed by night lighting.

37 It is good that developing countries now have brighter lighting.

38 Italians need not worry about reduced street lighting.

39 Bright lights along the road are necessary for safe driving.

Question 40

*Choose the correct letter, **A**, **B**, **C**, or **D**.*

Write the correct letter in box 40 on your answer sheet.

According to the writer, how much night lighting should there be in relation to what there is?

    A Much more

    B A little more

    C A little less

    D Much less

LISTENING
READING
WRITING
SPEAKING

TASK 1   TASK 2

LISTENING
READING
WRITING
SPEAKING

TASK 1   TASK 2

Writing

The Writing test lasts for 60 minutes. It has two tasks. Task 2 is worth twice as much as Task 1. Although candidates are assessed on four criteria for each task, an overall band, from 1-9, is awarded.

Task 1

Spend about 20 minutes on this task.

> **The chart below shows tea and coffee consumption in 2015.**
>
> **Write a summary of the information. Select and report the main features, and make comparisons where necessary.**

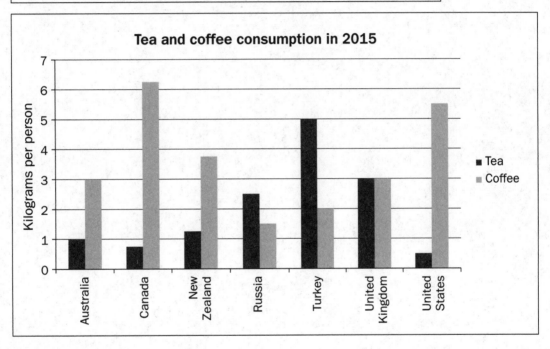

Write at least 150 words.

Task 2

Spend about 40 minutes on this task.

Write about the following topic:

> **In some countries at secondary or high school, there may be two streams of study: academic or vocational.***
>
> **What are the advantages for students and society of putting students into two streams at the age of fifteen?**

Provide reasons for your answer, including relevant examples from your own knowledge or experience.

Write at least 250 words.

---

*Vocational training is learning how to become a carpenter, chef, lab technician, mechanic, plumber, or some other tradesperson.

LISTENING
READING
WRITING
SPEAKING

| PART 1 | PART 2 | PART 3 |

Speaking

The Speaking test lasts for eleven to fourteen minutes. There are three parts, and a candidate answers around 25 questions in total. An overall band from 1-9 is awarded by the Speaking examiner although he or she assesses the candidate on four individual criteria: Fluency and Coherence; Vocabulary Range and Accuracy; Grammatical Range and Accuracy; and, Pronunciation.

PART 1

For four to five minutes, the examiner asks the candidate questions on familiar topics, such as where the candidate lives, and what he or she does. Then, the examiner asks questions on two topics of general interest.

How might you answer the following questions?

1   Could you tell me what you're doing at the moment: are you working or studying?

2   What do you do in your job?

3   Do you like your job?

4   What do you remember about your first day in this job?

5   Now, let's talk about taking photos. Do you mainly take photos with your phone, or do you use a camera?

6   Is there anything in particular you like to take photos of?

7   Typically, what do you do with your photos after you've taken them?

8   Would you like to take classes in photography?

9   Let's move on to talk about parks. Do you go to any parks near where you live?

10   Do you prefer a park with designated areas for leisure activities, or one that has mostly open space?

Play Audio   **PLAY RECORDING #5 TO HEAR PART ONE OF THE SPEAKING TEST.**

PART 2

The examiner gives the candidate a topic, which is often a recount of a personal experience. The candidate has one minute to think about this and may make notes. Then he or she should speak for two minutes. The examiner may ask one or two brief questions at the end.

How might you speak about the following topic for two minutes?

> **I'd like you to tell me about an embarrassing experience you have had with food.**
>
> * Where were you?
>
> * What happened?
>
> * How did you feel afterwards?
>
> And, what did other people think about this event?

PART 1	PART 2	PART 3

Play Audio | **PLAY RECORDING #6 TO HEAR PART TWO OF THE SPEAKING TEST.**

PART 3

For four to five minutes, the topic from Part 2 is developed more generally. Questions the examiner asks the candidate become more abstract, and the candidate should be able to do the following:

1   agree or disagree

2   identify and describe

3   compare or contrast

4   explain or defend

5   give reasons for

6   suggest or outline

7   evaluate or assess

8   speculate, and

9   predict.

Play Audio | **PLAY RECORDING #7 TO HEAR PART THREE OF THE SPEAKING TEST.**

Which of the above did Carla do?

How might you answer the following questions?

1   First of all, natural versus processed food.

Do people these days eat enough natural food?

To what extent are food producers responsible for the health of consumers?

2   Now, let's consider global food security.

There are predictions of serious global food insecurity within our lifetime. What do you think about these predictions, and what might be done to improve global food security?

Go to pp 65-67 for the recording scripts.

Answers

LISTENING:

Section 1: **1.** C; **2.** A; **3.** B; **4.** C; **5.** Wool; **6.** 7/seven; **7.** Tuesdays (*must have an 's' at the end*); **8.** river; **9.** exhibition; **10.** 0212 064 993. Section 2: **11.** E; **12.** A; **13.** C; **14.** F; **15.** Standardised/Standardized delivery; **16.** 1/One hour; **17.** 14/Fourteen; **18.** Iconic works; **19.** To alter misconceptions // To move on; **20.** Japanese. Section 3: **21.** B; **22.** A; **23.** B; **24.** A; **25.** proud; **26.** politics; **27.** development; **28-30.** BDF (*in any order*). Section 4: **31.** B; **32.** A; **33.** A; **34.** C; **35.** B; **36.** 60/sixty; **37.** food chain; **38.** China // Guangdong Province; **39.** 2020; **40.** electronic.

The highlighted text below is evidence for the answers above.

Narrator	Recording 1. Practice Listening Test 1. Section 1. Community College Classes. You will hear a receptionist and a teacher talking about classes at a community college. Read the example.
Receptionist	Good evening. How may I help you?
Amal	My name's Amal Nouri. I'm a new teacher.
Receptionist	Nice to meet you, Amal. You're teaching Arabic, aren't you?
Amal	Spanish, actually. I'm from Argentina.
Narrator	The answer is 'B'. On this occasion only, the first part of the conversation is played twice. Before you listen again, you have 30 seconds to read questions 1 to 4.
Receptionist	Good evening. How may I help you?
Amal	My name's Amal Nouri. I'm a new teacher.
Receptionist	Nice to meet you, Amal. You're teaching Arabic, aren't you?
Amal	Spanish, actually. I'm from Argentina. My relatives moved there a long time ago. You'd be surprised how big the Arab community is in Latin America.
Receptionist	But Spanish isn't on tonight – it's tomorrow, Wednesday.
Amal	I know. I just thought I'd introduce myself. When I came for my interview, I only met the principal.
Receptionist	Mr Andrews?
Amal	Yes, Trevor Andrews. I must say he made me feel welcome, especially since he speaks Spanish himself.
Receptionist	Trevor's a lovely guy. We're going to miss him when he leaves at the end of the term.
Amal	Oh, why's he leaving? Has he found another job?
Receptionist	(1) No, he's retiring. He wants to spend more time with his grandchildren.
Amal	Right. He did mention them to me.
Receptionist	Did Trevor also mention that he likes to sit in on new teachers' classes – just for a few minutes?
Amal	Umm…
Receptionist	It's the policy of the college that new teachers are observed either by Trevor or by the vice-principal. I'm sure it's in your contract.
Amal	Probably.
Receptionist	Don't worry, it's all quite informal – you won't need to submit a lesson plan. (2) In general, student feedback at the end of the term is taken more seriously.
Amal	I see.
Receptionist	One more piece of advice, Amal. (3) Don't be upset about the fact that you'll start the term with fifteen students, but end up with five. That's just what happens with evening classes. People sign up for things without really knowing what's involved, or something else comes up on that night. (3) The high dropout rate is no reflection on your teaching.
Amal	Thanks for the tip. Anyway, the real reason I'm here, tonight, is that I'd like to enroll in a class. I saw in the contract that (4) teachers can take one class themselves, paying only 10% of tuition, which seems a pretty good deal.

Receptionist	Indeed. When I was teaching Keyboarding Skills, I did Korean and Car Maintenance.
	However, for a few courses, like Life Drawing, where students have to pay for a model, or Cooking with Seafood, where the ingredients are expensive, I'm afraid teachers can't pay only (4) 10% – they have to pay the full fee.
Narrator	Before you listen to the rest of the conversation, you have 30 seconds to read questions 5 to 10.
Receptionist	So, Amal, what would you like to do?
Amal	I'm interested in Sally Burton's class called 'Working with (5) Wool'. I read about her in the local paper.
Receptionist	Yes, she's very popular.
Amal	She made those amazing sculptures near the Town Hall. I'd no idea that (5) wool could be used in such huge artworks. I'd always thought of it just in clothing or carpets.
Receptionist	Unfortunately, Sally's class is full. You see, she holds it in her studio, so she only accepts (6) seven students. And, we've already had (6) seven enrollments. I could put you on the waiting list.
Amal	It's all right. My second choice was Watercolour Painting on (7) Tuesdays and Fridays. Yikes! There's a class tonight.
Receptionist	Kostia's class is also popular, but someone's just cancelled, so there is a place for you.
Amal	Great.
Receptionist	For the first few nights, he's in Room 14, but later in the term, when it's lighter in the evening, he takes his class on excursions to the (8) river. There were some gorgeous paintings of the (8) river in our end-of-term (9) exhibition last year.
Amal	Sounds good.
	By the way, where will my class be, tomorrow?
Receptionist	I'm not sure yet. We've had to make a few changes, but I'll give you a call or send you a text when I know.
Amal	OK.
Receptionist	Ah… I don't think I've got your phone number.
Amal	(10) It's 0212 064 993.
Receptionist	Double *nine* three or double *five* three?
Amal	Double *nine* three.
Receptionist	Thanks.
	Lovely to meet you, Amal. I hope you'll enjoy your time with us.
Narrator	You now have 30 seconds to check your answers.
	That is the end of Section 1.
Narrator	Recording 2.
	Section 2. Voluntary Guiding.
	You will hear a woman talking to voluntary guides at an art gallery.
	Before you listen, you have 30 seconds to read questions 11 to 14.
Wendy McEwen	Good morning. (11) I'm Wendy McEwen. Please call me Wendy. I train volunteers at the gallery, and it's my great pleasure to meet you today.
	To begin, I'd like to quote from a speech made in 1882 by (12) our first director, Eliezer Montefiore. He said, 'The Australian public should be afforded every facility to avail themselves of the educational and civilising influence engendered by an exhibition of works, bought at the public expense.' We now live in a world where the notion of civilisation is seldom discussed, so let me mention some of its synonyms: enlightenment, refinement, and conformity with the standards of a highly developed society. In my view, this is what the creation and enjoyment of art can do for the public – conform, refine, and enlighten.
	The idea of civilisation may be unfashionable, but an interest in different civilisations has certainly grown. Australian art is well represented in our collection – we have some wonderful paintings by Grace Cossington-Smith and Arthur Boyd – but there are Asian and European works to rival those abroad. In fact, (13) the single most expensive purchase this gallery has ever made was a 16.2-million-dollar landscape, painted in 1888, by Paul Cézanne. Visitors will ask you for this figure, just as they'll be curious about Cézanne's career as a banker in France and his time with his lover in Tahiti. (14) Sometimes, it seems the public is more interested in trivia than in art, so it's your job to inform about the techniques of production, the themes an artwork deals with, as well as the culture from which it came. Elevate cultural discourse rather than stoop to the level of the popular press. Bear in mind those words of Eliezer Montefiore.

Narrator	Before you listen to the rest of the talk, you have 30 seconds to read questions 15 to 20.
Wendy McEwen	While guides are diverse, guiding is systematic. By this I mean, we adhere to (15) standardised delivery whether tours be for viewers on Saturday morning, for school groups, or for VIPs. (15) Standardised delivery means that guides give the public virtually the same information about the same artworks. Sure, we all have our personal styles, but the content needs to be the same. To that end, guides are tested on information before taking their first tour.
	Guides also have to keep an eye on the clock. Guided tours last (16) one hour. Since the building is large, part of that time is taken up in walking as well as mentioning the location of toilets, fire exists, and drinking fountains. After recent additions, the gallery is twice the size it was in 2013. So, ask your group where they'd like to go first, then calculate how many artworks you can see on each level. Aim for a total of (17) fourteen in your (16) hour. In each room, there's lots to see, but you'll only be talking about one or two items. By all means, when people in your group want to know about a work not on your list, go to it, but be brief. For the (18) iconic works by Australian painters, you'll need to take longer. Some of these (18) iconic works are part of the school curriculum, and many are known to international visitors, who come just to see them.
	In the past, guides stood beside an artwork and gave a short speech. To a certain extent, that's still what happens with an audio tour. However, we now try to involve the public. One technique is called elicitation: when a guide asks questions about an artwork to see what knowledge already exists among the visitors. That way, you don't appear as the ultimate authority, and often visitors know considerably more than you. On that note, there will be times when you need to intervene: to let others in the group speak, (19) to alter misconceptions, or, simply, (19) to move on.
	As I said earlier, before you're let loose on the public, each voluntary guide is evaluated.
	Oh, that reminds me, I recall from your applications that two of you are (20) Japanese speakers, so we'll probably ask you to take around groups of Japanese.
	Now, let's go into the gallery itself.
Narrator	You now have 30 seconds to check your answers. That is the end of Section 2.
Narrator	Recording 3. Section 3. Preparing for a Scholarship Interview. You will hear a woman who is going to be interviewed for a scholarship talking to a man who previously received one. Before you listen, you have 30 seconds to read questions 21 to 27.
Sovy	Hi, Vibol. Thanks for coming.
Vibol	No problem, Sovy. I hope I can help. When's the interview?
Sovy	On Thursday.
Vibol	Which course do you want to do?
Sovy	(21) A Master's in Development Studies.
Vibol	Whereabouts?
Sovy	In Australia – Melbourne, actually.
Vibol	Well, Melbourne's a great place. I visited in my semester break.
Sovy	(28-30) But you studied in Adelaide, didn't you?
Vibol	Yeah.
Sovy	Why Adelaide?
Vibol	I heard before I applied for the scholarship that most applicants want to go to Sydney or Melbourne, so by choosing Adelaide I thought I'd have a better chance.
Sovy	D'you think I should go to Adelaide? Or not do (21) Development Studies?
Vibol	I think the key is to choose a course you're really interested in, no matter where it is.
Sovy	Why's that?
Vibol	Because the workload is heavy. My Master's was probably the most difficult thing I've done in my whole life.
Sovy	I see. Anyway, I bet the interview panel asks the same questions every year. What did they ask you?

Vibol	Firstly, about why I wanted to go to Australia.
Sovy	What did you say?
Vibol	I told them I'd been there already, and I liked it.
Sovy	What else did the panel ask?
Vibol	About my undergraduate degree. About my job. About how a Master's would improve my performance and the performance of my organisation.
Sovy	Where *are* you working now?
Vibol	Oh, and they asked about my family – whether I'd take my wife with me.
Sovy	Well, I'm single, and planning to stay that way. As to the course's helping me at work, you know I quit my regular job, working in the university library.
Vibol	Yeah, I heard that. What are you doing now?
Sovy	(22) I'm a volunteer at a rehabilitation centre.
Vibol	How ever do you survive, financially?
Sovy	I teach English at night, and I live cheaply.
Vibol	Good for you. You could say an MA would improve your prospects of finding permanent work.
Sovy	(23) I wonder what the interview panel will think about my undergraduate degree. It's in Russian and History. I studied Russian so I could get a scholarship to Russia for a Master's degree, but I only lasted six months in Europe.
Vibol	If I were you, (23) I wouldn't mention you already have an incomplete Master's. I'd focus on the work you're doing now. Use phrases like 'grass roots activism' and 'capacity building'. The panel will love that.
Sovy	Oh? I do worry about my background. My family comes from a village on the coast. (24) I seem to recall that most people who were awarded scholarships in the last three years came from big cities and were socially successful.
Vibol	In the past, that was true. Indeed, all the interviews were held here, in the capital, but this year, they're also taking place in the provinces, so scholarships will go to a more diverse group of people. I don't think you should beg for assistance, Sovy, but you don't need to hide your background either. Be (25) proud of it.
Sovy	I am (25) proud of it.
Vibol	After all, it means you can empathise with the people you volunteer for. However, when you come back with a Master's degree, you'll be able to mix with more influential people – I mean, politically influential. I'd emphasise that if I were you.
Sovy	I'm not sure the selectors will want to know about my (26) politics, but they may want to see that I'm passionate about (27) development.
Narrator	Before you listen to the rest of the conversation, you have 30 seconds to read questions 28 to 30.
Sovy	By the way, (28-30) Vibol, in Adelaide, what did you do your Master's in?
Vibol	Taxation Law.
Sovy	And what are you doing now?
Vibol	(28-30) I, well, I-I set up a restaurant.
Sovy	A restaurant? With a Master's in *Taxation* Law?
Vibol	Taxation is a nightmare here. To be honest, Sovy, (28-30) I just want an easy life.
Narrator	You now have 30 seconds to check your answers. That is the end of Section 3.
Narrator	Recording 4. Section 4. E-Waste Disposal. You will hear a lecture on the disposal of electronic or e-waste. Before you listen, you have 45 seconds to read questions 31 to 40.
Lecturer	Normally in this class, we design and evaluate apps, and we'll get back to that tomorrow. This afternoon, (31) I'd like to raise your awareness about the issue of electronic waste disposal.

As some of you know, I've got twin daughters, who turn thirteen on Tuesday. Like many children their age, they're totally in love with electronic devices. My husband gave his old smartphone to one of them, and I was forced to give my newish phone to the other. That was two years ago. Now, they're both demanding brand-new smartphones of their own. As an anxious parent, I would've given in to this demand had I not just read an article about e-waste. Let me add that I read part of it on my tablet at home, the rest on my desktop computer at work, and, afterwards, I counted how many electronic items my family and I have at home, at school, and at work. And we've got 24. Yup, 24. (32) An average American family, no doubt.

Anyway, I finally agreed to birthday phones for my girls on condition that my husband and I shed some of our own devices as responsibly as we could. In the past, we've just put them out in the garbage as though they were banana peel or broken plates. This time, I decided to take two laptops and my girls' phones to a recycler accredited by the Environmental Protection Agency or EPA. I found an interactive map on the EPA website showing companies that sign up to recycling schemes, called E-Stewards and Responsible Recycling Practices. It's easy enough to drop stuff off at these companies, and receive cash in return. I do regret to say that (33) in the US the cash return is tiny because there are currently insufficient volumes of electronic trash for these companies to turn into treasure. Since I'd like to encourage this recycling practice among my students and colleagues, there's a web link on my Facebook page.

Frankly, I don't think Americans recycle enough. Yet, even with these companies that have popped up recently, there's still a huge problem. I mean, the collection of the e-waste is fine, but who knows how it's processed! (34) The EPA believes that only 20% is actually recycled, and the rest is incinerated or put in landfill. The auditing of this process has yet to begin. The majority of local e-waste, around eight million metric tons a year, is sent off abroad, mostly to Asia or Africa, where health and safety regulations scarcely exist.

One reason the US still banishes most of its e-waste is because it refused to sign the 1989 Basel Convention that controls the export of hazardous waste from rich countries to poorer ones. Needless to say, it wasn't the only rich country to spurn the convention. Neither Canada nor Japan consented to a 1995 amendment banning such trade completely. (35) However, European signatories to the Basel Convention may not, in reality, behave any better. Inspections at ports in Germany and the Netherlands have proven that e-waste, like much other cargo, is deliberately mislabelled, so it passes unnoticed through Customs.

So, what's inside e-waste, and who deals with most of it? Well, the list of chemicals is very long indeed. An average smartphone contains around (36) 60 different chemical elements. Heavy metals, like lead and mercury, exist alongside arsenic, beryllium, cadmium, and polyvinyl chloride – all toxic to humans in quite small amounts. When electronics are incinerated, unless at extremely high temperatures, many more toxins are produced, including halogenated dioxins and furans, which seriously contaminate the (37) food chain.

India and China are two major processors of e-waste. At present, the city of Guiyu in (38) Guangdong Province, in (38) China, is considered the world's e-waste capital. American, Japanese, and European containers loaded with e-waste arrive in Guiyu hourly, but these days there's also considerable waste from the rest of China, itself.

The EPA estimates that by (39) 2020, 100 million metric tons of e-waste will be produced globally each year, and, of that, only an infinitesimal amount will see its way back into more (40) electronic products.

So, designing apps for this digital age is important. As an extra assignment, I'd like those of you who are interested to create one that lets users responsibly end the lives of their many electronic devices.

Narrator   That is the end of the Listening test.
You now have ten minutes to transfer your answers to your answer sheet.

READING: Passage 1: **1.** vii; **2.** i; **3.** viii; **4.** ix; **5.** iv; **6.** D; **7.** B; **8.** C; **9.** A; **10.** G; **11.** B; **12.** A; **13.** F; **14.** E. Passage 2: **15.** T/True; **16.** T/True; **17.** F/False; **18.** NG/Not Given; **19.** F/False; **20.** NG/Not Given; **21.** A; **22.** D; **23.** B; **24.** C; **25.** C; **26.** D; **27.** D. Passage 3: **28.** B; **29.** F; **30.** E; **31.** C; **32.** A; **33.** artificial // night; **34.** 70; **35.** 500; **36.** Y/Yes; **37.** N/No; **38.** NG/Not Given; **39.** N/No; **40.** D.

> *The highlighted text below is evidence for the answers above.*
>
> *If there is a question where 'Not given' is the answer, no evidence can be found, so there is no highlighted text.*

The value of handwriting

A 'When I was in school in the 1970s,' says Tammy Chou, 'my end-of-term report included Handwriting as a subject alongside Mathematics and Physical Education, yet, by the time my brother started, a decade later, it had been subsumed into English. I learnt two scripts: printing and cursive,* while Chris can only print.'

The 2013 Common Core, a curriculum used throughout most of the US, requires the tuition of legible writing (generally printing) only in the first two years of school; thereafter, teaching keyboard skills is a priority.

B 'I work in recruitment,' continues (9) Chou. 'Sure, these days, applicants submit a digital CV and cover letter, but there's still information interviewees need to fill out by hand, and (9) I still judge them by the neatness of their writing when they do so. Plus (1) there's nothing more disheartening than receiving a birthday greeting or a condolence card with a scrawled message.'

C (10) Psychologists and neuroscientists may concur with Chou for different reasons. (*11 and 13 are inferred*; 12) They believe children learn to read faster when they start to write by hand, and they generate new ideas and retain information better. Karin James conducted an experiment at Indiana University in the US in which children who had not learnt to read were shown a letter on a card and asked to reproduce it by tracing, by drawing it on another piece of paper, or by typing it on a keyboard. Then, their brains were scanned while viewing the original image again. (2) Children who had produced the freehand letter showed increased neural activity in the left fusiform gyrus, the inferior frontal gyrus, and the posterior parietal cortex – areas activated when adults read or write, whereas all other children displayed significantly weaker activation of the same areas.

James speculates that in handwriting there is variation in the production of any letter, so the brain has to learn each personal font – each variant of 'F', for example, that is still 'F'. Recognition of variation may establish the eventual representation more permanently than recognising a uniform letter printed by computer.

(7) Victoria Berninger at the University of Washington studied children in the first two grades of school to demonstrate that printing, cursive, and keyboarding are associated with separate brain patterns. Furthermore, children who wrote by hand did so much faster than the typists, who had not been taught to touch type. (7) Not only did the typists produce fewer words but also the quality of their ideas was consistently lower. (2) Scans from the older children's brains exhibited enhanced neural activity when their handwriting was neater than average, and, importantly, the parts of their brains activated are those crucial to working memory.

(8) Pam Mueller and Daniel Oppenheimer have shown in laboratories and live classrooms that tertiary students learn better when they take notes by hand rather than inputting via keyboard. As a result, some institutions ban laptops and tablets in lectures, and prohibit smartphone photography of lecture notes. Mueller and Oppenheimer also believe handwriting aids contemplation as well as memory storage.

D Some learners of English whose native script is not the Roman alphabet have difficulty in forming several English letters: the lower case 'b' and 'd', 'p' and 'q', 'n' and 'u', 'm' and 'w' may be confused. This condition affects a tiny minority of first-language learners and sufferers of brain damage. Called dysgraphia, it appears less frequently when writers use cursive instead of printing, which is why (3) cursive has been posited as a cure for dyslexia.

E Berninger is of the opinion that (4) cursive, endangered in American schools, promotes self-control, which printing may not, and which typing – especially with the 'delete' function – unequivocally does not. In a world saturated with texting, where many have observed that people are losing the ability to filter their thoughts, a little more restraint would be a good thing.

A rare-book and manuscript librarian, Valerie Hotchkiss, worries about the cost to our heritage as knowledge of cursive fades. Her library contains archives from the literary giants Mark Twain, Marcel Proust, HG Wells, and others. (4) If the young generation does not learn cursive, its ability to decipher older documents may be compromised, and culture lost.

F (6) Paul Bloom, from Yale University, is (5) less convinced about the long-term benefits of handwriting. In the 1950s – indeed in Tammy Chou's idyllic 1970s – when children spent hours practising their copperplate, what were they doing with it? Mainly copying mindlessly. For Bloom, (5, 6 & 14) education, in the complex digital age, has moved on.

Growing up in New Zealand

It has long been known that the first one thousand days of life are the most critical in ensuring a person's healthy future; precisely what happens during this period to any individual has been less well documented. (15) To allocate resources appropriately, public health and education policies need to be based upon quantifiable data, so the New Zealand Ministry of Social Development began a longitudinal study of these early days, with the view to extending it for two decades. Born between March 2009 and May 2010, (16) the 6,846 babies recruited came from a densely populated area of New Zealand, and (17) it is hoped they will be followed until they reach the age of 21.

---

*A style of writing in which letters are joined, and the pen is lifted off the paper at the end of a word.

By 2014, four reports, collectively known as *Growing Up in New Zealand* (*GUiNZ*), had been published, (19) showing New Zealand to be a complex, changing country, with the participants and their families' being markedly different from those of previous generations.

Of the 6,846 babies, the majority were identified as European New Zealanders, but one quarter were Maori (indigenous New Zealanders), 20% were Pacific (originating in islands in the Pacific), and one in six were Asian. Almost 50% of the children had more than one ethnicity.

The first three reports of *GUiNZ* are descriptive, portraying the cohort before birth, at nine months, and at two years of age. Already, the first report, (21) *Before we are born*, has made history as it contains interviews with the children's mothers *and* fathers. (22) The fourth report, which is more analytical, explores the definition of vulnerability for children in their first one thousand days.

Before we are born, published in 2010, describes the hopes, dreams, and realities that prospective parents have. It shows that the average age of both parents having a child was 30, and around two-thirds of parents were in legally binding relationships. However, one-third of the children were born to either a mother or a father who did not grow up in New Zealand – a significant difference from previous longitudinal studies in which a vast majority of parents were New Zealanders born and bred. Around 60% of the births in the cohort were planned, and most families hoped to have two or three children. During pregnancy, some women changed their behaviour, with regard to smoking, alcohol, and exercise, but many did not. Such information will be useful for public health campaigns.

(23) *Now we are born* is the second report. Fifty-two percent of its babies were male and 48% female, with nearly a quarter delivered by caesarean section. The World Health Organisation and New Zealand guidelines recommend babies be breastfed exclusively for six months, but the median age for this in the *GUiNZ* cohort was four months, since almost one-third of mothers had returned to full-time work. By nine months, the babies were all eating solid food. While 54% of them were living in accommodation their families owned, (23) their parents had almost all experienced a drop in income, sometimes a steep one, mostly due to mothers' not working. Over 90% of the babies were immunised, and almost all were in very good health. Of the mothers, however, eleven percent had experienced post-natal depression – an alarming statistic, perhaps, but, once again, useful for mental health campaigns. Many of the babies were put in childcare while their mothers worked or studied, and the providers varied by ethnicity: children who were Maori or Pacific were more likely to be looked after by grandparents; European New Zealanders tended to be sent to day care.

(24) *Now we are two*, the third report, provides more insights into the children's development – physically, emotionally, behaviourally, and cognitively. Major changes in home environments are documented, like the socio-economic situation, and childcare arrangements. (24) Information was collected both from direct observations of the children and from parental interviews. Once again, a high proportion of New Zealand two-year-olds were in very good health. Two thirds of the children knew their gender, and used their own name or expressed independence in some way. The most common first word was a variation on 'Mum', and the most common favourite first food was a banana. Bilingual or multi-lingual children were in a large minority of 40%. (25) Digital exposure was high: one in seven two-year-olds had used a laptop or a children's computer, and 80% watched TV or DVDs daily; by contrast, 66% had books read to them each day.

(26) The fourth report evaluates twelve environmental risk factors that increase the likelihood of poor developmental outcomes for children, and draws on experiences in Western Europe, where the specific factors were collated. This, however, was the first time for their use in a New Zealand context. The factors include: (27) being born to an adolescent mother; having one or both parents on income-tested benefits; and, living in cramped conditions.

In addition to descriptive ones, future reports will focus on children who move in and out of vulnerability to see how these transitions affect their later life.

To date, *GUiNZ* has been highly successful with only a very small dropout rate for participants – even those living abroad, predominantly in Australia, have continued to provide information. The portrait *GUiNZ* paints of a country and its people is indeed revealing.

Let there be light?

A 'Incandescent light bulbs lit the 20th century; the 21st will be lit by LED lamps.' So stated the Nobel Prize Committee on awarding the 2014 prize for physics to the inventors of light-emitting diodes (LEDs).

Around the world, LED systems are replacing most kinds of conventional lighting since they use about half the electricity, and the US Department of Energy expects LEDs to account for 74% of US lighting sales by 2030.

(32) However, with lower running costs, LEDs may be left on longer, or installed in places that were previously unlit. (40) Historically, when there has been an improvement in lighting technology, far more outdoor illumination has occurred. Furthermore, many LEDs are brighter than other lights, and they produce a blue-wavelength light that animals misinterpret as dawn.

According to the American Medical Association, there has been a noticeable rise in obesity, diabetes, cancer, and cardio-vascular disease in people like shift workers exposed to too much (33) artificial light of any kind. (40) It is likely more pervasive LEDs will contribute to a further rise.

B In some cities, a brown haze of industrial pollution prevents enjoyment of the night sky; in others, a yellow haze from lighting has the same effect, and it is thought that almost (34) 70% of people can no longer see the Milky Way.

When a small earthquake disabled power plants in Los Angeles a few years ago, (28) the director of the Griffith Observatory was bombarded with phone calls by locals who reported an unusual phenomenon they thought was caused by the quake – a brilliantly illuminated night sky, in which around 7,000 stars were visible. In fact, this was just an ordinary starry night, seldom seen in LA due to light pollution!

Certainly, light pollution makes professional astronomy difficult, but it also endangers humans' age-old connection to the stars. It is conceivable that children who do not experience a true starry night may not speculate about the universe, nor may they learn about nocturnal creatures.

C (40) Excessive illumination impacts upon the nocturnal world. Around 30% of vertebrates and over 60% of invertebrates are nocturnal; many of the remainder are crepuscular – most active at dawn and dusk. (36) Night lighting, hundreds of thousands of times greater than its natural level, has drastically reduced insect, bird, bat, lizard, frog, turtle, and fish life, with even dairy cows producing less milk in brightly-lit sheds.

Night lighting has a vacuum-cleaner effect on insects, particularly moths, drawing them from as far away as 122 metres. As insects play an important role in pollination, and in providing food for birds, (36) their destruction is a grave concern. Using low-pressure sodium-vapour lamps or UV-filtered bulbs would reduce insect mortality, but an alternative light source does not help amphibians: frogs exposed to any (33) night light experience altered feeding and mating behaviour, making them easy prey.

Furthermore, birds and insects use the sun, the moon, and the stars to navigate. It is estimated that around (35) 500 million migratory birds are killed each year by collisions with brightly-lit structures, like skyscrapers or radio towers. In Toronto, Canada, the Fatal Light Awareness Program educates building owners about reducing such deaths by darkening their buildings at the peak of the migratory season. Still, over 1,500 birds may be killed within one night when this does not happen.

Non-migratory birds are also affected by light pollution – sleep is difficult, and waking up only occurs when the sun has overpowered artificial lighting, resulting in the birds' being too late to catch insects.

(31) Leatherback turtles, which have lived on Earth for over 150 million years, are now endangered as their hatchlings are meant to follow light reflected from the moon and stars to go from their sandy nests to the sea. Instead, they follow street lamps or hotel lights, resulting in death by dehydration, predation, or accidents, since they wander onto the road in the opposite direction from the sea.

D Currently, eight percent of all energy generated in the US is dedicated to public outdoor lighting, and much evidence shows that lighting and energy use are growing at around four percent a year, exceeding population growth. In some newly industrialised countries, lighting use is rising by 20%. (37 & 40) Unfortunately, as the developing world urbanises, it also lights up brightly, rather than opting for sustainability.

E There are several organisations devoted to restoring the night sky: one is the International Dark-Sky Association (IDA), based in Arizona, US. (30) The IDA draws attention to the hazards of light pollution, and works with manufacturers, planners, legislators, and citizens to encourage lighting only what is necessary when necessary.

With 58 chapters in sixteen countries, (30) the IDA has been the driving force behind the establishment of nine world reserves, most recently the 1,720-square-kilometre Rhon Biosphere Reserve in Germany. (30) IDA campaigns have also reduced street lighting in several US states, and changed national legislation in Italy.

F Except in some parks and observatory zones, the IDA does not defend complete darkness, acknowledging that urban areas operate around the clock. (39) For transport, lighting is particularly important. Nonetheless, there is an appreciable difference between harsh, glaring lights and those that illuminate the ground without streaming into the sky. The US Department of Transportation recently conducted research into highway safety, and found that a highway lit well only at interchanges was as safe as one lit along its entire length. In addition, reflective signage and strategic white paint improved safety more than adding lights.

(29) Research by the US Department of Justice showed that outdoor lighting may not deter crime. Its only real benefit is in citizens' perceptions: lighting reduces the fear of crime, not crime itself. Indeed, bright lights may compromise safety, as they make victims and property more visible.

Some dark-sky proponents suggest that where streetlights stay on all night, they have a lower lumen rating, or are controlled with dimmers; that they point downwards, or are fitted with directional metal shields. For private dwellings, low-lumen nightlights should be activated only when motion is detected.

G It is not merely the firefly, the fruit bat, or the frog that suffers from light pollution – many human beings no longer experience falling stars or any but the brightest stars, nor consequently ponder their own place in the universe. Hopefully, prize-winning LED lights will be modified and (40) used circumspectly to return to us all the splendour of the night sky.

WRITING: Task 1

The chart shows tea and coffee consumption per person in 2015 in the United Kingdom, New Zealand, Australia, Canada, the United States, Turkey, and Russia.

In general, more coffee was consumed in the seven countries than tea. The UK was the only place where tea and coffee were consumed equally, at 3 kg per person.

Elsewhere, there are nationalities that had similar consumption patterns. Australians and New Zealanders were moderate tea yet high coffee consumers, with the amounts being: in Australia, 1 kg of tea to 3 of coffee; in NZ, 1.25 kg of tea to 3.75 of coffee. Likewise, Canadians and Americans consumed similar amounts of both commodities. In Canada, 0.75 kg of tea was consumed, while 6.25 kg of coffee were consumed – the highest amount of all seven countries surveyed. In the US, a negligible amount of tea was consumed – 0.5 kg, while the second-highest amount of coffee was consumed – 5.5 kg.

In 2015, Turkey and Russia bucked the trend by preferring tea to coffee. Turks consumed 5 kg of tea but 2 kg of coffee; Russians consumed 2.5 kg of tea but 1.5 kg of coffee. (189 words)

Task 2

In some countries, fifteen-year-old school students are offered the choice of academic or vocational training. In this essay, I shall outline the reasons for adopting this two-stream system, and suggest its advantages.

As economies become more complex and more specialised, workers need a high degree of competence. Countries where there is an emphasis on vocational training hope to improve their economic competitiveness with a young skilled workforce. Those that have chosen to train prospective employees while still at school may have an even sharper competitive edge. In my view, an education system with a purely academic curriculum suits about 40% of students. Admittedly, people who go on to university generally find employment on graduation if not in their field, and successful post-graduates are almost invariably offered highly paid jobs. However, obtaining a degree takes time and dedication. For people who do not wish to do this, or who do not have the ability, they are far less likely to find work on leaving school where academic study has been the only option, particularly if their marks and self-esteem are low. A fortunate few do gain employment, but more commonly, even in the developed world, the majority of young school leavers are faced with unemployment – a scourge to society and a cause of distress to individuals. Therefore, countries like Germany have decided that all school students should be placed in either an academic or a vocational stream from fifteen. From an individual's perspective, being a plumber, for example, does not only mean that drainage functions well, but that the plumber belongs to an organisation of tradespeople and is part of a respected tradition. Starting this training at the age of fifteen ensures that an adolescent has a head start with regard to jobs as well as a clear focus and sense of personal worth.

I firmly believe there needs to be an alternative curriculum to the academic at secondary; otherwise, on leaving school, too many young people are adrift, and specialised industries lack a skilled workforce. (339 words)

SPEAKING:

Narrator	Recording 5. Test 1. Part 1 of the Speaking test. Listen to a candidate who is likely to be awarded a Nine answering questions in Part 1 of the Speaking test.
Examiner	Good afternoon. My name is Robert. Could you tell me your full name please?
Candidate	Carla Andrea Markulin Diaz.
Examiner	And where are you from?
Candidate	Colombia – a city called Buenaventura, on the Pacific coast.
Examiner	Could I check your ID, please? Thanks. First of all, Carla, I'd like to ask you a few questions about yourself. Could you tell me what you're doing at the moment: are you working or studying?
Candidate	I'm a student right now, but I've also got a part-time job.
Examiner	What do you do in your job?
Candidate	I'm a care assistant in an old people's home. I do all kinds of things: feeding, cleaning, washing the patients, chatting to them.
Examiner	Do you like your job?
Candidate	It's OK. I mean, it gives me enough money to live on while I'm studying, but I don't see myself doing it after I've graduated.
Examiner	What do you remember about your first day in this job?
Candidate	It was pretty stressful because I had to use English all day long. Back home in Colombia, I used English at work, but mainly for emails or when foreigners came for meetings. The other thing was that even though my name isn't hard to say, for some reason, my boss called me Carol, then Caroline, and finally, Carlee. It was kind of funny because I'd expected the elderly residents to be forgetful, but not her.

Examiner	Now, let's talk about taking photos. Do you mainly take photos with your phone, or do you use a camera?
Candidate	My phone's all right for snapshots, but my Nikon D300 has a lot more settings, and the size of the photo files is very large.
Examiner	Is there anything in particular you like to take photos of?
Candidate	Well, the Pacific coast in Colombia is beautiful, and you can see whales and dolphins at certain times of year. I've taken quite a few boat trips just for wildlife photography.
Examiner	Typically, what do you do with your photos after you've taken them?
Candidate	Honestly, I delete about 75%. Those that I do keep, I store on my laptop, and recently I've started leaving my laptop on with a slideshow playing when guests are at my place. I upload some of my pictures to Facebook, and a few really good ones to Flickr.
Examiner	Would you like to take classes in photography?
Candidate	Actually, I already have. I took a course at the ACP in architectural photography. I'm thinking of doing one in portraiture next.
Examiner	Let's move on to talk about parks. Do you go to any parks near where you live?
Candidate	I run around a little park called Bardon Park, at Coogee, almost every evening, and I sometimes go cycling in Centennial Park.
Examiner	Do you prefer a park with designated areas for leisure activities, or one that has mostly open space?
Candidate	I don't have a preference. When I was working in Beijing last year, there were very few large parks with greenery nearby, and none that was free, but there were little ones with all kinds of equipment like you have in the gym, and I joined in with some exercises there. In Sydney, we're spoilt for choice. There's any kind of park you want, including some national parks you can walk in for seven days without seeing another person.
Narrator	Recording 6. Part 2 of the Speaking test. Listen to Carla's two-minute topic.
Examiner	In this part, I'm going to give you a topic for you to speak about for two minutes. Before you speak, you'll have one minute to prepare, and you can write some notes on this paper if you like. Do you understand?
Candidate	Yes, I do.
Examiner	Here's your topic: I'd like you to tell me about an embarrassing experience you've had with food.
Narrator	One minute later.
Examiner	OK? Remember, you're going to speak for two minutes. Don't worry if I interrupt you to tell you when your time is up. Could you start speaking now, please, Carla?
Candidate	Right. Well, I've had quite a few uncomfortable experiences with food. I mean, I've had some pretty bad meals in restaurants, and I went to America when I was a kid, where I was too scared to eat anything. I'm sure I was an embarrassment to my parents. But, by far the most embarrassing food story I have is about my own cooking. When I was sixteen, my cousin and her French fiancé came to stay with my family because he was working at the port. Well, I decided to cook some French food for them to make him feel at home, or maybe just to show off. I dunno exactly; I *was* only sixteen. At the time, I couldn't really cook any Colombian food, let alone anything French! You see, in Colombia, it's common that children have so much homework that their parents don't let them cook, or that a maid or a cook does the cooking. Even in the holidays, every single meal was prepared for me. I guess I was spoilt. Anyway, my cousin and her husband were staying at our place, and on the fourth or fifth night, I made a French flan with custard and fresh strawberries. Basically what happened was that I didn't follow the recipe. The custard needed six eggs, but we only had four, and while I could've asked my mother to get some more, I thought it didn't matter if I only used four. I added some corn flour to make the custard set. When I put the flan into the oven, it was a bit wobbly, but I thought baking would help. When I took it out, it was still wobbly, and when I decorated it, the strawberries sank into the

custard, so I covered the whole thing up with whipped cream, sprayed on out of an aerosol. I didn't even know how to whip the cream.

When my mother served the dessert, my cousin said how lovely it looked, even though it was just a mountain of cream. Then, when my mother cut it – oh my God – the whole thing collapsed and dribbled all over the table. It was horrible. My cousin's husband burst out laughing, and I spent the rest of the night in my bedroom. *(378 words)*

Examiner	Did you ever cook the dish again?
Candidate	No. That was the end of French cuisine for me.

Narrator	Recording 7. Part 3 of the Speaking test. Listen to the rest of Carla's test.
Examiner	So you've told me about an embarrassing food story, and now I'd like to discuss some more general questions related to food and the food industry. First of all: natural versus processed food. Do people these days eat enough natural food?
Candidate	This depends on quite a few different things. It depends on where you live, what your budget is, or how much time you have, as well as on your level of education. For instance, at work, my colleagues who are nurses know what constitutes a healthy diet, but the women – especially the ones with families – just don't have time to prepare healthy lunches for themselves. They survive on instant noodles at work, and *that* kind of food is about as processed as you can get. In Colombia, the food is really wonderful, you can grow absolutely anything, but in big cities, people follow American trends, and eat a lot of junk. Obesity has risen dramatically in the past ten years.
Examiner	To what extent are food producers responsible for the health of consumers?
Candidate	That's a tricky question because on the one hand, food is a huge industry, but on the other, obesity, diabetes, or even gluten intolerance may be caused or exacerbated by processed food.
Examiner	So, is the industry responsible?
Candidate	Ultimately, no. But I think food labelling should be accurate.
Examiner	Now, let's consider global food security. There are predictions of serious global food insecurity within our lifetime. What do you think about these predictions, and what might be done to improve global food security?
Candidate	This isn't something I know much about, but I was on holiday in North Africa a few years ago when subsidies were taken off rice in one country, and there were riots. There were also tensions because people from a neighbouring country, where there were still subsidies, were smuggling cheap food over the border. I imagine a situation like this could escalate. What might be done? Well, international aid is one possibility in the North-African scenario. I think in South America, salty soil and erratic rainfall are meaning smaller rice crops. Maybe scientists could develop rice that doesn't mind so much salt or so little water. And researchers might work more regionally or internationally, rather than just for the good of their own economies.
Examiner	Thank you very much. That is the end of the Speaking test.

Before You Do Test 2

- Prepare some snacks and drinks.

- Find a reliable stopwatch or clock.

- Use an electronic device to access the online audio at www.mheIELTS6practicetests.com

- Find a place where you can work with no interruptions for four hours – three for the exam + one to go through the answers.

- Note: This time, there are fewer tips.

HOW TO GET A SEVEN

Section 1 Question 1	**Think logically.** If the total number of bedrooms in apartment #414 is three, the number of double bedrooms can only be one, two, or three.
	Listen for sentence stress. Jack says the virtual tour showed apartments with one double bedroom, but Peter says: '*Mostly*, that's true, but…'
Q2	**Spell a plural correctly.**
Q3	**Don't worry if an answer is easy.**
Q5-6	**Know your numbers.**
	To avoid a spelling mistake, **write a numeral** ('8 or 8th') **not a number** ('eighth').

TEST 2

Listening

Firstly, tear out the Test 2 Listening / Reading Answer Sheet at the back of this book.

The Listening test lasts for about 20 minutes.

Write your answers on the pages below as you listen. After Section 4 has finished, you have ten minutes to transfer your answers to your Listening Answer Sheet. You will need to time yourself for this transfer.

After checking your answers on pp 104-108, go to page 9 for the raw-score conversion table.

 PLAY RECORDING #8.

SECTION 1   Questions 1-10

RENTING AN APARTMENT

Questions 1-6

Complete the table below.

Write **ONE WORD OR A NUMBER** for each answer.

Address:	(**Example**) <u>96</u> Hobson Street
Apartment #414:	
Number of bedrooms:	3
Number of double bedrooms:	(**1**)………………..
Number of bathrooms:	1
Dishwasher and washing machine: Yes	
Other features:	Small (**2**)………………..
Weekly rental:	$450
Apartment #1520:	
Number of bedrooms:	3
Number of double bedrooms:	1
Number of bathrooms:	1
Dishwasher and washing machine: (**3**)………………..	
Other features:	• Large L-shaped living room • Views • Secure (**4**)………………..
Weekly rental:	(**5**) $………………..
Date lease commences:	(**6**)………………..March
Signed by the tenant:	Mr Peter Park

69

LISTENING	SECTION 1	SECTION 2	SECTION 3	SECTION 4
READING				
WRITING				
SPEAKING				

HOW TO GET A SEVEN

Q7	**Understand inference, especially negative concepts.** Peter does *not* say any of the words in the correct option. He talks about the desk, not the space. However, he uses the verb 'doubt', which is negative to talk about the desk.
	Ignore an option that is not mentioned at all.
Q8	**Understand inference.** Peter gives examples of the correct option.
	Ignore information that relates to someone else. Peter is the focus of the question *not* Jack.
Q9	**Ignore a partial answer.** While Jack's story is amusing, this is not mainly why he tells it.
Q10	**Listen for information *throughout* the section.** (See the highlighted evidence in the recording script.)
	Listen for sentence stress when Peter talks about his aunt.
Section 2 Q11	**Know your grammar.** The answer is a singular noun because it is preceded by 'the' and followed by 'is'.
	Listen for a cue *after* another part of speech. 'Threatened' is in the question, but 'under threat' is in the cue.
Q14	**Listen for the same word.**
	Listen for sentence stress. This is the first time you hear the word that is the answer, but, as the speaker has been talking about *male* honeybees, it's likely he's going to mention *female* bees next.
	Use your general knowledge. If you know about bees, you'll know the gender of the workers.
Q15	**Know your numbers.** This is a large one because the speaker says 'up to'.

Questions 7-10

Choose the correct letter, A, B, or C.

7   Peter suggests Jack's father's desk may not be useful because

    A   the space is limited.

    B   the apartment is furnished.

    C   the desk is the wrong style.

8   Peter objects to Jack's idea about lunch because

    A   the neighbours may not come.

    B   it will be inconvenient.

    C   he cannot cook.

9   Jack mentions his experience with the taxi

    A   to tell an amusing story.

    B   to warn Peter about staying out late.

    C   to suggest neighbours can be helpful.

10   Overall, Peter and Jack think help from relatives is……useful.

    A   always

    B   sometimes

    C   seldom

Play Audio PLAY RECORDING #9.

SECTION 2   Questions 11-20

BEEKEEPING FOR BEGINNERS

Questions 11-15

Complete the sentences below.

Write ONE WORD OR A NUMBER for each answer.

11   Currently, the ……………….. of bees is threatened.

12   In a biologically ……………….. society, one female mates with many males.

13   Ancient Egyptians cultivated bees at least ……………….. years ago.

14   ……………….. worker honeybees live the shortest time.

15   Queen honeybees can lay up to ……………….. eggs at a time.

HOW TO GET A SEVEN

Q16	**Predict before you listen.** It's likely the word 'clothing' or a type of clothing will be mentioned.
	Note: If you write 'clothes', you will not get a mark.
	You must include at least one adjective in your answer.
Q17	**Predict before you listen.** Since bees can be dangerous to humans, this answer will relate to humans' physical condition.
	The answer must be three words, including a pronoun that refers to the *people* not the bees.
Q18-20	**Take notes.** Some elements will be mentioned twice. Although you're asked for only three, if you take notes on *all* the elements, your answers will probably be correct.
	A = cover (top); **H** = _____ (bottom);
	B = _____; **C** = _____, below lid;
	D = two _____; **E** = screen below D; **F** = _____;
	G, above stand, = _____ preventing animals from getting inside.

LISTENING
READING
WRITING
SPEAKING

SECTION 1   SECTION 2   SECTION 3   SECTION 4

Questions 16-17

Answer the questions below.

*Write **THREE WORDS** for each answer.*

16   What should people wear when dealing directly with bees?

   ………………..………………..

17   What must people who would like to keep bees consider first?

   ………………..………………..

Questions 18-20

Label the diagram below.

*Write the correct letter, **A-H**, next to questions 18-20.*

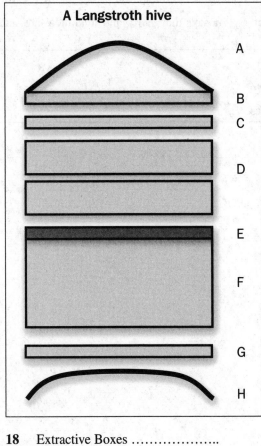

A Langstroth hive

A
B
C
D
E
F
G
H

18   Extractive Boxes ………………..

19   Optional Glass ………………..

20   Brood Chamber ………………..

HOW TO GET A SEVEN

Section 3 Q21	**Listen for paraphrases.** 'Overall' in the stem = 'On the whole' in the recording; and, 'impressive' = 'rather good'. **Beware of a distractor.** One speaker does say that the research for the essays came from 'reliable' sources, but that is not the essays' entire contents, and it's the view of one speaker only.
Q22	**Ignore false information.** Sylvia thinks the research is reliable. **Beware of a distractor.** Later, Jim says the essays lack paragraphs.
Q23	**Understand inference.** Jim says writers 'need to steer clear of …' while 'avoiding … is a good idea'. **Beware of distractors.** The professor talks about proving other academics wrong, and Sylvia mentions 'et cetera'.
Q24	**Listen for a synonym.** 'Inaccurate' in the option = '…' in the recording. **Beware of a distractor.** Sylvia says that 'nerd' and 'real men' are slang, *not* 'assigned'.
Q25-26	**Think logically.** **Beware of distractors.** **Listen for paraphrases.**

Play
Audio   PLAY RECORDING #10.

SECTION 3   Questions 21-30

RESEARCH INTO ESSAY-WRITING

Questions 21-26

Choose the correct letter, A, B, or C.

21   Overall, Sylvia and Jim think the content of the students' essays is

    A   reliable.

    B   impressive.

    C   predictable.

22   Sylvia, the female student, says that many of the essays she read

    A   had insufficient research.

    B   seemed like oral presentations.

    C   lacked paragraphing.

23   Jim, the male student, says that good academic writers

    A   avoid words like 'should' and 'never'.

    B   often prove other academic writers wrong.

    C   use expressions like 'et cetera'.

24   According to the professor, in: 'Men who avoid cigarettes may be assigned as nerds', the word 'assigned' is

    A   ambiguous.

    B   slang.

    C   inaccurate.

25   What is the problem with the word 'smocking' in the students' essays?

    A   It is wrongly spelt.

    B   It is rather old-fashioned.

    C   A spell checker won't find it.

26   What is 'smocking'?

    A   Decoration on clothing

    B   A kind of honeycomb

    C   A serious illness

LISTENING   SECTION 1   SECTION 2   SECTION 3   SECTION 4
READING
WRITING
SPEAKING

HOW TO GET A SEVEN

Q27-29	Avoid answering from your own belief.
	Ignore false information.
	Match a concept in the statement with examples in the recording.
	Listen for a paraphrase.
Section 4 Q31	Listen for the word *after* a cue, 'commercial'.
Q32	Listen for the word *after* a cue, 'develop or apportion'.

LISTENING
READING
WRITING
SPEAKING

| SECTION 1 | SECTION 2 | SECTION 3 | SECTION 4 |

Questions 27-29

In the professor's opinion, what do good academic writers do?

*Choose **THREE** answers from the box, and write the correct letter, A-H, next to questions 27-29.*

> **They:**
>
> | A | write a single draft. |
> |---|---|
> | B | write fewer words than poor writers. |
> | C | use unusual vocabulary. |
> | D | punctuate carefully. |
> | E | avoid personal pronouns. |
> | F | avoid giving opinions. |
> | G | do a lot of research. |
> | H | give their readers pleasure. |

Question 30

Choose the correct letter, A, B, or C.

30 The professor asks Sylvia to

  A limit her theoretical research.

  B collect some more student essays.

  C meet again in one month's time.

Play Audio **PLAY RECORDING #11.**

SECTION 4   Questions 31-40

ROAD CONGESTION AND MARKET FAILURE

Questions 31-35

Complete the sentences below.

*Write **NO MORE THAN TWO WORDS** for each answer.*

31 Road congestion, carbon emissions, and commercial ……………….. are examples of market failure.

32 The lecturer defines market failure as the inability of the free market to develop or apportion ……………….. efficiently.

33 Some markets fail completely because firms cannot seek profit within those markets. The lecturer gives the example of ……………….. .

34 Markets fail partially in many ways, one of which is ……………….. – when too many goods or services are produced.

35 Negative externalities are the failure of consumers or producers consider the results of their actions on third ……………….. .

LISTENING   SECTION 1   SECTION 2   SECTION 3   SECTION 4
READING
WRITING
SPEAKING

HOW TO GET A SEVEN

Q36	**Identify a function.** 'Back to business' suggests a …
Q37	**Listen for a synonym.** 'As incomes rise' = '…'
Q38	**Think logically.** It's unlikely traffic *went down* by 60%. **Ignore numbers that refer to other things.**
Q39	**Listen for a paraphrase.**
Q40	**Listen for intonation and stress.** The woman's pronunciation in her final sentence shows the attitude of many drivers.

Questions 36-40

*Choose the correct letter, **A**, **B**, or **C**.*

36   The speaker's story about London traffic in 1916 is

    A   an entertaining apology.

    B   a relevant digression.

    C   an amusing story.

37   What connection does the lecturer make between public transport and wealth?

    A   As public transport becomes more convenient, more people use it.

    B   Use of public transport declines as wealth increases.

    C   Like alcohol and vacations, there are fashions in public transport use.

38   Road traffic was reduced in central London from 2011 to 2014 by more than

    A   10%.

    B   30%.

    C   60%.

39   How does the lecturer evaluate new road building and congestion charging?

    A   They are equally ineffective.

    B   Road construction is less effective than congestion charging.

    C   Congestion charging is less effective than road construction.

40   The lecturer thinks most drivers who contribute to congestion are

    A   unaware.

    B   undecided.

    C   unconcerned.

LISTENING
READING
WRITING
SPEAKING

PASSAGE 1   PASSAGE 2   PASSAGE 3

Reading

Firstly, turn over the Test 2 Listening Answer Sheet you used earlier to write your Reading answers on the back.

The Reading test lasts exactly 60 minutes.

Certainly, make any marks on the pages below, but transfer your answers to the answer sheet <u>as you read</u> since there is no extra time at the end to do so.

After checking your answers on pp 111-113, go to page 9 for the raw-score conversion table.

PASSAGE 1

*Spend about 20 minutes on **Questions 1-14**, based on Passage 1 below.*

STAINLESS STEEL

Uses

In any ordinary kitchen, there are numerous items made from stainless steel, including cutlery, utensils, and appliances. 'Inox' or '18/10' may be stamped on the base of a good stainless steel pot: 'Inox' is short for the French *inoxydable*; while 18 refers to the percentage of chromium in the stainless steel, and 10 to its nickel content.

In hospitals, laboratories and factories, stainless steel is used for many instruments and pieces of equipment because it can easily be sterilised, and it remains relatively bacteria-free, thus improving hygiene. Since it is mostly rust-free, stainless steel also does not need painting, so proves cost-effective.

As a decorative element, stainless steel has been incorporated into skyscrapers, like the Chrysler Building in New York, and the Jin Mao Building in Shanghai, the latter considered one of the most stunning contemporary structures in China. Bridges, monuments, and sculptures are often stainless steel; and, cars, trains, and aircraft contain stainless steel parts.

Recent alloys

As most pure metals serve little practical purpose, they are often combined or alloyed. Some examples of ancient alloys are bronze (copper + tin) and brass (copper + zinc). Carbon steel (iron + carbon), first made in small quantities in China in the sixth century AD, was produced industrially only in mid-nineteenth-century Europe. Stainless steel, which retains the strength of carbon steel with some added benefits, consists of iron, carbon, chromium, and nickel, and may contain trace elements. Stainless steel is a new invention – Austenitic stainless steel was patented by German engineers in 1912, the same year that Americans created ferritic stainless steel, while Martensitic stainless steel was patented as late as 1919.

Properties

The name, stainless steel, is misleading since, where there is very little oxygen or a great amount of salt, the alloy will, indeed, stain. In addition, stainless steel parts should not be joined together with stainless steel nuts or bolts as friction damages the elements; another alloy, like bronze, or pure aluminium or titanium must be used.

In general, stainless steel does not deteriorate as ordinary carbon steel does, which rusts in air and water. Rust is a layer of iron oxide that forms when oxygen reacts with the iron in carbon steel. Because iron oxide molecules are larger than those of iron alone, they wear down the steel, causing it to flake and eventually snap. Stainless steel, however, contains between 13-26% chromium, and,

LISTENING
READING
WRITING
SPEAKING

PASSAGE 1   PASSAGE 2   PASSAGE 3

LISTENING
READING
WRITING
SPEAKING

PASSAGE 1   PASSAGE 2   PASSAGE 3

with exposure to oxygen, forms chromium oxide, which has molecules the same size as the iron ones beneath, meaning they bond strongly to form an invisible film that prevents oxygen or water from penetrating. As a result, the surface of stainless steel neither rusts nor corrodes. Furthermore, if scratched, the protective chromium-oxide layer of stainless steel repairs itself in a process known as passivation, which also occurs with aluminium, titanium, and zinc.

Varieties

There are over 150 grades of stainless steel with various properties, each distinguished by its crystalline structure. Austenitic stainless steel, comprising 70% of global production, is barely magnetic, but ferritic and Martensitic stainless steel function as magnets because they contain more nickel or manganese. Ferritic stainless steel – soft and slightly corrosive – is cheap to produce, and has many applications, while Martensitic stainless steel, with more carbon than the other types, is incredibly strong, so it is used in fighter jet bodies, but is also the costliest to produce.

Recyclability

Stainless steel can be recycled completely, and these days, the average stainless steel object comprises around 60% of recycled material.

Cutting-edge application

In the last few years, 3D printers have become widespread, and stainless steel infused with bronze is the hardest material that a 3D printer can currently use.

In 3D printing, an inkjet head deposits alternate layers of stainless steel powder and organic binder into a build box. After each layer of binder is spread, overhead heaters dry the object before another layer of powder is added. Upon completion of printing, the whole object, still in its build box, is sintered in an oven, which means the object is heated to just below melting point, so the binder evaporates. Next, the porous object is placed in a furnace so that molten bronze can replace the binder. To finish, the object is blasted with tiny beads that smooth the surface.

Appraisal

In less than a century, stainless steel has become essential due to its relatively cheap production cost, its durability, and its renewability. Used in the new manufacturing process of 3D printing, its future looks bright.

LISTENING
READING
WRITING
SPEAKING

PASSAGE 1　　PASSAGE 2　　PASSAGE 3

HOW TO GET A SEVEN

Passage 1 Question 2	**Look for synonyms.** **Beware of a distractor.** Although stainless steel is cost-effective, it is not necessarily cheap.
Q4	**Scan for a date.** **Look for a different part of speech.** There is a noun in the option, but an adjective in the passage.
Q5	**Read closely** to see that the statement contains a negative idea, but the passage has a positive one.
Q6	**Read closely** to see that the statement and the passage contain the same information.
Q8	**Match the type of stainless steel with a percentage produced in the passage.**
Q9	**Read closely** about Martensitic stainless steel. Is there information about its production? Is it produced in China?
Q10	**Read closely** about recycling. Is there information about where recycling takes place?

Questions 1-4

*Choose the correct letter, **A**, **B**, **C**, or **D**.*

Write the correct letter in boxes 1-4 on your answer sheet.

1   A stainless steel pot with '18/10' stamped on it contains

    A   18% carbon and 10% iron.

    B   18% iron and 10% carbon.

    C   18% chromium and 10% nickel.

    D   18% nickel and 10% chromium.

2   Hospitals and laboratories use stainless steel equipment because it

    A   is easy to clean.

    B   is inexpensive.

    C   is not disturbed by magnets.

    D   withstands high temperatures.

3   Stainless steel has been used in some famous buildings for its

    A   durability.

    B   beauty.

    C   modernity.

    D   reflective quality.

4   The first type of stainless steel was patented in

    A   China in 1912.

    B   Germany in 1912.

    C   the UK in 1919.

    D   the US in 1919.

Questions 5-11

Do the following statements agree with the information given in Passage 1?

In boxes 5-11 on your answer sheet, write:

    TRUE   *if the statement agrees with the information.*

    FALSE   *if the statement contradicts the information.*

    NOT GIVEN *if there is no information on this.*

5   Stainless steel does not stain.

6   Carbon steel rusts as its surface molecules are smaller than those of iron oxide.

7   Passivation is unique to stainless steel.

8   Austenitic stainless steel is the most commonly produced type.

9   These days, Martensitic stainless steel is mainly produced in China.

10   Currently, the recycling of stainless steel takes place in many countries.

11   Close to two-thirds of a stainless steel object is made up of recycled metal.

LISTENING
READING
WRITING
SPEAKING

PASSAGE 1   PASSAGE 2   PASSAGE 3

HOW TO GET A SEVEN

Q12-14	**Find the single paragraph about 3D printing.** **Read closely.**
Passage 2 Q15-18	**Skim the headings** *before* **you read the passage, but when reading each paragraph decide what it's about yourself**, then see what matches the list of headings. **Cross out the headings you choose**, so you don't choose them again later by mistake.
Q15	There are two headings about the GSL. Eliminate the one not connected to Paragraph B, but don't cross it out as you may need it later.
Q16	**Look for a synonym** for 'overhauling'. 'Overhauling' is negative, so look for a negative idea in Paragraph C.
Q17	**Scan for acronyms** (abbreviations made up of capital letters, eg: GSL). Find the paragraph with both NGSL and NAWL. **Beware of a distractor.** The origins of the NAWL are mentioned briefly in Paragraph D, but they are not what D is *mainly* about.
Q18	'Advent' means 'the arrival of someone or something important'. The CEC is a 'well-known' collection, and most of one paragraph is about corpora.
Q19	**Look for a signpost word.** 'Still' means a negative idea follows.

Questions 12-14

Label the diagrams below.

*Choose **NO MORE THAN TWO WORDS** from the passage for each answer.*

Write your answers in boxes 12-14 on your answer sheet.

3D printing using stainless steel and bronze

Sintering	Replacing the binder	Finishing
BUILD BOX in OVEN	OBJECT in (13)………………..	
Object heated to just below (12)……………….. to evaporate binder.	Binder replaced with molten bronze.	Object blasted with (14)……………….. .

PASSAGE 2

*Spend about 20 minutes on **Questions 15-27**, based on Passage 2 below.*

Questions 15-19

Passage 2 has six paragraphs: **A-F**.

*Choose the correct heading for paragraphs **B-F** from the list of headings below.*

*Write the correct number, **i-ix**, in boxes 15-19 on your answer sheet.*

List of Headings
i English vocabulary is hard to learn
ii Comparison of the NGSL and the NAWL
iii Description of the GSL
iv Utility and frequency should guide the choice of new lexis
v Reservations about lists and corpora
vi Learning the NAWL raises an IELTS candidate's score
vii Reasons for overhauling the GSL
viii Benefits of the NAWL
ix Advent of corpora

Example	*Answer*
Paragraph **A**	**iv**

15   Paragraph **B**

16   Paragraph **C**

17   Paragraph **D**

18   Paragraph **E**

19   Paragraph **F**

Word lists

A As any language learner knows, the acquisition of vocabulary is of critical importance. Grammar is useful, yet communication occurs without it. Consider the utterance: 'Me station.' Certainly, 'I'd like to go to the station' is preferable, but a taxi driver will probably head to the right place with 'Me station.' If the passenger uses the word 'airport' instead of 'station', however, the journey may well be fraught. Similarly, 'What time train Glasgow?' signals to a station clerk that a timetable is needed even though 'What time does the train go to Glasgow?' is correct. In both of these requests, nouns – 'station', 'time', 'train', and 'Glasgow' – carry most of the meaning; and, generally speaking, foreign-language learners, like infants in their mother tongue, acquire nouns first. Verbs also contain unequivocal meaning; for instance, 'go' indicates departure not arrival. Furthermore, 'Go' is a common word, appearing in both requests above, while 'the' and 'to' are the other frequent items. Thus, for a language learner, there may be two necessities: to acquire both useful *and* frequent words, including some that function grammatically. It is a daunting fact that English contains around half a million words, of which a graduate knows 25,000. So how does a language learner decide which ones to learn?

B The General Service List (GSL), devised by the American, Michael West, in 1953, was one renowned lexical aid. Consisting of 2,000 headwords, each representing a word family, GSL words were listed alphabetically, with definitions and example sentences, while a number alongside each word showed its number of occurrences per five million words, and a percentage beside each meaning indicated how often that meaning occurred. For 50 years, particularly in the US, the GSL wielded great influence: graded readers and other materials for primary schools were written with reference to it, and American teachers of English as a foreign language (EFL) relying heavily upon it.

C Understandably, West's 1953 GSL has been updated several times because, firstly, his list contained archaisms such as 'shilling', while lacking words that existed in 1953 but which were popularised later, like 'drug', 'OK', 'television', and 'victim'. Naturally, his list did not contain neologisms such as 'email'. However, around 80% of West's original inclusions were still considered valid, according to researchers Billuroğlu and Neufeld (2005). Secondly, what constituted a headword and a word family in the West's GSL was not entirely logical, and rules for this were formulated by Bauer and Nation (1995). Thirdly, technological advance has meant that billions of words can now be analysed by computer for frequency, context, and regional variation. West's frequency data was based on a 2.5-million-word corpus drawn from research by Thorndike and Lorge (1944), and some of it was unreliable. A 2013 incarnation of the GSL, called the New General Service List (NGSL), used a 273-million-word subsection of the Cambridge English Corpus (CEC), and research indicates this list provides a higher degree of coverage than West's.

HOW TO GET A SEVEN

Q20	**Scan for answers.** Remember, a list of items in a box follows the order of information in the passage, but the statements may not.
	Look for '**A West**', first, don't answer Q20 first. (It happens that West is at the beginning of the passage, but the answer for Q21 is some way down the passage.)
Q21	**Understand inference.** There is no phrase 'created the AWL' in the passage; you have to work out who created the AWL from other information.
Q22	**Check reference.** In 'rules for this', 'this' refers back to 'what constituted a headword and a word family'.
	Find a definition in the passage for a word in the question.

D A partner to the NGSL is the 2013 New Academic Word List (NAWL) with 2,818 headwords – a modification of Averill Coxhead's 2000 AWL. The NAWL excludes NGSL words, focusing on academic language, but, nevertheless, items in it are generally serviceable – they are merely not used often enough to appear in the NGSL. An indication of the difference between the two lists can be seen in just four words: the NGSL begins with 'a' and ends with 'zonings', whereas 'abdominal' and 'yeasts' open and close the NAWL.

E Over time, linguistics and EFL have become more dependent upon computerized statistical analysis, and large bodies of words have been collected to aid academics, teachers, and learners. One such body, known by the Latin word for body, 'corpus', is the CEC, created at Cambridge University in the UK. This well-known collection has two billion words of written and spoken, formal and informal, British, American, and other Englishes. Continually updated, its sources are very wide indeed – far wider than West's. Although the CEC is one of many English-language corpora, it is not the largest, but it was the one used by the creators of the NGSL and the NAWL.

F Still, a learner cannot easily access corpora, and even though the NGSL and NAWL are free online, a learner may not know how best to use them. Linguists have demonstrated that words should be learnt in a context (not singly, not alphabetically); that items in the same lexical set should be learnt together; that it takes at least six different sightings or hearings to learn one item; that written language differs significantly from spoken; and, that concrete language is easier to acquire than abstract. Admittedly, a list of a few thousand words is not so hard to learn, but language learning is not only about frequency and utility, but also about passion and poetry. Who cares if a word you like isn't in the top 5,000? If you like it or the way it sounds, you're likely to learn it. And, if you use it correctly, at least your IELTS examiner will be impressed.

Questions 20-24

Look at the following statements and the list of people on the following page.

*Match each statement with the correct person or people: **A-E**.*

*Write the correct letter, **A-E**, in boxes 20-24 on your answer sheet.*

20 He / She / They created the GSL.

21 He / She / They created the AWL.

22 He / She / They standardised headwords and word families.

HOW TO GET A SEVEN

Q23	**Understand inference.** Remember that West created the original GSL.
	Look for a different part of speech in the passage than that in the question.
Q24	**Understand connotation.** 'Narrow' is negative. Look for a negative adjective to describe research.
Q26	**Find a paraphrase** of 'at least'.
Q27	**Read the last five lines closely** as a writer's view is often found in the conclusion.
	Think logically. The instruction to this question asks for *NO MORE THAN THREE WORDS.* Your answers to Q25 and Q26 are short numbers, so this answer must have three words.

23 He / She / They reviewed the GSL for content validity.

24 His / Her / Their early research was narrow.

List of people
A West
B Billuroğlu and Neufeld
C Bauer and Nation
D Thorndike and Lorge
E Coxhead

Questions 25-27

Answer the questions below.

*Choose **NO MORE THAN THREE WORDS AND / OR A NUMBER** from the passage for each answer.*

Write your answers in boxes 25-27 on your answer sheet.

25 How many words are there in the complete Cambridge English Corpus?

....

26 At least how many times must a learner see or hear a new word before it can be learnt?

....

27 According to the writer, what else must there be a sense of for a person to learn a new word?

....

PASSAGE 3

*Spend about 20 minutes on **Questions 28-40**, based on Passage 3 below.*

● ●

WORLD HERITAGE DESIGNATION

Almost all cultures raise monuments to their own achievements or beliefs, and preserve artefacts and built environments from the past.

There has been considerable interest in saving cultural sites valuable to all humanity since the 1950s. In particular, an international campaign to relocate pharaonic treasures from an area in Egypt where the Aswan Dam would be built was highly successful, with more than half the project costs borne by 50 different countries. Later, similar projects were undertaken to save the ruins of Mohenjoh-daro in Pakistan and the Borobodur Temple complex in Indonesia.

The idea of listing world heritage sites (WHS) that are cultural or natural was proposed jointly by an American politician, Joseph Fisher, and a director of an environmental agency, Russell Train, at a White House conference in 1965. These men suggested a programme of cataloguing, naming, and conserving outstanding sites, under what became the World Heritage Convention, adopted by UNESCO* in November 1972, and effective from December 1975. Today, 191 states and territories have ratified the

*The United Nations Educational, Scientific, and Cultural Organisation, based in Paris, France.

LISTENING   PASSAGE 1   PASSAGE 2   PASSAGE 3
READING
WRITING
SPEAKING

convention, making it one of the most inclusive international agreements of all time. The UNESCO World Heritage Committee, composed of representatives from 21 UNESCO member states and international experts, administers the programme, albeit with a limited budget and few real powers, unlike other international bodies, like the World Trade Organisation or the UN Security Council.

In 2014, there were 1,007 WHS around the world: 779 of them, cultural; 197 natural; and, 31 mixed properties. Italy, China, and Spain are the top three countries by number of sites, followed by Germany, Mexico, and India.

Legally, each site is part of the territory of the state in which it is located, and maintained by that entity, but as UNESCO hopes sites will be preserved in countries both rich and poor, it provides some financial assistance through the World Heritage Fund. Theoretically, WHS are protected by the Geneva Convention, which prohibits acts of hostility towards historic monuments, works of art, or places of worship.

Certainly, WHS have encouraged appreciation and tolerance globally, as well as proving a boon for local identity and the tourist industry. Moreover, diversity of plant and animal life has generally been maintained, and degradations associated with mining and logging minimised.

Despite good intentions, significant threats to WHS exist, especially in the form of conflict. The Garamba National Park in the Democratic Republic of Congo is one example, where militias kill white rhinoceros, selling their horns to purchase weapons; and, in 2014, Palmyra – a Roman site in northern Syria – was badly damaged by a road built through it, as well as by shelling and looting. In fact, theft is a common problem at WHS in under-resourced areas, while pollution, nearby construction, or natural disasters present further dangers.

But most destructive of all is mass tourism. The huge ancient city of Angkor Wat, in Cambodia, now has over one million visitors a year, and the nearby town of Siem Reap – a village 20 years ago – now boasts an international airport and 300 hotels. Machu Picchu in Peru has been inundated by tourists to the point where it may now be endangered. Commerce has altered some sites irrevocably. Walkers along the Great Wall near Beijing are hassled by vendors flogging every kind of item, many unrelated to the wall itself, and extensive renovation has given the ancient wonder a Disneyland feel.

In order for a place to be listed as a WHS, it must undergo a rigorous application process. Firstly, a state takes an inventory of its significant sites, which is called a Tentative List, from which sites are put into a Nomination File. Two independent international bodies, the International Council on Monuments and Sites, and the World Conservation Union, evaluate the Nomination File, and make recommendations to the World Heritage Committee. Meeting once a year, this committee determines which sites should be added to the World Heritage List by deciding that a site meets at least one criterion out of ten, of which six are cultural, and four are natural.

In 2003, a second convention, effective from 2008, was added to the first. The Convention for the Safeguarding of Intangible Cultural Heritage has so far been ratified by 139 states – a notable exception being the US. Aiming to protect traditions rather than places, 267 elements have already been enshrined, including: Cambodia's Royal Ballet; the French gastronomic meal; and, watertight-bulkhead technology of Chinese junks.

The World Heritage Committee hopes that the states that agree to list such elements will also promote and support them, although, once again, commercialisation is problematic. For instance, after the French gastronomic meal was listed in 2010, numerous French celebrity chefs used the designation in advertising, and UNESCO debated delisting the element. The US has chosen not to sign the second convention due to implications to intellectual property rights. As things stand, with the first treaty, the US has far fewer nominated sites than its neighbour Mexico, partly because some Mexican sites are entire towns or city centres, and the US has no desire for its urban planning to be restricted by world-heritage status. St Petersburg, in Russia, which has its entire historic centre as a WHS, introduced strict planning regulations to maintain its elegant 18th-century appearance, only to discover thousands of minor infringements by owners preferring to do what they pleased with their properties.

LISTENING

READING

WRITING

SPEAKING

PASSAGE 1   PASSAGE 2   PASSAGE 3

HOW TO GET A SEVEN

Passage 3 Q28-31	**Scan for answers.** Circle all the countries in the passage while reading. **Remember, the items in the box are in the order of the passage, but questions are not.** Also, there are six countries, but only four answers.
Q30	**Look for a synonym** for 'put forward'.
Q31	Go to the beginning of the passage since you're looking for support *'prior to* the convention'.

With intangible elements, changes over time, due to modernisation or globalization, may be greater than those threatening buildings. Opponents of the second convention believe traditions should not be frozen in time, and are equally unconcerned if traditions dwindle or die.

Although the 1972 World Heritage Convention lacks teeth, and many of its sites are suffering, and although the 2003 Convention for the Safeguarding of Intangible Cultural Heritage has proven less popular, it would seem that the overall performance of these two instruments has been very good.

• •

Questions 28-31

Look at the following statements and the list of countries below.

*Match each statement with the correct country, **A-F**, below.*

*Write the correct letter, **A-F**, in boxes 28-31 on your answer sheet.*

28   It has the most world heritage sites.

29   Mass tourism has seriously threatened one of its sites.

30   Two men from here put forward the idea of a convention.

31   There was international support for a project here prior to the convention.

List of countries	
A	Pakistan
B	the US
C	Italy
D	China
E	Peru
F	France

LISTENING
READING
WRITING
SPEAKING

PASSAGE 1   PASSAGE 2   PASSAGE 3

HOW TO GET A SEVEN

Q32	**Mark the paragraph with the information for the flowchart.** **Copy an answer correctly** from the passage if a word is new to you.
Q33	**Copy a plural correctly.**
Q34	**Don't worry if an answer is easy.**
Q39	**Understand inference and connotation.** The focus of the passage is on planning regulations, but the focus of the question is on property owners. 'Infringements' and '[doing] what they please' are negative, so find a negative ending from the list.

LISTENING
READING
WRITING
SPEAKING

PASSAGE 1   PASSAGE 2   PASSAGE 3

Questions 32-35

Complete the flowchart below.

*Choose **ONE WORD OR A NUMBER** from the passage for each answer.*

Write your answers in boxes 32-35 on your answer sheet.

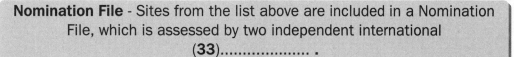

SITE REGISTRATION
Inventory - A state or territory takes an inventory of its important sites, called a (**32**)....................List.

Nomination File - Sites from the list above are included in a Nomination File, which is assessed by two independent international (**33**).................... .

Exernal File Evaluation - To be listed as a WHS, a site must meet at least (**34**)....................out of ten criteria. Most of these are (**35**).................... , but there are some natural and mixed ones too.

Questions 36-40

*Complete each sentence with the correct ending, **A-G**, below.*

*Write the correct letter, **A-G**, in boxes 36-40 on your answer sheet.*

36   The Convention for the Safeguarding of Intangible Cultural Heritage is designed to

37   The World Heritage Committee worries about

38   The US refused to sign the 2003 convention due to concerns about

39   Russian property owners have been annoyed by what they see as

40   Critics of the 2003 convention are not disturbed by

A	changes to or disappearance of traditions.
B	price rises due to world-heritage listing.
C	over-regulation connected to world-heritage listing.
D	protect traditions.
E	protect built environments.
F	intellectual property rights.
G	the commercial exploitation of listed traditions.

LISTENING
READING
WRITING
SPEAKING

TASK 1   TASK 2

LISTENING
READING
WRITING
SPEAKING

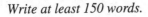
TASK 1   TASK 2

Writing

The Writing test lasts for 60 minutes. It has two tasks. Task 2 is worth twice as much as Task 1. Although candidates are assessed on four criteria for each task, an overall band, from 1-9, is awarded.

Task 1

Spend about 20 minutes on this task.

> **The two plans below show Pancha Village in 2005 and 2015.**
>
> **Write a summary of the information. Select and report the main features, and make comparisons where necessary.**

Write at least 150 words.

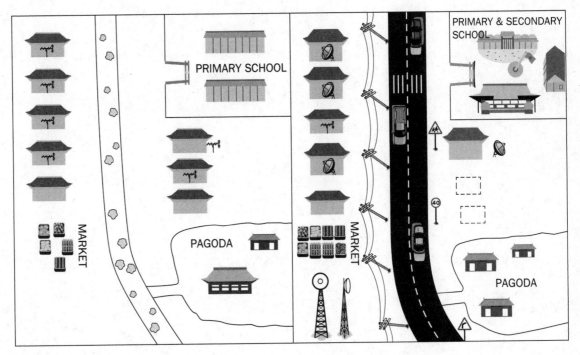

Task 2

Spend about 40 minutes on this task.

Write about the following topic:

> **Many developed countries now have large numbers of people over the age of 65.**
>
> **What problems might this cause?**
>
> **How can the problems be solved?**

Provide reasons for your answer, including relevant examples from your own knowledge or experience.

Write at least 250 words.

Speaking

PART 1

How might you answer the following questions?

1 Tell me about the accommodation you're currently living in.

2 Do you have a favourite part of the house?

3 Do you think you'll stay where you're living for a while?

4 Let's move on to talk about hats and caps. Do you ever wear a hat or a cap?

5 Why do some people wear hats or caps?

6 Do you think headgear was more popular in the past? Why?

7 Now, let's talk about time. When was the last time you were rather late?

8 How do you feel when other people are late?

9 Do you think people these days have enough time?

10 How do you think children perceive time?

Play Audio **PLAY RECORDING #12 TO HEAR PART ONE OF THE SPEAKING TEST.**

PART 2

How might you speak about the following topic for two minutes?

> **I'd like you to tell me about someone you think is attractive.**
>
> * Who is this person?
> * Why is he or she attractive?
> * How does this person dress?
>
> And, what do other people think about this person's looks?

Play Audio **PLAY RECORDING #13 TO HEAR PART TWO OF THE SPEAKING TEST.**

PART 3

How might you answer the following questions?

1 First of all, physical appearance and societal pressure.

Do you think these days, there's an over-emphasis on conforming to a norm, or on looking beautiful?

What are some of the dangers of this pressure to be attractive?

2 Let's talk about concepts of beauty throughout time.

Do you think our idea of beauty has changed over time, or basically stayed the same?

Play Audio **PLAY RECORDING #14 TO HEAR PART THREE OF THE SPEAKING TEST.**

Go to pp 112-114 for the recording scripts.

Answers

The highlighted text below is evidence for the answers above.

Narrator	Recording 8. Practice Listening Test 2. Section 1. Renting an Apartment. You will hear two men talking about renting an apartment with a third man. Read the example.
Peter	Hi Jack. Sorry I'm late.
Jack	No problem, Peter. We're still waiting for Mike. So, what did you think about 96 Hobson Street?
Peter	It's great.
Narrator	The answer is '96'. On this occasion only, the first part of the conversation is played twice. Before you listen again, you have 30 seconds to read questions 1 to 6.
Peter	Hi Jack. Sorry I'm late.
Jack	No problem, Peter. We're still waiting for Mike. So, what did you think about 96 Hobson Street?
Peter	It's great.
Jack	You don't think the building's too noisy, so close to the motorway?
Peter	It depends which apartment we take.
Jack	What are our options?
Peter	At the moment, there are two apartments available: one on the fourth floor; the other, higher up.
Jack	Do they get views?
Peter	Apartment 1520 does.
Jack	Last night, I went online and took a virtual tour of the building. One thing I noticed was that three-bedroom apartments have only one double bedroom.
Peter	Mostly, that's true, but apartment 414 has (1) two.
Jack	What about bathrooms?
Peter	A single bathroom in each apartment.
Jack	And (2) balconies?
Peter	Four fourteen has two small (2) balconies off the bedrooms.
Jack	The kitchens in the tour looked good, but I can't remember whether they come with a dishwasher and a washing machine.
Peter	(3) Yes, they do. The kitchen in 1520 is quite small, but there's a large L-shaped living room to compensate.
Jack	I know Mike's got a car. Is there a (4) garage?
Peter	Secure (4) parking is limited to tenants who pay over $600 a week.
Jack	How much *is* the rental on the apartments you saw?
Peter	Four Fourteen is $450, and 1520 is (5) $610.
Jack	That's quite a difference.
Peter	Yeah.
Jack	And 1520's only got one double bedroom, right?
Peter	Uh huh. But it's facing away from Hobson Street, so it'll be quiet, and Mike's car would be safe.

Jack	Right.
Peter	I'm planning to sign the lease on Friday. The agent wants it to start in the second or third week of March.
Jack	I'll be away until the seventh.
Peter	All right. Let's have it start on the (6) ninth.
Jack	The (6) ninth sounds fine.
Narrator	Before you listen to the rest of the conversation, you have 30 seconds to read questions 7 to 10.
Jack	Looks like Mike won't be here for another 20 minutes.
Peter	That's a pity. I wonder if we could use his car to move?
Jack	I'm sure we'll be able to. (10 *useful & useless*) My dad said he'd lend a hand too, and he's got a truck.
Peter	That'd be good. With a truck we could move everything in one go.
Jack	(10) He's also got lots of stuff he doesn't need anymore – plates bowls, pots and pans, and a big old wooden desk.
Peter	(7) I doubt that a large desk would fit in any of the bedrooms. What we really need is a couch and some things to decorate the living room.
Jack	When I rented last year, we spent lots of time before we moved in choosing nice furniture and decorations, but we neglected the basics, like rubbish bins and cleaning supplies. (10 *useless*) Then, there was the problem that some people gave us weird things, like a device my aunt bought for chopping onions. I mean, all you need is a sharp knife, right?
Peter	Yeah.
Jack	But we did do one great thing, which we should try again: we invited the neighbours to lunch one Saturday.
Peter	Complete strangers? (8) What about the cost?
Jack	The meal doesn't have to be fancy, and not everyone we ask will come.
Peter	Why bother? Especially when (8) I'll miss the football.
Jack	It's just a way to show that, even though we're students, we're generous and approachable.
Peter	OK.
Jack	And it does pay off. One night I came home in a taxi very late. Suddenly, I realised (9) I couldn't pay the driver because I'd left my wallet somewhere, so I ran upstairs, knocked on my neighbour's door, and he lent me some money.
Peter	Lucky you. All right. To sum up: we're borrowing your dad's truck; (10 *useful*) we're accepting some *useful* things from relatives; and, we're getting to know our neighbours.
Narrator	You now have 30 seconds to check your answers. That is the end of Section 1.
Narrator	Recording 9. Section 2. Beekeeping for beginners. You will hear a man talking about beekeeping for beginners. Before you listen, you have 30 seconds to read questions 11 to 15.
Beekeeper	Good morning.
	As you may be aware, all over the world, bees are under threat. For their (11) survival, the goodwill and hard work of enthusiasts like you is vital.
	Today, I'll present some facts about bees and beekeeping. Then, I'll show you a Langstroth hive, which is a type commonly used by beekeepers.
	Bees and bee products can be eaten, and beeswax used to make candles and cosmetics. And of course, bees pollinate plants, so are essential in agriculture.
	There are many kinds of bees: solitary and social. Social bees live in colonies in the wild, and can be cultivated in hives.
	The word (12) eusocial describes the organisation of bee society. It's spelt (12) EU plus social. It means there's one single reproductively active female to several males. It also signals a division of labour, and co-operative care of the young by non-breeding individuals. In addition to honeybees, there are (12) eusocial ants, termites, and naked vole rats.

Before humans cultivated honeybees, wild colonies were raided, and sadly, this continues today. In Spain, 8,000-year-old rock drawings depict such raids while Egyptian tomb paintings from (13) 4,500 years ago show domesticated bees. However, the ancient Egyptians did not understand bee society, and killed most of their insects in the quest for honey. Hives with moveable parts that ensure continual honey collection and the safety of the queen were designed just 170 years ago by the American, Lorenzo Langstroth.

It is only in the last 300 years that the functions of the different parts of a bee colony and of the three types of honeybees, themselves, have been understood.

A queen honeybee is the largest and most important member of honeybee society. She lives far longer than the other bees, up to three years; and, her pheromones control the colony. Drones, or *male* honeybees, make up around ten percent of a colony, and live for just four months. They mate with queens and forage, but do little else. (14) *Female* worker honeybees, constituting 90% of a colony, have a mere six-week lifespan, yet they are the busiest creatures: guarding, cleaning, nursing, fanning, and foraging.

The queen lays eggs after she has been inseminated by a drone while flying in the open air. She can lay up to (15) 2,000 eggs at one time. When unmated queens hatch from those 2,000 eggs, they will fight to the death, or one will fly away with a swarm to form her own colony elsewhere. The beauty of a Langstroth hive is that a beekeeper can separate out the laying queen, and easily kill egg cells containing potential queens.

Before you listen to the rest of the conversation, you have 30 seconds to read questions 16 to 20.

So let's look at some slides of a Langstroth hive. I can't open my own outside as it's winter, and not much is happening, but also because we'd all need to be wearing (16) good protective clothing. Bees sting, remember, and their venom is poisonous. Two percent of people who are stung experience an uncomfortable allergic reaction, and, without medical intervention, a tiny minority die from toxic shock. Anyone who'd like to keep bees must first determine (17) their allergic reaction first.

OK. Here's a Langstroth hive with nine elements. It stands at 1.5 metres, and contains (18) extractive boxes, from where you take the honey, and (20) a brood chamber, where the queen breeds. This hive's got two extractive boxes, but you can build it up to five.

The hive is wooden, with a cover and a stand at top and bottom. There's always a wooden lid, letter B on your diagram, and, (19) if keepers collect venom, there's a sheet of glass below the lid. (18) The extractive boxes are shallow because they're frequently handled. They hold 30 kilos of honey each, and a beekeeper couldn't lift one if it were any deeper. The thin screen beneath (18) the lower extractive box has holes that drones and worker bees can crawl through, but which are too small for the queen. She, therefore, remains in (20) the deep brood chamber, where the eggs are laid. The final element, above the stand, is a board that prevents other animals from getting inside.

Narrator	You now have 30 seconds to check your answers. That is the end of Section 2.

Narrator	Recording 10. Section 3. Research into essay-writing. You will hear two post-graduate students talking to their professor about their research into academic essay-writing. Before you listen, you have 30 seconds to read questions 21 to 26.
Professor	Come in, Sylvia. Come in Jim. How are you?
Sylvia	A bit tired, actually. I read 75 of the essays about smoking over the weekend.
Professor	And you, Jim?
Jim	I'm fine. I've read 20 so far. They're pretty interesting – a really good sample for our research.
Sylvia	Yes, I found them stimulating. (21) On the whole, their content is rather good. The students have done a fair bit of research.
Jim	That's true.
Sylvia	And they quote from reliable sources. The problems are more with style. (22) Many of the ones I read seemed like oral presentations instead of academic essays.
Jim	I'd agree with that.
Sylvia	For a start, some of the vocabulary was inappropriate. Take this sentence from a conclusion: 'To get smokers to cut down or give up, there should be more ads on TV about the health problems et cetera.'
Professor	Yes. Students forget that 'get' and most phrasal verbs are spoken.

evaporates. Next, the porous object is placed in a (13) furnace so that molten bronze can replace the binder. To finish, the object is blasted with (14) tiny beads that smooth the surface.

Appraisal

In less than a century, stainless steel has become essential due to its relatively cheap production cost, its durability, and its renewability. Used in the new manufacturing process of 3D printing, its future looks bright.

Word lists

A As any language learner knows, the acquisition of vocabulary is of critical importance. Grammar is useful, yet communication occurs without it. Consider the utterance: 'Me station.' Certainly, 'I'd like to go to the station' is preferable, but a taxi driver will probably head to the right place with 'Me station.' If the passenger uses the word 'airport' instead of 'station', however, the journey may well be fraught. Similarly, 'What time train Glasgow?' signals to a station clerk that a timetable is needed even though 'What time does the train go to Glasgow?' is correct. In both of these requests, nouns – 'station', 'time', 'train', and 'Glasgow' – carry most of the meaning; and, generally speaking, foreign-language learners, like infants in their mother tongue, acquire nouns first. Verbs also contain unequivocal meaning; for instance, 'go' indicates departure not arrival. Furthermore, 'Go' is a common word, appearing in both requests above, while 'the' and 'to' are the other frequent items. Thus, for a language learner, there may be two necessities: to acquire both useful *and* frequent words, including some that function grammatically. It is a daunting fact that English contains around half a million words, of which a graduate knows 25,000. So how does a language learner decide which ones to learn?

B (15) The General Service List (20) (GSL), devised by the American, Michael West, in 1953, was one renowned lexical aid. Consisting of 2,000 headwords, each representing a word family, GSL words were listed alphabetically, with definitions and example sentences, while a number alongside each word showed its number of occurrences per five million words, and a percentage beside each meaning indicated how often that meaning occurred. For 50 years, particularly in the US, the GSL wielded great influence: graded readers and other materials for primary schools were written with reference to it, and American teachers of English as a foreign language (EFL) relying heavily upon it.

C (16) Understandably, West's 1953 GSL has been updated several times because, firstly, his list contained archaisms such as 'shilling', while lacking words that existed in 1953 but which were popularised later, like 'drug', 'OK', 'television', and 'victim'. Naturally, his list did not contain neologisms such as 'email'. (23) However, around 80% of West's original inclusions were still considered valid, according to researchers Billuroğlu and Neufeld (2005). Secondly, (22) what constituted a headword and a word family in the West's GSL was not entirely logical, and rules for this were formulated by Bauer and Nation (1995). Thirdly, technological advance has meant that billions of words can now be analysed by computer for frequency, context, and regional variation. West's frequency data was based on a 2.5-million-word corpus (24) drawn from research by Thorndike and Lorge (1944), and some of it was unreliable. A 2013 incarnation of the GSL, called the New General Service List (NGSL), used a 273-million-word subsection of the Cambridge English Corpus (24) (CEC), and research indicates this list provides a higher degree of coverage than West's.

D (17) A partner to the NGSL is the 2013 New Academic Word List (NAWL) with 2,818 headwords – a modification of (21) Averill Coxhead's 2000 AWL. The NAWL excludes NGSL words, focusing on academic language, but, nevertheless, items in it are generally serviceable – they are merely not used often enough to appear in the NGSL. An indication of the difference between the two lists can be seen in just four words: the NGSL begins with 'a' and ends with 'zonings', whereas 'abdominal' and 'yeasts' open and close the NAWL.

E (18) Over time, linguistics and EFL have become more dependent upon computerized statistical analysis, and large bodies of words have been collected to aid academics, teachers, and learners. One such body, known by the Latin word for body, 'corpus', is the CEC, created at Cambridge University in the UK. This well-known collection has (25) two billion words of written and spoken, formal and informal, British, American, and other Englishes. Continually updated, its sources are very wide indeed – far wider than West's. Although the CEC is one of many English-language corpora, it is not the largest, but it was the one chosen by the creators of the NGSL and the NAWL.

F (19) Still, a learner cannot easily access corpora, and even though the NGSL and NAWL are free online, a learner may not know how best to use them. Linguists have demonstrated that words should be learnt in a context (not singly, not alphabetically); that items in the same lexical set should be learnt together; that it takes at least (26) six different sightings or hearings to learn one item; that written language differs significantly from spoken; and, that concrete language is easier to acquire than abstract. Admittedly, a list of a few thousand words is not so hard to learn, but language learning is not only about frequency and utility, but also about (27) passion and poetry. Who cares if a word you like isn't in the top 5,000? If you like it or the way it sounds, you're likely to learn it. And, if you use it correctly, at least your IELTS examiner will be impressed.

World heritage designation

Almost all cultures raise monuments to their own achievements or beliefs, and preserve artefacts and built environments from the past.

There has been considerable interest in saving cultural sites valuable to all humanity since the 1950s. In particular, an international campaign to relocate pharaonic treasures from an area in Egypt where the Aswan Dam would be built was highly successful, with more than half the project costs borne by 50 different countries. (31) Later, similar projects were undertaken to save the ruins of Mohenjo-daro in Pakistan and the Borobudur Temple complex in Indonesia.

(30) The idea of listing world heritage sites (WHS) that are cultural or natural was proposed jointly by an American politician, Joseph Fisher, and a director of an environmental agency, Russell Train, at a White House conference in 1965. These men suggested

Jim	Also, (23) they need to steer clear of 'should' and 'must'. When a writer has a hypothesis to prove, he or she doesn't want to put the readers off with such strong language.
	A writer needs to use verbs like 'could' or 'might' instead. (23) And avoiding adverbs like 'always' and 'never' is a must. After all, you never know when you'll be proven wrong!
Professor	Absolutely. Over the years, many colleagues have challenged my academic papers. I see you've circled 'et cetera', Sylvia, on several essays.
Sylvia	'Et cetera' is OK in note taking but not in academic writing.
Jim	Here's something else related to vocabulary. It's part of an argument about why people start smoking. At least, I *think* the student's written 'smoking'. Maybe it's 'smocking'?
Sylvia	Go on.
Jim	'Men who avoid cigarettes may be assigned as nerds. This ideology makes them dare to join in smocking activities to let us know they're real men.'
Professor	That is interesting. I mean, there's an attempt at sophistication, (24) with 'assigned' and 'ideology', but they're both used incorrectly.
Jim	And 'nerd' and 'real men' are slang.
Sylvia	Going back to the word 'smocking'. I read five essays out of 75 in which students wrote about 'smocking'. I must say it made me chuckle!
Professor	(25) What it does reveal is the danger of spell checkers – they can't alert a writer to words that really do exist.
Jim	What exactly is 'smocking'?
Sylvia	Here's a dictionary definition: (26) 'Ornamentation on a garment made by gathering together a section of material into tight pleats and sewing across it to make a pattern similar to a honeycomb.'
Jim	It sounds old-fashioned to me.
Sylvia	Yes, I had it on a dress when I was a girl.
Jim	Whatever was it doing in an essay on *smoking*?
Narrator	Before you listen to the rest of the conversation, you have 30 seconds to read questions 27 to 30.
Professor	So, let's discuss what good academic writers do. How do they avoid the embarrassment of writing about 'smocking'?
Sylvia	Simple. They check their work. They write second and third drafts.
Professor	In redrafting, (27-29) they also reduce redundancy.
Jim	Redundancy is a major issue. Listen to this: 'Second-hand smoke not only affects smokers but also people around them, even loved ones, like wives and children, and it can lead to illness.'
Professor	What would *you* have written?
Jim	'Second-hand smoke can lead to illness.'
Professor	(27-29) Six words instead of 24.
	(27-29) Good writers also avoid personal pronouns, like 'I' or 'me'. After all, they're trying to construct universal arguments, not just give their opinions.
Jim	Some of the essays I read certainly needed more paragraphs. They were hard for me to follow.
Professor	Indeed. An essay is not just about showing what the writer knows; (27-29) it's about giving the reader an enjoyable experience. So, when do you two think you'll be ready to start the theoretical part of your research?
Jim	I'm not sure. I'll see you next week about that.
Sylvia	I've already started, but I've got *so* much to read!
Professor	It seems to me, Sylvia, you've collected more than enough essays to analyse, and now you're in danger of reading too many academic articles. (30) I'd limit the time for your theoretical research to one month. OK?
Sylvia	Thanks. That's sound advice.
Narrator	You now have 30 seconds to check your answers. That is the end of Section 3.
Narrator	Recording 11. Section 4. Road Congestion and Market Failure. You will hear a lecture on road congestion as an example of market failure. Before you listen, you have 45 seconds to read questions 31 to 40.
Lecturer	Sorry I'm late – the traffic was unbelievable. However, my lateness is pertinent to today's topic: road congestion as an example of market failure. Next weeks' examples will be carbon emissions and commercial (31) fishing.

But what is market failure? Broadly speaking, it's when the free market fails to develop or apportion (32) resources efficiently. A market may fail completely or partially.

In the case of complete failure, resources cannot be allocated to satisfy need or want because there are insufficient incentives for profit-seeking firms to enter the market. Take (33) street lighting: without state intervention, there probably wouldn't be any, as it's unlikely private individuals would pay for it themselves. With no revenue generated and no profit earned, no firm would enter the street-lighting market either. That's why taxes are set aside for public goods.

There are many ways in which partial market failure occurs, but I'd like to focus on (34) over-supply, which is when markets produce too many goods or services. It commonly occurs with demerit goods, like alcohol or tobacco, and with negative externalities.

What are negative externalities? Well, the inability of consumers or producers to account for the effects of their actions on third (35) parties. Road congestion is a classic case.

(36) Oh, let me tell you something I read last night. The speed of traffic in central London has remained fairly constant over the past 100 years. Really? How can that be? Wasn't most traffic horse-drawn in 1916? Indeed, it was. But the fact remains: in central London, giant four-wheel drives and sleek sports cars travel about as fast as wagons pulled by horses!

Back to business. There are four main ways of dealing with congestion. One, a city increases the amount of road space. Two, it improves public transport. Three, it reduces the demand for travel. Or four, it increases the cost of private travel.

In the case of London, the first measure is counter-productive. There are enormous costs associated with construction, and a long delay between planning and availability. Once built, more roads only encourage more driving, and very soon, congestion rears its ugly head again.

On the surface, improving (37) public transport seems a great idea, but even when it's reliable, cheap, and convenient, (37) it's viewed as an inferior good. As incomes rise, most of us leave inferior goods behind. I mean, we used to drink beer; now we drink *boutique* beer. We used to holiday, locally, at the seaside; now we fly to Thailand!

What about reducing the demand for travel? Unfortunately, no one seems to know how to do this.

The fourth option, raising the cost of private travel has also had limited success. In London, we've experienced higher vehicle and fuel taxes, more expensive parking and licence fees, no-parking routes, and a raised driving age, but we've kept on driving. Other big cities have taken a different approach. Some Chinese cities limit drivers to four days a week, based on the final number of their licence plate; but, the rich just buy two cars. Sydney and Singapore have tolls on bridges and tunnels, yet people pay up, or drive longer routes to avoid tolls, creating traffic jams elsewhere.

In 2003, London opted for a congestion charge in the central city. Back then, the charge was £5 a day; it's now £11.50. From its inception, there was a discernible decrease in traffic. Estimates in 2004 by Transport for London, or TFL, were that traffic flow was reduced by almost 20% or 50,000 cars per day. Journeys were 15% faster. The number of bus journeys rose by 15%, and cycle usage by 30. (38) TFL stated that road traffic reduced a further 10% between 2011 and 14. However, a recent report has concluded that, by 2031, (39) congestion will have worsened by a staggering 60% even if strict measures are adopted immediately. It seems as though the cycle is similar to building more roads – a sharp initial improvement, a slower improvement over time, followed by stasis and decline.

So, to conclude: part of the reason for road congestion is an unquantifiable negative externality, exemplary of partial market failure. The free market is incapable of allocating resources efficiently. No matter what authorities do, people continue to drive. On some level, we all know congestion leads to more noise, pollution, accidents, and slower travel times, but cars are cheap and their outlay is fixed. Principally, we drive because we don't consider our actions in relation to anyone else's. (40) And, even if we did, I'm not sure most people would care!

Narrator   That is the end of the Listening test.
You now have ten minutes to transfer your answers to your answer sheet.

READING: Passage 1: **1.** C; **2.** A; **3.** B; **4.** B; **5.** F/False; **6.** T/True; **7.** F/False; **8.** T/True; **9.** NG/Not Given; **10.** NG/No **11.** T/True; **12.** melting point; **13.** Furnace; **14.** tiny beads. Passage 2: **15.** iii; **16.** vii; **17.** ii; **18.** ix; **19.** v; **20.** A; **21.** E; **22. 24.** D; **25.** 2/Two billion; **26.** 6/Six; **27.** Passion and poetry. Passage 3: **28.** C; **29.** E; **30.** B; **31.** A; **32.** Tentative; **33.** bodies **35.** cultural; **36.** D; **37.** G; **38.** F; **39.** C; **40.** A.

> *The highlighted text below is evidence for the answers above.*
>
> *If there is a question where 'Not given' is the answer, no evidence can be found, so there is no highlighted text.*

Stainless steel

Uses

In any ordinary kitchen, there are numerous items made from stainless steel, including cutlery, utensils, and appliances. 'Ino '18/10' may be stamped on the base of a good stainless steel pot: 'Inox' is short for the French *inoxydable*; (1) while 18 refe percentage of chromium in the stainless steel, and 10 to its nickel content.

(2) In hospitals, laboratories and factories, stainless steel is used for many instruments and pieces of equipment because it can be sterilised, and it remains relatively bacteria-free, thus improving hygiene. Since it is mostly rust-free, stainless steel also do need painting, so proves cost-effective.

(3) As a decorative element, stainless steel has been incorporated in skyscrapers, like the Chrysler Building in New York, and th Mao Building in Shanghai, the latter considered one of the most **stunning** contemporary structures in China. Bridges, monumer and sculptures are often stainless steel; and, cars, trains, and aircraft contain stainless steel parts.

Recent alloys

As most pure metals serve little practical purpose, they are often combined or alloyed. Some examples of ancient alloys are bronz (copper + tin) and brass (copper + zinc). Carbon steel (iron + carbon), first made in small quantities in China in the sixth century AD, was produced industrially only in mid-nineteenth-century Europe. Stainless steel, which retains the strength of carbon steel with some added benefits, consists of iron, carbon, chromium, and nickel, and may contain trace elements. (4) Stainless steel is a new invention – Austenitic stainless steel was patented by German engineers in 1912, the same year that Americans created ferritic stainless steel, while Martensitic stainless steel was patented as late as 1919.

Properties

(5) The name, stainless steel, is misleading since, where there is very little oxygen or a great amount of salt, the alloy will, indeed, stain. In addition, stainless steel parts should not be joined together with stainless steel nuts or bolts as friction damages the elements; another alloy, like bronze, or pure aluminium or titanium must be used.

In general, stainless steel does not deteriorate as ordinary (6) carbon steel does, which rusts in air and water. Rust is a layer of iron oxide that forms when oxygen reacts with the iron in carbon steel. Because iron oxide molecules are larger than those of iron alone they wear down the steel, causing it to flake and eventually snap. Stainless steel, however, contains between 13-26% chromium, ar with exposure to oxygen, forms chromium oxide, which has molecules the same size as the iron ones beneath, meaning they bond strongly to form an invisible film that prevents oxygen or water from penetrating. As a result, the surface of stainless steel neither rusts nor corrodes. Furthermore, if scratched, the protective chromium-oxide layer of stainless steel repairs itself in (7) a process known as passivation, which also occurs with aluminium, titanium, and zinc.

Varieties

There are over 150 grades of stainless steel with various properties, each distinguished by its crystalline structure. (8) Austeniti stainless steel, comprising 70% of global production, is barely magnetic, but ferritic and Martensitic stainless steel function as magnets because they contain more nickel or manganese. Ferritic stainless steel – soft and slightly corrosive – is cheap to prod and has many applications, while (9) Martensitic stainless steel, with more carbon than the other types, is incredibly strong, sc used in fighter jet bodies, but is also the costliest to produce.

Recyclability

Stainless steel can be recycled completely, and these days, (11) the average stainless steel object comprises around 60% of r material.

Cutting-edge application

In the last few years, 3D printers have become widespread, and stainless steel infused with bronze is the hardest material t printer can currently use.

In 3D printing, an inkjet head deposits alternate layers of stainless steel powder and organic binder into a build box. Afte of binder is spread, overhead heaters dry the object before another layer of powder is added. Upon completion of printin object, still in its build box, is sintered in an oven, which means the object is heated to just below (12) melting point, so

a programme of cataloguing, naming, and conserving outstanding sites, under what became the World Heritage Convention, adopted by UNESCO* in November 1972, and effective from December 1975. Today, 191 states and territories have ratified the convention, making it one of the most inclusive international agreements of all time. The UNESCO World Heritage Committee, composed of representatives from 21 UNESCO member states and international experts, administers the programme, albeit with a limited budget and few real powers, unlike other international bodies, like the World Trade Organisation or the UN Security Council.

In 2014, there were 1,007 WHS around the world: 779 of them, cultural; 197 natural; and, 31 mixed properties. (28) Italy, China, and Spain are the top three countries by number of sites, followed by Germany, Mexico, and India.

Legally, each site is part of the territory of the state in which it is located, and maintained by that entity, but as UNESCO hopes sites will be preserved in countries both rich and poor, it provides some financial assistance through the World Heritage Fund. Theoretically, WHS are protected by the Geneva Convention, which prohibits acts of hostility towards historic monuments, works of art, or places of worship.

Certainly, WHS have encouraged appreciation and tolerance globally, as well as proving a boon for local identity and the tourist industry. Moreover, diversity of plant and animal life has generally been maintained, and degradations associated with mining and logging minimised.

Despite good intentions, significant threats to WHS exist, especially in the form of conflict. The Garamba National Park in the Democratic Republic of Congo is one example, where militias kill white rhinoceros, selling their horns to purchase weapons; and, in 2014, Palmyra – a Roman site in northern Syria – was badly damaged by a road built through it, as well as by shelling and looting. In fact, theft is a common problem at WHS in under-resourced areas, while pollution, nearby construction, or natural disasters present further dangers.

But most destructive of all is mass tourism. The huge ancient city of Angkor Wat, in Cambodia, now has over one million tourists a year, and the nearby town of Siem Reap – a village 20 years ago – boasts an international airport and 300 hotels. (29) Machu Picchu in Peru has been inundated by visitors to the point where it may now be endangered. Commerce has altered some sites irrevocably. Walkers along the Great Wall near Beijing are hassled by vendors flogging every kind of item, many unrelated to the wall itself, and extensive renovation has given the ancient wonder a Disneyland feel.

In order for a place to be listed as a WHS, it must undergo a rigorous application process. Firstly, a state takes an inventory of its significant sites, which is called a (32) Tentative List, from which sites are put into a Nomination File. Two independent international (33) bodies, the International Council on Monuments and Sites, and the World Conservation Union, evaluate the Nomination File, and make recommendations to the World Heritage Committee. Meeting once a year, this committee determines which sites should be added to the World Heritage List by deciding that a site meets at least (34) one criterion out of ten, of which six are (35) cultural, and four are natural.

In 2003, a second convention, effective from 2008, was added to the first. (36) The Convention for the Safeguarding of Intangible Cultural Heritage has so far been ratified by 139 states – a notable exception being the US. Aiming to protect traditions rather than places, 267 elements have already been enshrined, including: Cambodia's Royal Ballet; the French gastronomic meal; and, water-tight-bulkhead technology of Chinese junks.

(37) The World Heritage Committee hopes that the states that agree to list such elements will also promote and support them, although, once again, commercialisation is problematic. For instance, after the French gastronomic meal was listed in 2010, numerous French celebrity chefs used the designation in advertising, and UNESCO debated delisting the element. (38) The US has chosen not to sign the second convention due to implications to intellectual property rights. As things stand, with the first treaty, the US has far fewer nominated sites than its neighbour Mexico, partly because some Mexican sites are entire towns or city centres, and the US has no desire for its urban planning to be restricted by world-heritage status. (39) St Petersburg, in Russia, which has its entire historic centre as a WHS, introduced strict planning regulations to maintain its elegant 18th-century appearance, only to discover thousands of minor infringements by owners preferring to do what they pleased with their properties. With intangible elements, changes over time, due to modernisation or globalization, may be greater than those threatening buildings. (40) Opponents of the second convention believe traditions should not be frozen in time, and are equally unconcerned if traditions dwindle or die.

Although the 1972 World Heritage Convention lacks teeth, and many of its sites are suffering, and although the 2003 Convention for the Safeguarding of Intangible Cultural Heritage has proven less popular, it would seem that the overall performance of these two instruments has been very good.

WRITING: Task 1

Pancha Village changed markedly from 2005 to 2015. While both sides of its main road were built up in 2005, they were more so a decade later. Only two totally new buildings in the pagoda complex, one in the school, and some stalls in the market had been added by 2015, but redevelopment and technological improvement were noticeable.

What, in 2005, was solely a primary school, was, in 2015, both a primary and a secondary school. The two school buildings that were originally huts were rebuilt in concrete, one new building was constructed, and a flagpole erected in the playground.

Technological improvements in 2015 included: a sealed road with lane markings, a pedestrian crossing, and signage. Poles along the road brought electricity to the village. Two large antennae for mobile communications had been built next to the market, and

---

* The United Nations Educational, Scientific, and Cultural Organisation, based in Paris, France.

four houses that formerly had only had TV aerials now boasted satellite dishes. The road had been widened, and there was three vehicles on it.

The only sign of destruction in 2015 was the removal of two houses near the pagoda. (171 words)

Task 2

Today, there is an imbalance in the populations of developed countries. Declining birth rates and low immigration mean there are many more people over 65 years of age than those below. Despite a high standard of living, the ageing population is causing social and economic problems.

An ageing population, with many medical needs, may be a drain on health services. Where a developed country has a subsidised health service, this means that public funds are channelled more towards the aged than towards younger people. As a result, there may be reduced public funding of sectors such as education.

Those over 65 are usually eligible for state pensions, which they see as their right because they paid taxes when employed. However, this can cause tension between the young and the old.

Employment, too, is another area where the aged often benefit at the expense of those younger. Elderly people who are able, may work much longer than those who retired at 65. Some work from need; others because they are mentally, and in some cases physically, fit enough to continue. In the past, the older generation made way for the younger ones.

I suggest the following solutions. Firstly, through technological and medical advances, health care of the aged will continue to improve, making them less of a burden. To ensure that the public is not responsible for others' health care, a national health insurance scheme should be compulsory.

Secondly, the pension age should be raised to match the fitness of the aged. Since many over 65 are already still working, this should not be too problematic. Also if a personal pension scheme is made obligatory from the age of 21, then later aged generations will not be a burden on the young.

Lastly, if more immigrants are encouraged to enter a developed country, they could not only fill in the generation gap, but also bring skills that may be lost as the workforce ages. Mechanics, technicians, doctors, nurses, engineers, and teachers all would be beneficial. (334 words)

SPEAKING:

Narrator	Recording 12. Test 2. Part 1 of the Speaking test. Listen to a candidate who is likely to be awarded a Nine answering questions in Part 1 of the Speaking test.
Examiner	Good afternoon. My name is Lucy. Could you tell me your full name please?
Candidate	Gao Nan, but my English name is Stephen.
Examiner	And where are you from, Stephen?
Candidate	Tianjin – a big city not far from Beijing.
Examiner	Could I check your ID, please? Thanks. First of all, Stephen, I'd like to ask you a few questions about yourself. Could you tell me about the accommodation you're currently living in?
Candidate	Right now, I'm living with my cousin in a house in Hillsdale. We're sharing with three other people – another guy from China, and a married couple from Iran.
Examiner	And do you have a favourite part of the house?
Candidate	I'd say my bedroom or perhaps the back yard. Yeah – the back yard. We've got a small yard that's mostly brick. I like to sit out there in a rusty old chair. It's peaceful. I like to look at the blue sky. You almost never see blue sky in Tianjin.
Examiner	Do you think you'll stay where you're living for a while?
Candidate	I guess so. It's close to the uni I'm hoping to go to next year, and it's great for shopping and public transport.
Examiner	Now, let's move on to talk about hats and caps.
Candidate	Hats and caps?
Examiner	Yes, hats and caps. Do you ever wear a hat or a cap?
Candidate	Not really. Not in Sydney. I know the sun's really bad here, and I occasionally wear a baseball cap in summer, but otherwise, no.
Examiner	Why do some people wear hats or caps?

Candidate	Well, to keep the sun off, to cover up their bald patches – I had an uncle who did that – and, of course in Tianjin it snows in winter, so lots of people wear hats then. I've also noticed that most schoolchildren in Sydney wear hats as part of their uniform.
Examiner	Do you think headgear was more popular in the past?
Candidate	Probably. In my grandfather's photos from the 1960s, lots of people in Tianjin are wearing hats. In the 1970s, there was a cap, like the one Chairman Mao wore, that was kind of obligatory.
Examiner	Why was headgear more popular in the past?
Candidate	I'm not sure exactly. Perhaps hats showed your occupation or your social status, or, as I said, they were obligatory. You can still see old guys in Xinjiang – that's a western province of China – wearing tall black woollen hats because they're farmers. And some headgear belongs to certain ethnic groups.
Examiner	Now, let's talk about time: When was the last time you were rather late?
Candidate	Actually, I'm almost always on time, but a few weeks ago, my cousin and I drove up to the Blue Mountains—we'd been invited to a party at Mount Wilson. We've both got Google maps on our phones, but we still got lost. By the time we found the party, almost everyone else'd gone home.
Examiner	How do you feel when other people are late?
Candidate	Depends on the situation. I don't mind if it's a friend or a relative, and they send a text or something. But at work, it does annoy me because I'm not paid extra to do the work of a latecomer.
Examiner	Do you think people these days have enough time?
Candidate	Yes, I do. They *say* they don't, but everyone I know who makes a schedule and sticks to it, or makes some kind of long-term plan manages, pretty much, to fit everything in. I believe you can make time if you want to.
Examiner	How do you think children perceive time?
Candidate	How do I think children perceive time? Well, some children are impatient. And some children think the future is never gonna happen. I know when I was a kid I couldn't believe I'd get to high school, let alone university. Maybe time goes more slowly for children?
Narrator	Recording 13. Part 2 of the Speaking test. Listen to Stephen's two-minute topic.
Examiner	In this part, Stephen, I'm going to give you a topic for you to speak about for two minutes. Before you speak, you'll have one minute to prepare, and you can write some notes on this paper if you like. Do you understand?
Candidate	Sure.
Examiner	Here's your topic: I'd like you to tell me about someone you think is attractive.
Narrator	One minute later.
Examiner	OK? Remember, you're going to speak for two minutes. Don't worry if I interrupt you to tell you when your time is up. Could you start speaking now, please, Stephen?
Candidate	Right. Well, I'm going to tell you about my mother. Perhaps that's kinda corny, but when I look at her in photos taken when she was a teenager or in her twenties, she was, in fact, very attractive. Firstly, she's quite tall. Her family comes from Heilongjiang Province, where there are quite a lot of tall people. Her own mother was taller than average for a woman of her time. So, my mother's tall, and she's always had a good figure. Even now, in her fifties, she's slim and fit. She's always maintained excellent posture, which I put down to the fact that she's been a dancer since she was a child. She's tall, she's got a good figure, and, most noticeably, she's got a lovely smile. Her facial features aren't classically beautiful or completely regular, but that's also part of her charm. When she smiles, she's got two little dimples in her cheeks, and her nickname was 'Dimple' when she was a kid. She's got very narrow eyes and high cheekbones and a small chin. Her face is sort of triangular. Once, when I was about twelve, we were on an overnight train trip, and a woman sharing our carriage insisted my mother looked like a famous singer. It turned out that when my father first met my mother, he'd thought the same. But, in my eyes, what's particularly attractive about my mother is her gentleness. I mean, I haven't been what you'd call a model son. I scored pretty badly in the Gaokao – that's the Chinese university entrance exam – and I took almost five years to get my bachelor's degree. But, in all that time, she still believed in me.

What else? Oh, the way she dresses. In the past, our family didn't have much money, and Mum hardly ever bought any new clothes for herself, but I remember she always looked elegant in comparison to the mothers of my school friends. Even today, she usually wears fitted dresses in plain colours – not patterns, whereas lots of Chinese women of her generation like floral clothes. Yes, I'd say she's got flair.

Examiner Thank you.

Narrator Recording 14.
Part 3 of the Speaking test.
Listen to the rest of Stephen's test.

Examiner So you've told me about someone you think is attractive, and now I'd like to discuss some more general questions related to beauty.
First of all: Physical appearance and societal pressure.
Do you think these days, there's a lot of pressure to conform to a norm, or to look beautiful?

Candidate Absolutely.

Think of all the gyms and products that are meant to make you thin in some places and muscular in others. We're bombarded with these products.

Before I came to Sydney, I was working in South Korea, and I've never seen anyone so obsessed with plastic surgery as the Koreans. Women *and* men. My boss'd had about five procedures, and he claimed that the only way to get promoted was to look more handsome than the other guy.

Examiner Do you think he was right?
Candidate Maybe.
Examiner So, what are some of the dangers of this pressure to be attractive?
Candidate Well, there'll be people who are less physically attractive who find it hard to get jobs even though they've got the skills, and that's a waste for society. In Busan, I met people who'd borrowed money from banks to pay for their plastic surgery, and I'm sure that money could've been better invested elsewhere.

But the world is so competitive now. I dunno what the answer is. Maybe people were less judgmental in the past, more tolerant?

Examiner Let's talk about concepts of beauty throughout time.
Do you think our idea of beauty has changed over time, or basically stayed the same?

Candidate Some things change. I mean, the big lip thing. My grandmother said that when she was young, women wanted to have thin lips because that looked aristocratic. These days, all the movie stars and singers have suddenly got huge lips. Also, height and shape. In the past, in China, it was considered feminine to be petite and girlish. Now, men and women think being tall is cool, and they want a more western body shape.

But equally, some things do remain the same. A round face and pale skin are thought to be most attractive in China. If you read Chinese literature from three or four hundred years ago, those were also important then.

Examiner Thank you very much. That is the end of the Speaking test.

TEST 3

- Prepare some snacks and drinks.

- Find a reliable stopwatch or clock.

- Use an electronic device to access the audio at www.mheIELTS6practicetests.com.

- Find a place where you can work with no interruptions for four hours – three for this whole test + one to go through the answers.

Listening

Firstly, tear out the Test 3 Listening / Reading Answer Sheet at the back of this book.

The Listening test lasts for about 20 minutes.

Write your answers on the pages below as you listen. After Section 4 has finished, you have ten minutes to transfer your answers to your Listening Answer Sheet. You will need to time yourself for this transfer.

After checking your answers on pp 134-138, go to page 9 for the raw-score conversion table.

Play Audio **PLAY RECORDING #15.**

SECTION 1   Questions 1-10

INSURANCE

Questions 1-6

Complete the form below.

Write **NO MORE THAN TWO WORDS OR A NUMBER** for each answer.

(**Example**) *Travel* **Insurance**	
Type	(**1**)....................Comprehensive
Section 1 – Baggage and Personal Effects	
Single (**2**)...................	$1,500
Cameras & portable electronic (**3**)...................	$2,500
Emergency personal effects	$1,500
Money	(**4**) $...................
Documents	$3,000
Section 2 – Disrupted Travel	
Loss of deposits	$50,000
Travel delay	$5,000
Missed connections or early return (as verified by the (**6**)...................)	(**5**)...................
Resumed travel	Economy fare

Questions 7-8

Choose the correct letter, A, B, or C.

7   The woman will buy

    A   a new car.

    B   an old car.

    C   a new motorbike.

8   The woman does not want to insure her vehicle with a Multi-saver policy because it

    A   benefits homeowners.

    B   has too many conditions.

    C   is rather expensive.

Questions 9-10

*Choose **TWO** letters, A-E.*

    Which **TWO** of the following relate to the Top Cover policy?

    A   It is cheaper than many other policies.

    B   There is a stand-down period before it takes effect.

    C   It covers storm damage.

    D   It covers vehicles of any age.

    E   It includes an agreement on the value of a holder's vehicle.

Play Audio **PLAY RECORDING #16.**

SECTION 2   Questions 11-20

TOURING DEVONPORT ON A SEGWAY

Questions 11-16

Complete the sentences below.

*Write **NO MORE THAN THREE WORDS AND/OR A NUMBER** for each answer.*

11   The company does not allow children, pregnant women, or people recovering

    from…………………..to ride Segways.

12   The Segway tour of Devonport lasts for……………….. .

13   Unlike a cyclist, a Segway rider barely needs………………..to remain in motion.

14   A Segway weighs……………….. .

15   Accidents happen due to jumping off, or jerking instead of………………..to move the Segway.

16   The gyroscope monitors a rider's………………..., and adjusts the post to maintain balance.

Questions 17-20

Label the map below.

*Write the correct letter, **A-I**, next to questions 17-20.*

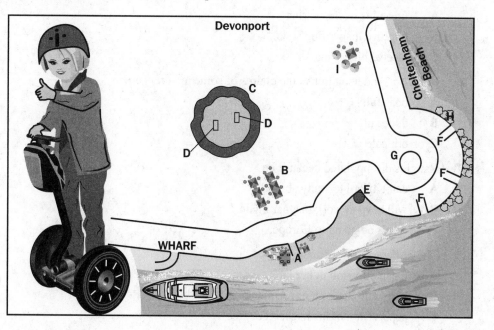

17   North Head   ....

18   French Café   ....

19   Yacht club   ....

20   Remains from pre-European settlement   ....

 PLAY RECORDING #17.

SECTION 3   Questions 21-30

STUDY OPTIONS

Questions 21-24

Answer the questions below.

*Write **NO MORE THAN TWO WORDS** for each answer.*

21   What was Professor Anderson attending in Massachusetts and New York?

....

22   What mark did Rangi receive for Classical Mechanics?

....

23   Which degree has Rangi decided to abandon?

....

24   How does Professor Anderson describe the Science Faculty?

....

LISTENING
READING
WRITING
SPEAKING

| SECTION 1 | SECTION 2 | SECTION 3 | SECTION 4 |

Questions 25-30

Choose the correct letter, A, B, or C.

25   A benefit of Rangi's decision is that he will
    A   finish his degree earlier.
    B   improve his writing style.
    C   receive higher marks.

26   Professor Anderson thinks the claims of some lecturers are
    A   boastful.
    B   doubtful.
    C   critical.

27   Rangi is disappointed because he
    A   can't afford to study abroad.
    B   will have to work in a bar again.
    C   won't be going to Europe.

28   The professor offers Rangi
    A   a part-time job in her lab.
    B   help with his laser experiments.
    C   supervision of his master's degree.

29   In the professor's opinion, Rangi is …… to win a scholarship.
    A   not so likely
    B   quite likely
    C   highly likely

30   Rangi feels …… by the end of the conversation.
    A   a little apprehensive
    B   relieved and grateful
    C   thrilled but nervous

Play Audio **PLAY RECORDING #18.**

SECTION 4   Questions 31-40

THE UGLY FRUIT MOVEMENT

Questions 31-35

Choose FIVE answers from the box, and write the correct letter, A-H, next to questions 31-35.

A	Consumers like food that tastes as good as it looks.
B	Every year, approximately 40% of food fit for humans is wasted.
C	Harvesting and processing need substantial improvement.
D	Food wastage causes an annual loss of $870 million.
E	Food production uses 80% of available fresh water.
F	Use-by-date labelling is being challenged.
G	Supermarkets sell fruit and vegetables in virtually any condition.
H	Newspapers mocked strict European Union regulations.

31   Globally ………………..

32   In the US ………………..

33   In Bolivia ………………..

34   In Portugal ………………..

35   In the UK ………………..

Questions 36-38

Complete the sentences below.

Write NO MORE THAN TWO WORDS OR A NUMBER for each answer.

36   Portugal was affected by a……………crisis.

37   Isabel Soares hopes to subvert notions about what food is…………… .

38   José Dias used to dump a……………of his tomato crop before he sold to *Fruta Feia*.

39   Tomatoes bought by members of *Fruta Feia* cost……………than those at supermarkets.

Question 40

40   What does the lecturer think of *Fruta Feia*?

A   He supports it wholeheartedly.

B   He supports it with some reservations.

C   He does not really support it.

LISTENING
READING
WRITING
SPEAKING

PASSAGE 1　　PASSAGE 2　　PASSAGE 3

Reading

Firstly, turn over the Test 3 Listening Answer Sheet you used earlier to write your Reading answers on the back.

The Reading test lasts exactly 60 minutes.

Certainly, make any marks on the pages below, but transfer your answers to the answer sheet <u>as you read</u> since there is no extra time at the end to do so.

After checking your answers on pp 139-141, go to page 9 for the raw-score conversion table.

PASSAGE 1

*Spend about 20 minutes on **Questions 1-13**, based on Passage 1 below.*

MÁRQUEZ AND MAGICAL REALISM

A When Gabriel García Márquez died in 2014, he was mourned around the world, as readers recalled his 1967 novel, *One hundred years of solitude*, which has sold more than 25 million copies, and led to Márquez's receipt of the 1982 Nobel Prize for Literature.

B Born in 1927, in a small town on Colombia's Caribbean coast called Aracataca, Márquez was immersed in Spanish, black, and indigenous cultures. In such remote places, religion, myth, and superstition hold sway over logic and reason, or perhaps operate as parallel belief systems. Certainly, the ghost stories told by his grandmother affected the young Gabriel profoundly, and a pivotal character in his 1967 epic is indeed a ghost.

Márquez's family was not wealthy: there were twelve children, and his father worked as a postal clerk, a telegraph operator, and an occasional pharmacist. Márquez spent much of his childhood in the care of his grandparents, which may account for the main character in *One hundred years of solitude* resembling his maternal grandfather. Although Márquez left Aracataca aged eight, the town and its inhabitants never seemed to leave him, and suffuse his fiction.

C *One hundred years of solitude* was the fourth of fifteen novels, but Márquez was an equally passionate and prolific journalist.

In Bogotá, during his twenties and thirties, Márquez experienced La Violencia, a period of great political and social upheaval, when around 300,000 Colombians were killed. Certainly, life was never safe for journalists, and after writing an article on corruption in the Colombian navy in 1955, Márquez was forced to flee to Europe. Incidentally, in Paris, he discovered that European culture was not richer than his own, and he was disappointed by Europeans who were patronising towards Latin Americans. On return to the southern hemisphere, Márquez wrote for Venezuelan newspapers and the Cuban press agency.

D In terms of politics, Márquez was leftwing. In Chile, he campaigned against the dictatorship of General Augusto Pinochet; in Venezuela, he financed a political party; and, in Nicaragua, he defended revolutionaries. He considered Fidel Castro, the President of Cuba, as a dear friend. Since the US was hostile towards Castro's communist regime, which Márquez supported, the writer was banned from visiting the US until invited by President Clinton in 1995. The novels of Márquez are imbued with his politics, but this does not prevent readers from enjoying a good yarn.

E Márquez maintained that in Latin America so much that is real would seem fantastic elsewhere, while so much that is magical seems real. He was an exponent of a genre known as Magical Realism.

'If you can explain it,' said the Mexican critic, Luis Leal, 'then it's not Magical Realism.' This demonstrates the difficulty of determining what the genre encompasses and which writers belong to it.

LISTENING
READING
WRITING
SPEAKING

PASSAGE 1   PASSAGE 2   PASSAGE 3

The term Magical Realism is usually applied to literature, but its first use was probably in 1925, when a German art critic reviewed paintings similar to those of Surrealism.

Many critics define Magical Realism by what it is not. Realism describes lives that could be real; Magical Realism uses the detail and the tone of a realist work, but includes the magical as though it were real. The ghosts in *One hundred years of solitude* and in the American Toni Morrison's *Beloved* are presented by their narrators as normal, so readers accept them unhesitatingly. Likewise, a character can live for 200 years in a Magical Realist novel. Surrealism explores dream states and psychological experiences; Magical Realism does not. Science Fiction describes a new or an imagined world, as in Aldous Huxley's *Brave New World*, but Magical Realism depicts the real world. Nor is Magical Realism fantasy, like Franz Kafka's *Metamorphosis*, in which an ordinary man awakens to find he has transformed into a cockroach. This is because the writer and the reader of that story cannot decide whether to ascribe natural or supernatural causes to the event. In contrast, in a work by Márquez, the world is both natural *and* supernatural, both rational *and* irrational, and this binary nature fascinates readers.

Magical Realism does share some common ground with post-modernism since the acts of writing and reading are self-reflexive. A narrative may not be linear, but may double back on itself, or be discontinuous, and the notion of character is more illusive than in other genres.

Naturally, some of these elements disturb a reader although the enormous success of *One hundred years of solitude* and the hundreds of other Magical Realist works from authors as far apart as Norway, Nigeria, and New Zealand would seem to belie it.

F Latin America has had a long history of conquest, revolution, and dictatorship; of hunger, poverty, and chaos, yet, at the same time, is endowed with rich cultures, with warm, emotional people, many of whom, like Márquez, remain optimistically utopian. Gabriel García Márquez has passed away, but his fiction will certainly endure.

Questions 1-7

Passage 1 has six sections, **A-F**.

Which section contains the following information?

Write the correct letter, A-F, in boxes 1-7 on your answer sheet.

NB: You may use any letter more than once.

1   Márquez's background

2   how Márquez felt about Europe

3   influences on Márquez

4   the extent of Márquez's fame

5   why the US did not welcome Márquez

6   what constitutes a Magical Realist work

7   other writing important to Márquez

Questions 8-13

Complete the summary below using the dates or words, A-L, below.

Write the correct letter, A-L, in boxes 8-13 on your answer sheet.

A	accept	B	adapting	C	adopting
D	believes	E	fantasy	F	non-linear
G	novel	H	rational	I	supernatural
J	use	K	1925	L	1927

What is Magical Realism?

The genre of Márquez's fiction is known as Magical Realism, a term first applied to painting in
(**8**)...................... . Magical Realism is often described in negative terms, as not being Realism,
Surrealism, Science Fiction, or (**9**)..................... .

In a Magical Realist novel, the world people live in – which is the real world – is described in detail,
but magical or (**10**)..................... elements intrude. These are treated like real ones, so that a reader
(**11**)..................... them. For instance, characters live longer than natural lives, and ghosts exist.
Time, in a Magical Realist work, may also be (**12**)..................... .

Despite requiring a suspension of disbelief by readers, Magical Realism has enjoyed great success,
with writers from all over the world (**13**)..................... the style.

PASSAGE 2

*Spend about 20 minutes on **Questions 14-27**, based on Passage 2 below.*

Recent stock-market crashes

For as long as there have been financial markets, there have been financial crises. Most economists agree, however, that from 1994 to 2013 crashes were deeper and the resultant troughs longer-lasting than in the 20-year period leading up to 1994. Two notable crashes, the Nifty Fifty in the mid-1970s and Black Monday in 1987, had an average loss of about 40% of the value of global stocks, and recovery took 240 days each, whereas the Dot-com and credit crises, post-1994, had an average loss of about 52%, and endured for 430 days. What economists do not agree upon is why recent crises have been so severe or how to prevent their recurrence.

John Coates, from the University of Cambridge in the UK and a former trader for Goldman Sachs and Deutsche Bank, believes three separate but related phenomena explain the severity. The first is dangerous but predictable risk-taking on the part of traders. The second is a lack of any risk-taking when markets become too volatile. (Coates does not advocate risk-aversion since risk-taking may jumpstart a depressed market.) The last is a new policy of transparency by the US Federal Reserve – known as the Fed – that may have encouraged stock-exchange complacency, compounding the dangerous risk-taking.

Many people imagine a trader to have a great head for maths and a stomach for the rollercoaster ride of the market, but Coates downplays arithmetic skills, and doubts traders are made of such stern stuff. Instead, he draws attention to the physiological nature of their decisions. Admittedly, there are women in the industry, but traders are overwhelmingly male, and testosterone appears to affect their choices.

Another common view is that traders are greedy as well as thrill-seeking. Coates has not researched financial incentive, but blood samples taken from London traders who engaged in simulated risk-taking exercises for him in 2013 confirmed the prevalence of testosterone, cortisol, and dopamine – a neurotransmitter precursor to adrenalin associated with raised blood pressure and sudden pleasure.

Certainly anyone faced with danger has a stress response involving the body's preparation for impending movement – for what is sometimes called 'Fight or flight', but, as Coates notes, any physical act at all produces a stress response: even a reader's eye movement along words in this line requires cortisol and adrenalin. Neuroscientists now see the brain not as a computer that acts neutrally, involved in a process of pure thought, but as a mechanism to plan and carry out movement, since every single piece of information humans absorb has an attendant pattern of physical arousal.

For muscles to work, fuel is needed, so cortisol and adrenalin employ glucose from other muscles and the liver. To burn the fuel, oxygen is required, so slightly deeper or faster breathing occurs. To deliver fuel and oxygen to the body, the heart pumps a little harder and blood pressure rises. Thus, the stress response is a normal part of life, as well as a resource in fighting or fleeing. Indeed, it is a highly pleasurable experience in watching an action movie, making love, or pulling off a multi-million-dollar stock-market deal.

Cortisol production also increases during exposure to uncertainty. For example, people who live next to a train line adjust to the noise of passing trains, but visitors to their home are disturbed. The phenomenon is equally well-known of anticipation being worse than an event itself: sitting in the waiting room thinking about a procedure may be more distressing than occupying the dentist's chair and having one. Interestingly, if a patient does not know approximately when he or she will be called for that procedure, cortisol levels are the most elevated of all. This appeared to happen with the London traders participating in some of Coates' gambling scenarios.

When there is too much volatility in the stock market, Coates suspects adrenaline levels decrease while cortisol levels increase, explaining why traders take fewer risks at that time. In fact, typically traders freeze, becoming almost incapable of buying or selling anything but the safest bonds. In Coates' opinion, the market needs investment as it falls and at rock bottom – at such times, greed is good.

The third matter – the behaviour of the Fed – Coates thinks could be controlled, albeit counter-intuitively. Since 1994, the US Federal Reserve has adopted a policy called Forward Guidance. Under this, the public is informed at regular intervals of the Fed's plans for short-term interest rates. Recently, rates have been raised by small but predictable increments. By contrast, in the past, the machinations of the Fed were largely secret, and its interest rates fluctuated apparently randomly. Coates hypothesises this meant traders were on guard and less likely to indulge in wild speculation. In introducing Forward Guidance, the Fed hoped to lower stock and housing prices; instead, before the crash of 2008, the market surged from further risk-taking, like an unleashed pit bull terrier.

There are many economists who disagree with Coates, but he has provided some physiological evidence for both traders' recklessness *and* immobilisation, and made the radical proposal of greater opacity at the Fed. Although, as others have noted, we could just let more women onto the floor.

- -

Questions 14-19

*Choose the correct letter, **A, B, C,** or **D**.*

Write the correct letter in boxes 14-19 on your answer sheet.

14   What do most economists agree about the financial crashes from 1994 to 2013?

    A   They were the worst global markets had ever experienced.

    B   Global stocks fell around 40% for a period of 240 days.

    C   They were particularly acute in the US.

    D   They were more severe than those between 1974 and 1993.

15   What does John Coates think about risk-taking among stock-market traders?

    A   It is almost invariably dangerous.

    B   It was prevalent at Goldman Sachs and Deutsche Bank.

    C   It should be regulated by the US Federal Reserve.

    D   It can sometimes assist a weak market.

16   What are some popular beliefs about traders?

    A   They are clever, calm, and acquisitive.

    B   They are usually men who are good at maths.

    C   They love danger and seek it out.

    D   They do not deserve their high salaries.

17   What did Coates find in blood samples from London traders in 2013?

    A   They had high levels of testosterone and dopamine.

    B   They produced excessive glucose and oxygen.

    C   They experienced high blood pressure.

    D   They drank large amounts of alcohol.

126   6 IELTS Practice Tests

LISTENING
READING
WRITING
SPEAKING

| PASSAGE 1 | PASSAGE 2 | PASSAGE 3 |

18   How do neuroscientists now view the brain?

A   As an extraordinary computer.

B   As an organ to control movement.

C   As the main producer of adrenaline and cortisol.

D   As a significant enhancer of pleasure.

19   Why might a person waiting to see a dentist have extremely high cortisol levels?

A   He or she may dislike going to the dentist.

B   He or she may be worried about the procedure.

C   He or she may not have a specific appointment.

D   He or she may not be able to afford the consultation.

Questions 20-24

Complete the flowchart below.

*Choose **ONE WORD ONLY** from the passage for each answer.*

Write your answers in boxes 20-24 on your answer sheet.

COATES' REASONS FOR THE SEVERITY OF RECENT CRASHES		
1. Increased risk-taking by traders	**2.** Increased risk-aversion by traders	**3.** US Federal Reserve policy
This occurs when the market is rising.	This occurs when there is too much (**20**) .... in the market.	Known as (**22**) .... Guidance, this was supposed to calm the market.
A rise in traders' adrenaline levels	A rise in traders' (**21**) .... levels	Traders' disregard for small, regular interest-rate rises and their (**23**) .... speculation
Further risk-taking	Immobilisation of traders	(**24**) .... risk-taking
Market collapse		

Questions 25-27

Do the following statements agree with the claims of the writer in Passage 2?

In boxes 25-27 on your answer sheet, write:

YES	*if the statement agrees with the claims of the writer.*
NO	*if the statement contradicts the claims of the writer.*
NOT GIVEN	*if it is impossible to say what the writer thinks about this.*

25   Coates' views are held by many other economists.

26   Coates' suggestion of less transparency at the Fed is sound.

27   Raising the number of female traders may solve the problem.

PASSAGE 3

*Spend about 20 minutes on **Questions 28-40**, which are based on Passage 3 below.*

ANIMAL PERSONHOOD

Aristotle, a 4th-century-BC Greek philosopher, created the Great Chain of Being, in which animals, lacking reason, ranked below humans. The Frenchman, René Descartes, in the 17th century AD, considered animals as more complex creatures; however, without souls, they were merely automatons. One hundred years later, the German, Immanuel Kant, proposed animals be treated less cruelly, which might seem an improvement, but Kant believed this principally because he thought acts of cruelty affect their human perpetrators detrimentally. The mid-19th century saw the Englishman, Jeremy Bentham, questioning not their rationality or spirituality, but whether animals could suffer *irrespective* of the damage done to their victimisers; he concluded they could; and, in 1824, the first large organisation for animal welfare, the Royal Society for the Prevention of Cruelty to Animals, was founded in England. In 1977, the Australian, Peter Singer, wrote the highly influential book *Animal liberation*, in which he debated the ethics of meat-eating and factory farming, and raised awareness about inhumane captivity and experimentation. Singer's title deliberately evoked other liberation movements, like those for women, which had developed in the post-war period.

More recently, an interest in the cognitive abilities of animals has resurfaced. It has been known since the 1960s that chimpanzees have sophisticated tool use and social interactions, but research from the last two decades has revealed they are also capable of empathy and grief, and they possess self-awareness and self-determination. Other primates, dolphins, whales, elephants, and African grey parrots are highly intelligent too. It would seem that with each new proof of animals' abilities, questions are being posed as to whether creatures so similar to humans should endure the physical pain or psychological trauma associated with habitat loss, captivity, or experimentation. While there may be more laws protecting animals than 30 years ago, in the eyes of the law, no matter how smart or sentient an animal may be, it still has a lesser status than a human being.

Steven Wise, an American legal academic, has been campaigning to change this. He believes animals, like those listed above, are autonomous – they can control their actions, or rather, their actions are not caused purely by reflex or from innateness. He wants these animals categorized legally as non-human persons because he believes existing animal-protection laws are weak and poorly enforced. He famously quipped that an aquarium may be fined for cruel treatment of its dolphins but, currently, the dolphins can't sue the aquarium.

While teaching at Vermont Law School in the 1990s, Wise presented his students with a dilemma: should an anencephalic baby be treated as a legal person? (Anencephaly is a condition where a person is born with a partial brain and can breathe and digest, due to reflex, but otherwise is barely alert, and not autonomous.) Overwhelmingly, Wise's students would say 'Yes'. He posed another question: could the same baby be killed and eaten by humans? Overwhelmingly, his students said 'No'. His third question, always harder to answer, was: why is an anencephalic baby legally a person yet not so a fully functioning bonobo chimp?

Wise draws another analogy: between captive animals and slaves. Under slavery in England, a human was a chattel, and if a slave were stolen or injured, the thief or violator could be convicted of a crime, and compensation paid to the slave's owner though not to the slave. It was only in 1772 that the chief justice of the King's Bench, Lord Mansfield, ruled that a slave could apply for habeas corpus, Latin for: 'You must have the body', as free men and women had done since ancient times. Habeas corpus does not establish innocence or guilt; rather, it means a detainee can be represented in court by a proxy. Once slaves had been granted habeas corpus, they existed as more than chattels within the legal system although it was another 61 years before slavery was abolished in England. Aside from slaves, Wise has studied numerous cases in which a writ of habeas corpus had been filed on behalf of those unable to appear in court, like children, patients, prisoners, or the severely intellectually impaired. In addition, Wise notes there are entities that are *not* living people that have legally become non-human persons, including: ships, corporations, partnerships, states, a Sikh holy book, some Hindu idols and the Wanganui River in New Zealand.

In conjunction with an organisation called the Non-human Rights Project (NhRP), Wise has been representing captive animals in US courts in an effort to have their legal status reassigned. Thereafter, the NhRP plans to apply, under habeas corpus, to represent the animals in other cases. Wise and the NhRP believe a new status will discourage animal owners or nation states from neglect or abuse, which current laws fail to do.

Richard Epstein, a professor of Law at New York University, is a critic of Wise's. His concern is that if animals are treated as independent holders of rights there would be little left of human society, in particular, in the food and agricultural industries. Epstein agrees some current legislation concerning animal protection may need overhauling, but he sees no underlying problem.

Other detractors say that the push for personhood misses the point: it focuses on animals that are similar to humans without addressing the fundamental issue that *all* species have an equal right to exist. Thomas Berry, of the Gaia Foundation, declares that rights do not emanate from humans but from the universe itself, and, as such, all species have the right to existence, habitat, and role (be that predator, plant, or decomposer). Dramatically changing human behaviour towards other species is necessary for their survival – and that doesn't mean declaring animals as non-human persons.

To date, the NhRP has not succeeded in its applications to have the legal status of chimpanzees in New York State changed, but the NhRP considers it some kind of victory that the cases have been heard. Now, the NhRP can proceed to the Court of Appeals, where many emotive cases are decided, and where much common law is formulated.

Despite setbacks, Wise doggedly continues to expose brutality towards animals. Thousands of years of perceptions may have to be changed in this process. He may have lost the battle, but he doesn't believe he's lost the war.

• •

Questions 28-33

*Choose the correct letter, **A, B, C,** or **D**.*

Write the correct letter in boxes 28-33 on your answer sheet.

28   Why did Aristotle place animals below human beings?

    A   He doubted they behaved rationally.

    B   He thought them less intelligent.

    C   He considered them physically weaker.

    D   He believed they did not have souls.

29   Why did Kant think humans should not treat animals cruelly?

    A   Animals were important in agriculture.

    B   Animals were used by the military.

    C   Animals experience pain in the same way humans do.

    D   Humans' exposure to cruelty was damaging to themselves.

30   What concept of animals did Bentham develop?

    A   The existence of their suffering

    B   The magnitude of their suffering

    C   Their surprising brutality

    D   Their surprising spirituality

31   Where and when was the RSPCA founded?

    A   In Australia in 1977

    B   In England in 1824

    C   In Germany in 1977

    D   In the US in 1824

32   Why might Singer have chosen the title *Animal liberation* for his book?

    A   He was a committed vegetarian.

    B   He was concerned about endangered species.

    C   He was comparing animals to other subjugated groups.

    D   He was defending animals against powerful lobby groups.

33   What has recent research shown about chimpanzees?

    A   They have equal intelligence to dolphins.

    B   They have superior cognitive abilities to most animals.

    C   They are rapidly losing their natural habitat.

    D   They are far better protected now than 30 years ago.

Questions 34-40

Complete the summary below.

*Choose **NO MORE THAN TWO WORDS** from the passage for each answer.*

Write your answers in boxes 34-40 on your answer sheet.

A new legal status for animals?	
Arguments for:	• Steven Wise believes some highly intelligent animals that are (**34**)……………….. should have a new legal status. While animals are not humans, the law has a status for (**35**)……………….., already applied to ships, companies, and a river in New Zealand. • If the legal status of animals were changed, Wise and the NhRP could file for (**36**)……………….., where a detainee is represented by someone else. Then, they could take more effective action against animal abusers.
Arguments against:	• Richard Epstein believes the (**37**)……………….. of animals is important, but if animals had rights, the cost to human society would be too great. • Others, like Thomas Berry, argue that rights are bestowed by the universe and not by humans. Furthermore, (**38**)……………….. species have an equal right to exist.
Current situation in the US:	• Although the NhRP has not (**39**)……………….. in having the legal status of any animals altered, it continues its struggle. Changing two millennia's worth of (**40**)……………….. could prove difficult.

Writing

The Writing test lasts for 60 minutes.

Task 1

Spend about 20 minutes on this task.

> **The diagram belows shows French blue mussel culture.**
>
> **Write a summary of the information. Select and report the main features, and make comparisons where necessary.**

Write at least 150 words.

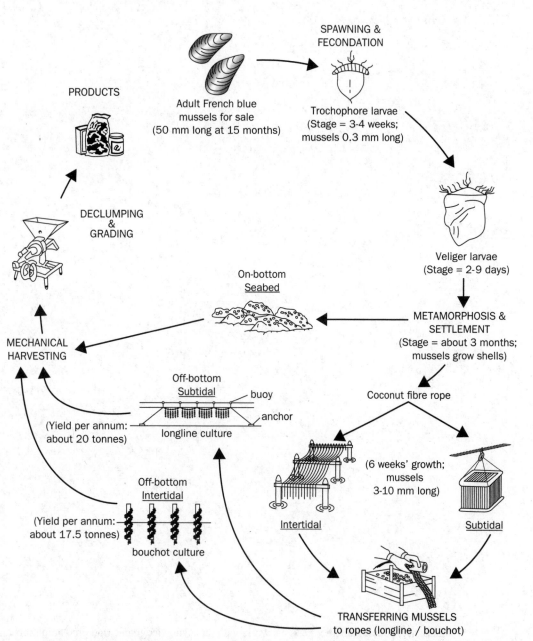

SPAWNING & FECONDATION

PRODUCTS

Adult French blue mussels for sale (50 mm long at 15 months)

Trochophore larvae (Stage = 3-4 weeks; mussels 0.3 mm long)

DECLUMPING & GRADING

Veliger larvae (Stage = 2-9 days)

On-bottom
Seabed

MECHANICAL HARVESTING

METAMORPHOSIS & SETTLEMENT (Stage = about 3 months; mussels grow shells)

Off-bottom
Subtidal
buoy
anchor
(Yield per annum: about 20 tonnes)
longline culture

Coconut fibre rope

(6 weeks' growth; mussels 3-10 mm long)

Off-bottom
Intertidal
(Yield per annum: about 17.5 tonnes)
bouchot culture

Intertidal

Subtidal

TRANSFERRING MUSSELS to ropes (longline / bouchot)

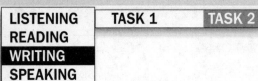

TASK 1   TASK 2

Task 2

Spend about 40 minutes on this task.

Write about the following topic:

Plagiarism* in all kinds of writing is becoming more frequent.

Why is this happening?

Some people think plagiarism causes problems, but others accept it. Discuss both views, and give your own opinion.

Provide reasons for your answer, including relevant examples from your own knowledge or experience.

Write at least 250 words.

---

*Plagiarism is copying another person's work, without acknowledgment, and pretending it is one's own.

Speaking

PART 1

How might you answer the following questions?

1   Could you tell me what you're doing at the moment: are you working or studying?

2   What do you find easy or difficult about your job?

3   Do you think you'll stay in the same job for a long time?

4   Now, let's talk about music. Have you ever played a musical instrument?

5   Do you think some people are naturally good at music?

6   Could you compare performing in a choir or orchestra with performing alone?

7   Do you agree or disagree: the music industry these days is less about music than about style?

8   Let's move on to talk about visiting people. How often do you have visitors to your home? What do you do?

9   How do you feel about staying the night at the homes of friends or relatives?

10   How has visiting others changed in your country in the last 20 years?

PART 2

How might you speak about the following topic for two minutes?

> **I'd like you to tell me about a game (not a sport) you used to play as a child.**
>
> * What was the game?
>
> * Who did you play it with?
>
> * What did you like about the game?
>
> And, do you still play this kind of game now?

PART 3

1   First of all, games children play.

Could you compare the kinds of games children in your country play outdoors, with those they play indoors?

What skills do children learn from playing games?

How does playing games develop a child's imagination?

2   Now, let's consider being competitive.

In what ways are people competitive at work in your country?

Do you think it is possible these days not to be competitive? Why?

Answers

<u>Section 1</u>: **1.** Individual; **2.** item; **3.** equipment; **4.** 700/seven hundred; **5.** Reasonable costs; **6.** airline; **7.** B; **8.** A; **9-10.** CE (*in either order*). <u>Section 2</u>: **11.** (leg) surgery; **12.** 2½ / two-and-a-half hours; **13.** to exert energy // exertion; **14.** 36 / thirty-six kg/kilograms/kilogrammes; **15.** leaning; **16.** centre / center of gravity; **17.** G; **18.** I; **19.** A; **20.** D. <u>Section 3</u>: **21.** (Physics) conferences; **22.** A+/plus; **23.** Arts (*must end in 's'*); **24.** disorganised/disorganized; **25.** A; **26.** B; **27.** C; **28.** A; **29.** C; **30.** B. <u>Section 4</u>: **31.** B; **32.** E; **33.** C; **34.** F; **35.** H; **36.** debt; **37.** edible // visually acceptable; **38.** ¼ / quarter; **39.** less; **40.** A.

The highlighted text below is evidence for the answers above.

Narrator	Recording 15. Practice Listening Test 3. Section 1. Insurance. You will hear a woman asking a sales assistant about insurance policies. Read the example.
Sales Assistant	Good morning. Take a seat. I see you've picked up some of our brochures.
Customer	Yes. I've been reading the one on travel.
Sales Assistant	Would the travel insurance be for you, or for your family as well?
Narrator	The answer is 'travel'. On this occasion only, the first part of the conversation is played twice. Before you listen again, you have 30 seconds to read questions 1 to 6.
Sales Assistant	Good morning. Take a seat. I see you've picked up some of our brochures.
Customer	Yes. I've been reading the one on travel.
Sales Assistant	Would the travel insurance be for you, or for your family as well?
Customer	Just for me.
Sales Assistant	So, (1) Individual?
Customer	That's right.
Sales Assistant	Are you looking for a basic or a comprehensive policy?
Customer	To be honest, I've had basic in the past, but it didn't pay out very much.
Sales Assistant	That's often true. With our company, you can be insured for different amounts. For instance, in Section 1: Baggage and personal effects, you can be insured for all five subsections or for as few as two.
Customer	I think I'd like insurance for all five since I'm going to some unsafe places.
Sales Assistant	Wise decision.
Customer	By the way, can a camera be counted as a single (2) item, or must it be included in Cameras and portable electronic (3) equipment?
Sales Assistant	If you have an expensive camera, you can nominate it as a single (2) item. Our maximum payout is $1,500. Occasionally, people have their camera and computer stolen together. If insurance is only taken out on Subsection 2, this may not cover the replacement of both things.
Customer	That's what happened with my previous policy. However, in that one, there was a higher limit for lost or stolen money: yours is only (4)$700.
Sales Assistant	These days, with credit cards, people don't carry much cash, so we've set the limit accordingly. Still, we pay out well for Documents.
Customer	Indeed. In the Disrupted travel section, (5) 'reasonable costs' is written for a missed connection or an early return, instead of an amount of money. What exactly are (5) 'reasonable costs'?

Sales Assistant	Put it this way: if you miss your flight due to poor weather that is verifiable, we pay $300 per day of lost time. If you arrive at check-in as the aircraft is leaving because you overslept, we still pay out, but only $100 a day. We rely on information from the (6) airline to determine this.
Narrator	Before you listen to the rest of the conversation, you have 30 seconds to read questions 7 to 10.
Sales Assistant	Are you also interested in vehicle insurance?
Customer	Yes, I am. I'm about to buy a nice (7) old car – a vintage Jaguar XJ6.
Sales Assistant	Hey, I used to have one of those although, nowadays, I prefer old motorbikes. Did you know you can insure a vehicle on its own, or you can include it in our Multi-saver policy, along with your house and contents?
Customer	Yes, I saw that. It's true I'm buying an expensive car, (8) but I rent my house, so I'm not ready for Multi-saver.
Sales Assistant	I understand. Have you decided which level of cover you'd like for your car?
Customer	Top cover.
Sales Assistant	Are you sure? It is pricey.
Customer	I know, but last time I had insurance, I wasn't covered for storm damage.
Sales Assistant	Don't tell me that was just before the November hailstorm!
Customer	Uh huh. (9-10) So, I need storm damage insurance. Also, I'd like my policy to start as soon as I've paid for it. With my old one, there was a stand-down period of two weeks. Would you believe, I backed into a wall just three days after I'd taken out the policy.
Sales Assistant	Oh dear.
Customer	Then, I spent months fighting with the insurance company over the value of my car. I know it wasn't worth much, but it was relatively new.
Sales Assistant	(9-10) If you choose Top Cover, we agree on a value for your car, and renegotiate each year to avoid disputes. Again, it's not as cheap as some, but the policy works out better in the long run.
Narrator	You now have 30 seconds to check your answers. That is the end of Section 1.
Narrator	Recording 16. Section 2. Touring Devonport on a Segway. You will hear a guide giving information on how to ride a Segway, and on places to see in Devonport. Before you listen, you have 30 seconds to read questions 11 to 16.
Guide	Hi folks. Before we start, I'd like to check if there's anyone here under the age of thirteen. No? Anyone who's pregnant, or who's just had (11) leg surgery? Good. Our company isn't insured for these users. Now, I can see you're all eyeing your Segways with interest. They're curious beasts, aren't they? Battery-driven two-wheeled vehicles often used in crowd control or postal delivery. I'll be giving detailed operating instructions in a moment, and then I'll outline our route. In (12) 2½ hours, we won't see everything in Devonport, but we'll take in much more than if we were on foot. In fact, the maximum speed of a Segway is eighteen kilometres per hour. Right-o. Safety gear. Here are your helmets. Please keep them on while riding. I hope you're wearing flat enclosed shoes as well. Actually, you can operate a Segway in any footwear, but our company insists on sturdy shoes because we explore tunnels, and walk around rocks at North Head. So. Riding a Segway is marvellously easy once you know how. It's important *not* to think of a Segway as similar to a bicycle or a scooter since a Segway rider barely needs (13) to exert energy to move. This concept of movement with minimal (13) exertion seems foreign to some beginners, and most mishaps are the result of riders' jerking backwards and losing their balance. Another mistake learners make is to hop off a Segway when they've stopped, but a Segway is as steady when stationary as when in motion, so don't dismount unless there's a place you can't ride into, like the tunnels in (17) North Head or (18) the French Café, where we end our tour.

A Segway is also robust. It's quite light at (14) 36 kilograms, and its low centre of gravity and wide tyres mean it can handle many different surfaces. In fact, I've been in the snow with mine.

However, a Segway does have a delicate internal mechanism. It contains a gyroscope – a device that's constantly moving to keep itself, and you, upright.

OK. Using the controls. The first thing you'll notice is that there are hardly any. There's an on-off button, and a screen indicating battery life and operational mode; we'll be using 'Normal'. So, let's turn on our Segways. Now, hold the post upright, and place one foot on the platform. Push the on-off button. You'll see the red lights rotating while the gyroscope is calibrating. When the lights turn green, release the kickstand, and place both feet on the platform. Now, lean forward slowly, and the machine will start; lean further forward, and it will speed up. In fact, (15) leaning is the way to control your Segway. (15) *Leaning* remember, not jerking – that'll make you fall off. Lean backwards, and the Segway slows down; keep leaning backwards, and it stops. Twist the *left* handle to go left; twist the *right* to go right. Simple. With the internal gyroscope constantly monitoring your (16) centre of gravity, and adjusting the post accordingly, you'll always keep your balance.

Narrator	Before you listen to the rest of the talk, you have 30 seconds to read questions 17 to 20.
Guide	As I said earlier, we're in this lovely harbour suburb of Devonport for (12) 2½ hours, beginning at the wharf and (18) ending up at the French Café. On the way, we'll pass (19) a yacht club, quite a famous club in fact, and a church and graveyard that are the oldest in this part of the city. We'll also climb two volcanoes. (20) The first volcano has remains from pre-European settlement in the form of storage pits and terraces, but there are no buildings left. (17) The second volcano, called North Head, has a museum at its base and some disused tunnels. The museum is devoted to naval history, but I'm afraid we won't have time to visit. Where do we go next? Oh yes – (17) the rocks below North Head. The rocks below North Head lead to Cheltenham Beach. We'll leave our Segways above the rocks while we explore. It's too cold to swim at this time of year, but people do in summer.
	Throughout our tour, I'll be guiding you on your Segway adventure, and recounting some amazing tales of this historic suburb.
Narrator	You now have 30 seconds to check your answers. That is the end of Section 2.
Narrator	Recording 17. Section 3. Study options. You will hear a professor talking to her student about his study options. Before you listen, you have 30 seconds to read questions 21 to 24.
Proffesor Anderson	Come in, Rangi.
Rangi	Thank you, Professor Anderson.
Prof Anderson	I've been meaning to contact you, but I just got back last night.
Rangi	Where've you been?
Prof Anderson	(21) Conferences in Massachusetts and New York.
Rangi	For (21) Physics?
Prof Anderson	Yes.
Rangi	Great. I'm looking forward to attending (21) conferences one day.
Prof Anderson	I imagine that won't be so far away. I was extremely impressed with your Classical Mechanics exam. In fact, you were one of only two students out of 180 to get an (22) A+.
Rangi	Wow. I really did enjoy the course.
Prof Anderson	So, how can I help you?
Rangi	I'm sorry to say it's a bit of a long story. You see, I've had to rethink my studies completely, and I wonder if I'm making the right decision.
Prof Anderson	You're doing two degrees, aren't you – Science and (23) Arts?
Rangi	I *was* doing two. I've decided to focus on Science.
Prof Anderson	Oh?

Rangi	It all came about because I wanted to study abroad for a year. I was thinking about Edinburgh. Firstly, I sought approval from the Maths and Physics Departments. I wanted to take Quantum Mechanics and Computer Simulations at Edinburgh.
Prof Anderson	Those are third-year courses, right?
Rangi	Yeah. So, I received approval from Maths and Physics. The stumbling block was the higher authority – the Science Faculty. When I submitted my application, it was rejected.
Prof Anderson	What?
Rangi	It turns out that students who study abroad for a year can only do first- or second-year courses, or third-year courses in a subject that's *not* their major.
Prof Anderson	I've never heard that before.
Rangi	Needless to say, the lecturers who approved my transfer hadn't either, and nor does the regulation appear on the Science Faculty website.
Prof Anderson	That'd be right. This faculty *is* (24) disorganised.
Rangi	So, then I thought I'd take Arts courses at Edinburgh, and leave the third-year Maths until I came back. I quickly got approval for second-year History and Philosophy from the Arts Faculty.
Prof Anderson	When are you heading off?
Rangi	That's just it. During this process I began to think carefully about my studies. To be honest, the Arts courses I've done were less challenging than the Science ones, so I've decided to drop (23) Arts.
Narrator	Before you listen to the rest of the conversation, you have 30 seconds to read questions 25 to 30.
Prof Anderson	Where do I figure in all this?
Rangi	The first week after I'd made my decision, I felt fine. (25) Without doing the Arts courses, I could finish my Science degree earlier. But this week, I've had some doubts. When I started the two degrees, lecturers in the Science Faculty assured me that, these days, scientists need a rounded education, which they get if they take some Arts courses. I was even told I'd learn to write and think better if I did Philosophy.
Prof Anderson	(26) I do think the claims made by some lecturers are dubious.
Rangi	Then, there's the fact that (27) now I'm going to be stuck here next year. I was so excited about going to Europe.
Prof Anderson	It is disappointing to give that up. Still, the reason I wanted to contact you, Rangi, is that (28) I'm looking for students to work six hours a week in my lab. It's paid work – not highly paid, but probably better than working in a bar. Also, we've just bought a new laser, which you'd learn to use.
Rangi	That sounds excellent.
Prof Anderson	As to going abroad, why not do your post-graduate studies in the US? There's some amazing Physics being done in Massachusetts. If you like, I can send you the papers from the conference.
Rangi	Thanks.
Prof Anderson	Of course I'd be sad to lose you if you did go abroad, (29) but an (22) A+ student, like you, has a very good chance of winning a major scholarship.
Rangi	Goodness. I've never even considered that.
Prof Anderson	Personally, I think committing yourself to Science is the way to go.
Rangi	(30) Thanks, Professor Anderson. You've taken a load off my mind. Now, I don't have to deal with Hegel or Leibnitz, I've plenty of time to read those conference papers.
Narrator	You now have 30 seconds to check your answers. That is the end of Section 3.

Narrator	Recording 18. Section 4. The ugly fruit movement. You will hear a lecture on the ugly fruit movement as an effort to prevent food wastage. Before you listen, you have 45 seconds to read questions 31 to 40.
Lecturer	Good Afternoon. I was in such a hurry I didn't have breakfast. I'd like to show you these apples that my neighbour grew. This one's fine, but this one's an odd shape; you certainly wouldn't find it on sale at a supermarket in this country. But, it tastes great. Today, I'd like to discuss food wastage, and a movement attempting to address the issue. There are ugly-fruit exponents throughout Europe, but I'll focus on a group in Portugal, called *Fruta Feia*, which means 'ugly fruit'. But first, some statistics. According to the Food and Agricultural Organisation of the United Nations, or the FAO, (31) around 40% of food for human consumption is wasted globally. The direct economic impact of this is a loss of $750 billion dollars each year. Meanwhile, every day, 870 million people worldwide go hungry. The environmental effects of food production are also astounding. (32) In the US, it's estimated that the transportation of food uses ten percent of the total US energy budget. At the same time, (32) food production consumes 50% of our land and (32) 80% of our available fresh water. The single largest component of solid municipal waste – around 40% – is rotting food, and the gases that produces increase global warming. Surprisingly, food wastage in developing countries is *as* high as in developed ones; what differs is where the wastage occurs. (33) In a country like Bolivia, Laos, or Zambia, food loss occurs after harvesting and during processing, due to inadequate storage, poor transportation infrastructure, and warm climatic conditions, whereas in the developed world, wastage occurs at the retail and consumer level – consumers seldom plan their shopping, which leads to over-purchasing; or, the enormous variety of supermarket food encourages impulse buying. Furthermore, consumers are strongly advised by regulatory authorities to dispose of food that may well be edible but which has passed its use-by date. (34) This overly-cautious labelling with use-by dates is something *Fruta Feia* has campaigned against. (35) The complex food rules of the European Union began in 1992, and have fuelled great discontent, especially in the UK, where journalists famously lampooned bureaucrats for banning bent bananas and curved cucumbers. After such criticism, the EU did reduce its list of rules for selling fruit and vegetables from 36 to ten. The difficulty lies with retailers that reject large amounts of food due to aesthetic considerations, believing spinach has to be completely green, and tomatoes perfectly spherical. Any blemish, even one that doesn't affect the edible contents, signals an item's destruction. To reduce wastage, the FAO recommends three things. Priority should be given to preventing wastage in the first place to by balancing production with demand. Where there is surplus, re-use by donation to needy people or to farm animals should take place. Lastly, if re-use is impossible, recycling and recovery should be pursued. Back to Portugal and *Fruta Feia*. Portugal, in Western Europe, is a developed nation of 10.5 million people. It joined the EU 30 years ago. In 2011, however, it was severely affected by a (36) debt crisis, and its economy is still shaky. As a result of the (36) debt crisis, unemployment is high, and hundreds of thousands of people have left the country. In these hard times, many Portuguese are hunting for bargains. So, enter the co-operative *Fruta Feia*, set up in Lisbon in 2013 by Isabel Soares. *Fruta Feia* has three aims: to feed people cheaply; to encourage EU rule-makers to overhaul use-by dates; and, to subvert notions of both what is (37) visually acceptable and what is (37) edible. When surveyed, most people who join *Fruta Feia* also support local agriculture. Isabel Soares estimates that one-third of Portugal's farm produce is thrown out due to artificial standards set by supermarkets. A farmer, José Dias, who supplies *Fruta Feia*, said that from his annual production of tomatoes, one (38) quarter did not meet supermarket standards, so were dumped. Now, *Fruta Feia* buys his 'reject' tomatoes at half the price he would sell them to a supermarket. Consequently, *Fruta Feia*'s members also pay (39) less for tomatoes than supermarket shoppers do. As to the myriad of regulations set by the EU, *Fruta Feia* does not contravene any: its own produce is unlabelled and unpackaged. Despite this somewhat unglamorous look, it has sold more than 20 metric tons of food in Lisbon alone. (40) Personally, even while the contribution of *Fruta Feia* and its 1,000 members is tiny, they are still, literally and metaphorically, eating away at the mountains of food that otherwise go to waste. And I salute that.
Narrator:	That is the end of the Listening test. You now have ten minutes to transfer your answers to your answer sheet.

READING: <u>Passage 1:</u> **1.** B; **2.** C; **3.** B; **4.** A; **5.** D; **6.** E; **7.** C; **8.** K; **9.** E; **10.** I; **11.** D; **12.** F; **13.** C. <u>Passage 2:</u> **14.** D; **15.** D; **16.** C; **17.** A; **18.** B; **19.** C; **20.** volatility; **21.** cortisol; **22.** Forward; **23.** wild; **24.** Further; **25.** N/No; **26.** NG/Not Given; **27.** Y/Yes. <u>Passage 3:</u> **28.** A; **29.** D; **30.** A; **31.** B; **32.** C; **33.** B; **34.** autonomous; **35.** non-human persons; **36.** habeas corpus; **37.** protection; **38.** all; **39.** succeeded; **40.** perceptions.

The highlighted text below is evidence for the answers above.

If there is a question where 'Not given' is the answer, no evidence can be found, so there is no highlighted text.

Márquez and Magical Realism

A (4) When Gabriel García Márquez died in 2014, he was mourned around the world, as readers recalled his 1967 novel, *One hundred years of solitude*, which has sold more than 25 million copies, and led to Márquez's receipt of the 1982 Nobel Prize for Literature.

B (1) Born in 1927, in a small town on Colombia's Caribbean coast called Aracataca, Márquez was immersed in Spanish, black, and indigenous cultures. (3) In such remote places, religion, myth, and superstition hold sway over logic and reason, or perhaps operate as parallel belief systems. Certainly, the ghost stories told by his grandmother affected the young Gabriel profoundly, and a pivotal character in his 1967 epic is indeed a ghost.

(1) Márquez's family was not wealthy: there were twelve children, and his father worked as a postal clerk, a telegraph operator, and an occasional pharmacist. Márquez spent much of his childhood in the care of his grandparents, (3) which may account for the main character in *One hundred years of solitude* resembling his maternal grandfather. Although Márquez left Aracataca aged eight, the town and its inhabitants never seemed to leave him, and suffuse his fiction.

C *One hundred years of solitude* was the fourth of fifteen novels, (7) but Márquez was an equally passionate and prolific journalist.

In Bogotá, during his twenties and thirties, Márquez experienced La Violencia, a period of great political and social upheaval, when around 300,000 Colombians were killed. Certainly, life was never safe for journalists, and after writing an article on corruption in the Colombian navy in 1955, Márquez was forced to flee to Europe. (2) Incidentally, in Paris, he discovered that European culture was not richer than his own, and he was disappointed by Europeans who were patronising towards Latin Americans. On return to the southern hemisphere, Márquez wrote for Venezuelan newspapers and the Cuban press agency.

D In terms of politics, Márquez was leftwing. In Chile, he campaigned against the dictatorship of General Augusto Pinochet; in Venezuela, he financed a political party; and, in Nicaragua, he defended revolutionaries. (5) He considered Fidel Castro, the President of Cuba, as a dear friend. Since the US was hostile towards Castro's communist regime, which Márquez supported, the writer was banned from visiting the US until invited by President Clinton in 1995. The novels of Márquez are imbued with his politics, but this does not prevent readers from enjoying a good yarn.

E Márquez maintained that in Latin America so much that is real would seem fantastic elsewhere, while so much that is magical seems real. He was an exponent of a genre known as Magical Realism.

'If you can explain it,' said the Mexican critic, Luis Leal, 'then it's not Magical Realism.' This demonstrates the difficulty of determining what the genre encompasses and which writers belong to it.

The term Magical Realism is usually applied to literature, but its first use was probably in (8) 1925, when a German art critic reviewed paintings similar to those of Surrealism.

(6) Many critics define Magical Realism by what it is not. Realism describes lives that could be real; Magical Realism uses the detail and the tone of a realist work, but includes the magical as though it were real. The ghosts in *One hundred years of solitude* and in the American Toni Morrison's *Beloved* are presented by their narrators as normal, (11) so readers accept them unhesitatingly. Likewise, a character can live for 200 years in a Magical Realist novel. Surrealism explores dream states and psychological experiences; Magical Realism does not. Science Fiction describes a new or an imagined world, as in Aldous Huxley's *Brave New World*, but Magical Realism depicts the real world. Nor is Magical Realism (9) fantasy, like Franz Kafka's *Metamorphosis*, in which an ordinary man awakens to find he has transformed into a cockroach. This is because the writer and the reader of that story cannot decide whether to ascribe natural or (10) supernatural causes to the event. In contrast, in a work by Márquez, the world is both natural *and* (10) supernatural, both rational *and* irrational, and this binary nature fascinates readers.

Magical Realism does share some common ground with post-modernism since the acts of writing and reading are self-reflexive. A narrative may (12) not be linear, but may double back on itself, or be discontinuous, and the notion of character is more illusive than in other genres.

Naturally, some of these elements disturb a reader although the enormous success of *One hundred years of solitude* and the hundreds of (13) other Magical Realist works from authors as far apart as Norway, Nigeria, and New Zealand would seem to belie it.

F Latin America has had a long history of conquest, revolution, and dictatorship; of hunger, poverty, and chaos, yet, at the same time, is endowed with rich cultures, with warm, emotional people, many of whom, like Márquez, remain optimistically utopian. Gabriel García Márquez has passed away, but his fiction will certainly endure.

Recent stock-market crashes

For as long as there have been financial markets, there have been financial crises. (14) Most economists agree, however, that from 1994 to 2013 crashes were deeper and the resultant troughs longer-lasting than in the 20-year period leading up to 1994. Two notable crashes, the Nifty Fifty in the mid-1970s and Black Monday in 1987, had an average loss of about 40% of the value of global stocks, and recovery took 240 days each, whereas the Dot-com and credit crises, post-1994, had an average loss of about 52%, and endured for 430 days. What economists do not agree upon is why recent crises have been so severe or how to prevent their recurrence.

John Coates, from the University of Cambridge in the UK and a former trader for Goldman Sachs and Deutsche Bank, believes three separate but related phenomena explain the severity. The first is dangerous but predictable risk-taking on the part of traders. The second is a lack of any risk-taking when markets become too volatile. (15) (Coates does not advocate risk-aversion since risk-taking may jumpstart a depressed market.) The last is a new policy of transparency by the US Federal Reserve – known as the Fed – that may have encouraged stock-exchange complacency, compounding the dangerous risk-taking.

Many people imagine a trader to have a great head for maths and a stomach for the rollercoaster ride of the market, but Coates downplays arithmetic skills, and doubts traders are made of such stern stuff. Instead, he draws attention to the physiological nature of their decisions. Admittedly, there are women in the industry, but traders are overwhelmingly male, and testosterone appears to affect their choices.

(16) Another common view is that traders are greedy as well as thrill-seeking. Coates has not researched financial incentive, (17) but blood samples taken from London traders who engaged in simulated risk-taking exercises for him in 2013 confirmed the prevalence of testosterone, cortisol, and dopamine – a neurotransmitter precursor to adrenalin associated with raised blood pressure and sudden pleasure.

Certainly anyone faced with danger has a stress response involving the body's preparation for impending movement – for what is sometimes called 'Fight or flight', but, as Coates notes, any physical act at all produces a stress response: even a reader's eye movement along words in this line requires cortisol and adrenalin. (18) Neuroscientists now see the brain not as a computer that acts neutrally, involved in a process of pure thought, but as a mechanism to plan and carry out movement, since every single piece of information humans absorb has an attendant pattern of physical arousal.

For muscles to work, fuel is needed, so cortisol and adrenalin employ glucose from other muscles and the liver. To burn the fuel, oxygen is required, so slightly deeper or faster breathing occurs. To deliver fuel and oxygen to the body, the heart pumps a little harder and blood pressure rises. Thus, the stress response is a normal part of life, as well as a resource in fighting or fleeing. Indeed, it is a highly pleasurable experience in watching an action movie, making love, or pulling off a multi-million-dollar stock-market deal.

Cortisol production also increases during exposure to uncertainty. For example, people who live next to a train line adjust to the noise of passing trains, but visitors to their home are disturbed. The phenomenon is equally well-known of anticipation being worse than an event itself: sitting in the waiting room thinking about a procedure may be more distressing than occupying the dentist's chair and having one. (19) Interestingly, if a patient does not know approximately when he or she will be called for that procedure, cortisol levels are the most elevated of all. This appeared to happen with the London traders participating in some of Coates' gambling scenarios.

When there is too much (20) volatility in the stock market, Coates suspects adrenaline levels decrease while (21) cortisol levels increase, explaining why traders take fewer risks at that time. In fact, typically traders freeze, becoming almost incapable of buying or selling anything but the safest bonds. In Coates' opinion, the market needs investment as it falls and at rock bottom – at such times, greed is good.

The third matter – the behaviour of the Fed – Coates thinks could be controlled, albeit counter-intuitively. Since 1994, the US Federal Reserve has adopted a policy called (22) Forward Guidance. Under this, the public is informed at regular intervals of the Fed's plans for short-term interest rates. Recently, rates have been raised by small but predictable increments. By contrast, in the past, the machinations of the Fed were largely secret, and its interest rates fluctuated apparently randomly. Coates hypothesises this meant traders were on guard and less likely to indulge in (23) wild speculation. In introducing (22) Forward Guidance the Fed hoped to lower stock and housing prices; instead, before the crash of 2008, the market surged from (24) further risk-taking, like an unleashed pit bull terrier.

(25) There are many economists who disagree with Coates, but he has provided some physiological evidence for both traders' recklessness *and* immobilisation, and made the radical proposal of greater opacity at the Fed. (27) Although, as others have noted, we could just let more women onto the floor.

Animal personhood

(28) Aristotle, a 4th-century-BC Greek philosopher, created the Great Chain of Being, in which animals, lacking reason, ranked below humans. The Frenchman, René Descartes, in the 17th century AD, considered animals as more complex creatures; however, without souls, they were merely automatons. One hundred years later, the German, (29) Immanuel Kant, proposed animals be treated less cruelly, which might seem an improvement, but Kant believed this principally because he thought acts of cruelty affect their human perpetrators detrimentally. The mid-19th century saw the Englishman, (30) Jeremy Bentham, questioning not their rationality or spirituality, but whether animals could suffer *irrespective* of the damage done to their victimisers; he concluded they could; and, (31) in 1824, the first large organisation for animal welfare, the Royal Society for the Prevention of Cruelty to Animals, was founded in England. In 1977, the Australian, Peter Singer, wrote the highly influential book *Animal liberation*, in which he debated the ethics of meat-eating and factory farming, and raised awareness about inhumane captivity and experimentation. (32) Singer's title deliberately evoked other liberation movements, like those for women, which had developed in the post-war period.

More recently, an interest in the cognitive abilities of animals has resurfaced. It has been known since the 1960s that (33) chimpanzees have sophisticated tool use and social interactions, but research from the last two decades has revealed they are also capable of empathy and grief, and they possess self-awareness and self-determination. Other primates, dolphins, whales, elephants, and African grey parrots are highly intelligent too. It would seem that with each new proof of animals' abilities, questions are being posed as to whether creatures so similar to humans should endure the physical pain or psychological trauma associated with habitat loss, captivity, or experimentation. While there may be more laws protecting animals than 30 years ago, in the eyes of the law, no matter how smart or sentient an animal may be, it still has a lesser status than a human being.

Steven Wise, an American legal academic, has been campaigning to change this. He believes animals, like those listed above, are (34) autonomous – they can control their actions, or rather, their actions are not caused purely by reflex or from innateness. He wants these animals categorized legally as (35) non-human persons because he believes existing animal-protection laws are weak and poorly enforced. He famously quipped that an aquarium may be fined for cruel treatment of its dolphins but, currently, the dolphins can't sue the aquarium.

While teaching at Vermont Law School in the 1990s, Wise presented his students with a dilemma: should an anencephalic baby be treated as a legal person? (Anencephaly is a condition where a person is born with a partial brain and can breathe and digest, due to reflex, but otherwise is barely alert, and not autonomous.) Overwhelmingly, Wise's students would say 'Yes'. He posed another question: could the same baby be killed and eaten by humans? Overwhelmingly, his students said 'No'. His third question, always harder to answer, was: why is an anencephalic baby legally a person yet not so a fully-functioning bonobo chimp?

Wise draws another analogy: between captive animals and slaves. Under slavery in England, a human was a chattel, and if a slave were stolen or injured, the thief or violator could be convicted of a crime, and compensation paid to the slave's owner though not to the slave. It was only in 1772 that the chief justice of the King's Bench, Lord Mansfield, ruled that a slave could apply for habeas corpus, Latin for: 'You must have the body', as free men and women had done since ancient times. Habeas corpus does not establish innocence or guilt; rather, it means a detainee can be represented in court by a proxy. Once slaves had been granted habeas corpus, they existed as more than chattels within the legal system although it was another 61 years before slavery was abolished in England. Aside from slaves, Wise has studied numerous cases in which a writ of (36) habeas corpus had been filed on behalf of those unable to appear in court, like children, patients, prisoners, or the severely intellectually impaired. In addition, Wise notes there are entities that are *not* living people that have legally become non-human persons, including: ships, corporations, partnerships, states, a Sikh holy book, some Hindu idols and the Wanganui River in New Zealand.

In conjunction with an organisation called the Non-human Rights Project (NhRP), Wise has been representing captive animals in US courts in an effort to have their legal status reassigned. Thereafter, the NhRP plans to apply, under habeas corpus, to represent the animals in other cases. Wise and the NhRP believe a new status will discourage animal owners or nation states from neglect or abuse, which current laws fail to do.

Richard Epstein, a professor of Law at New York University, is a critic of Wise's. His concern is that if animals are treated as independent holders of rights there would be little left of human society, in particular, in the food and agricultural industries. Epstein agrees some current legislation concerning animal (37) protection may need overhauling, but he sees no underlying problem.

Other detractors say that the push for personhood misses the point: it focuses on animals that are similar to humans without addressing the fundamental issue that (38) *all* species have an equal right to exist. Thomas Berry, of the Gaia Foundation, declares that rights do not emanate from humans but from the universe itself, and, as such, all species have the right to existence, habitat, and role (be that predator, plant, or decomposer). Dramatically changing human behaviour towards other species is necessary for their survival – and that doesn't mean declaring animals as non-human persons.

To date, the NhRP has not (39) succeeded in its applications to have the legal status of chimpanzees in New York State changed, but the NhRP considers it some kind of victory that the cases have been heard. Now, the NhRP can proceed to the Court of Appeals, where many emotive cases are decided, and where much common law is formulated.

Despite setbacks, Wise doggedly continues to expose brutality towards animals. Thousands of years of (40) perceptions may have to be changed in this process. He may have lost the battle, but he doesn't believe he's lost the war.

WRITING: Task 1

The diagram shows the 15-month process of French blue mussel production from spawning to sale.

After spawning and fecondation, mussel larvae spend three to four weeks in the trochophore stage, at which time they are around 0.3 millimetres in length. During the veliger larval stage that follows (2-9 days), they double in size. Metamorphosis occurs at around three months, when the creatures grow shells and settle either on-bottom or off-bottom.

On-bottom mussels attach themselves to rocks on the seabed as in nature.

Off-bottom mussels live on artificial structures: intertidal racks with coconut fibre ropes, or suspended subtidal cages. After six weeks, these 3-10-millimetre mussels are manually transferred to bouchot ropes or longlines, where most of their growth takes place.

The bouchot culture method is intertidal. Mussel-covered ropes spiral around poles fixed in rows to the seabed. Annual yield is 17.5 tonnes. The longline method is subtidal, with clusters of mussels hanging from buoyant ropes just below the surface of the sea. Annual yield is around 20 tonnes.

Mussel harvesting is mechanical.

On shore, mussels are separated, and processed for sale. The average length of a marketable French blue mussel is 50 millimetres. (194 words)

Task 2

Although plagiarism is stealing other people's ideas, thoughts and words, and considered unacceptable by most, it is becoming more and more a fact of life. As the world population increases, and millions are using the Worldwide Web to search for information and to communicate in general, it becomes much harder to police what is on the Web itself. Checking the originality of the vast amount of material that is written on the Web is difficult; deciding whether a student's essay or a journalist's article is original and praiseworthy, can be equally difficult.

Authors, journalists, students and researchers are all still supposed to offer original work, and provide their sources if they use someone else's ideas. But some do not do either. Simply by going online, a writer can copy and paste from various websites and blogs, and change a word here, a word there, without being detected. Whether a writer's work is original or not can often be difficult to ascertain. Today, citing books and journal articles often comes second to using the information on the Web.

However, not all is lost for those people who consider plagiarists to be cheats. There are now online plagiarism checkers that are used by teachers, students and others. Essays can be transferred to the chosen site and checked for originality. Not only can writers' words be scrutinised, but their sources can also be checked for possible uncited borrowings. Self-checking one's own writings undoubtedly provides relief.

Nevertheless, there is nothing new about plagiarism. For example, if William Shakespeare had not used the Holinshed Chronicles as the basis for his history plays, and a work such as Macbeth, English literature would be poorer. Yet although Shakespeare uses the plots for his plays, the language, thoughts, and characterisations are very much his.

Today, the main problem with plagiarism is that some writers cheat their way to success without offering originality. However, even though there are ways of checking for plagiarism, it is understandable why some do not see plagiarism as a problem since our technological world is putting everything out there for all to do what they like with, thus making it more and more impossible to police.

Despite the power of the Worldwide Web, I believe that writers should avoid cheating, and instead, rigorously uphold the conventions of good writing. They must acknowledge their sources, avoid plagiarising others, and show some originality. (397 words)

TEST 4

Listening

Firstly, tear out the Test 4 Listening / Reading Answer Sheet at the back of this book.

The Listening test lasts for about 20 minutes.

Write your answers on the pages below as you listen. After Section 4 has finished, you have ten minutes to transfer your answers to your Listening Answer Sheet. You will need to time yourself for this transfer.

After checking your answers on pp 162-167, go to page 9 for the raw-score conversion table.

PLAY RECORDING #19.

SECTION 1   Questions 1-10

CHILDREN'S DAY CARE

Questions 1-3

Answer the questions below.

*Write **ONE WORD OR A NUMBER** for each answer.*

Example   What are Angela and Sanjit going to drink before Tom arrives?

   Coffee

1   What is Sanjit's son called?

   …………………..……………..

2   What is the meaning of the name Zoe?

   …………………..……………..

3   What is the maximum daily rate in dollars at Zoe's day care?

   …………………..……………..

Questions 4-5

*Choose **TWO** letters, **A-E**.*

Which **TWO** of the following happen at Zoe's day care?

   A   Parents must provide diapers and food for their children.

   B   Children's birthdays are celebrated with songs and games.

   C   Children are divided by age into rooms named after animals.

   D   Parents who collect their children fifteen minutes late are fined.

   E   The centre reserves the right to send home children who are ill.

143

Questions 6-10

Complete the table below.

*Write **NO MORE THAN TWO WORDS** for each answer.*

	Advantages	**Disadvantages**
East Lindsay Day Care	• Very hygienic • Caring, responsible staff • Adequate (**6**)………………..	• No obvious tuition; too much (**7**)………………..
Zoe's Day Care	• Some structured tuition • Fairly hygienic • Free sick days or (**9**)………………. • Parents are kept (**10**)……………….	• (**8**)………………. Eg: parents' supply of birthday snacks & tablets

Play Audio   **PLAY RECORDING #20.**

SECTION 2   Questions 11-20

A VERY SMALL HOUSE

Questions 11-15

*Choose the correct letter, **A**, **B**, or **C**.*

11   What size is Charlotte's house?

    A   8 square metres

    B   80 square metres

    C   800 square metres

12   In the past, what did people think about Charlotte's lifestyle?

    A   They were curious.

    B   They were hostile.

    C   They were uninterested.

13   What does Charlotte's story about smoking show?

    A   Her mother is a keen supporter.

    B   Attitudes and behaviours do change.

    C   Americans approve of a ban on smoking in public.

14   How have American family and house sizes changed from 1945 to the present?

    A   Families and houses have shrunk.

    B   Families and houses have grown.

    C   Families have shrunk; houses have grown.

15   Who inspired Charlotte to live in a very small house?

    A   Her mother in France

    B   Her neighbours in Vietnam

    C   Her partner in Chicago

Questions 16-20

Complete the sentences below.

Write **NO MORE THAN THREE WORDS OR A NUMBER** *for each answer.*

16   Since living in Mozambique, Charlotte has not used a fridge or a..................... .

17   Charlotte believes children who live in small houses tend to................... more.

18   Now, every item Charlotte owns must be both................... .

19   Charlotte used to have 4,000 possessions; she now has................... .

20   Charlotte thinks the greatest saving from her lifestyle is she now has more................... .

Play
Audio   **PLAY RECORDING #21.**

SECTION 3   Questions 21-30

A BUSINESS ASSIGNMENT

Questions 21-26

*Choose the correct letter, **A**, **B**, or **C**.*

21   How many words has Luca written of his short essay so far?

    A   450

    B   560

    C   800

22   A business plan often includes information about a company's

    A   past performance and potential problems.

    B   present situation and its growth forecast.

    C   current state and a three-year sales projection.

23   According to Luca, a business plan might be written for

    A   future investors.

    B   tax authorities.

    C   a company's CEO.

24   What do the students think about design controls to measure the success of a business?

    A   They think controls are desirable.

    B   They think controls are essential.

    C   They are not sure what controls are.

25   A company usually makes separate

    A   Marketing and Production Plans.

    B   Finance and Purchasing Plans.

    C   plans for each section of a master plan.

26   How does Luca feel about detailed business plans?

    A   Surprised

    B   Inspired

    C   Uninterested

Questions 27-30

Complete the information below.

Write **NO MORE THAN TWO WORDS** *for each answer.*

A BUSINESS PLAN				
I. Business Profile				
II. Business Functions				
Marketing	Purchasing	Production	(27)………………..	Finance
III. Appendices or (28)………………..				

Business Profile in detail:

- Business Name
- Location
- Ownership (**29**)………………..
- Business Activity
- Market Entry Strategy
- Future Objectives
- Legal (**30**)………………..

Play Audio   **PLAY RECORDING #22.**

SECTION 4   Questions 31-40

THE BENEFITS OF LITERATURE

Questions 31-34

Complete the sentences below.

Write **NO MORE THAN TWO WORDS** *for each answer.*

31   The speaker, Kidd, and Castano believe………………..is the most useful kind to read for cognitive and emotional intelligence.

32   Theory of Mind is a person's capacity to understand that other people's mental states may be………………..from their own.

33   Austen, Fitzgerald, and al Aswany are examples of………………..literary authors.

34   A major disadvantage of popular literature is that it leaves a reader's worldview……………. .

Questions 35-40

*Choose the correct letter, **A**, **B**, or **C**.*

35 Kidd and Castano's experimental volunteers read from

  A   fiction and non-fiction.

  B   texts of their own choice.

  C   different genres or nothing at all.

36 According to the speaker, …… may benefit from a literature-focused approach.

  A   prisoners

  B   delinquents

  C   illiterate adults

37 The speaker compares reading the Harry Potter series to watching TV for the same amount of time to imply that

  A   they are both entertaining and educational.

  B   watching TV causes more neural activity.

  C   reading creates deeper emotional attachment.

38 According to the Common Sense Media report, how many teens read for pleasure daily in 1984 and 2014?

  A   17% and 9%

  B   31% and 27%

  C   31% and 17%

39 Why did the teenagers in the Common Sense report say they read less?

  A   They didn't enjoy reading.

  B   They lacked reading skills.

  C   They didn't have time.

40 The speaker gave her neighbour a copy of *The Little Prince* because

  A   reading literature helps people cope with a complex world.

  B   this French classic is one of her personal favourites.

  C   she believes literary fiction is neglected.

LISTENING
READING
WRITING
SPEAKING

PASSAGE 1   PASSAGE 2   PASSAGE 3

Reading

Firstly, turn over the Test 4 Listening Answer Sheet you used earlier to write your Reading answers on the back.

The Reading test lasts exactly 60 minutes.

Certainly, make any marks on the pages below, but transfer your answers to the answer sheet <u>as you read</u> since there is no extra time at the end to do so.

After checking your answers on pp 167-169, go to page 9 for the raw-score conversion table.

PASSAGE 1

*Spend about 20 minutes on **Questions 1-14**, based on Passage 1 below.*

Questions 1-6

Reading Passage 1 on the following page has seven sections: **A-G**.

*Choose the correct heading for sections **B-G** from the list of headings below.*

*Write the correct number, **i-x**, in boxes 1-6 on your answer sheet.*

List of Headings
i   The uses of red
ii   Russian and English views of red
iii   Red and beauty
iv   The optics of red
v   Red and religion
vi   The hazards of red
vii   Red and politics
viii Portrait painters who copied icons
ix   Red and art
x   Revolutionary painters

Example	*Answer*
Section A	**iii**

1   Section **B**

2   Section **C**

3   Section **D**

4   Section **E**

5   Section **F**

6   Section **G**

RED IN RUSSIAN ART

A In Old Slavonic, a language that precedes Russian, 'red' has a similar root to the words 'good' and 'beautiful'. Indeed, until the 20th century, *Krasnaya Ploshchad*, or Red Square, in central Moscow, was understood by locals as 'Beautiful Square'. For Russians, red has great symbolic meaning, being associated with goodness, beauty, warmth, vitality, jubilation, faith, love, salvation, and power.

B Because red is a long-wave colour at the end of the spectrum, its effect on a viewer is striking: it appears closer than colours with shorter waves, like green, and it also intensifies colours placed alongside it, which accounts for the popularity of red and green combinations in Russian painting.

C Russians love red. In the applied arts, it predominates: bowls, boxes, trays, wooden spoons, and distaffs for spinning all feature red, as do children's toys, decorative figurines, Easter eggs, embroidered cloths, and garments. In the fine arts, red, white, and gold form the basis of much icon painting.

D In pre-Christian times, red symbolised blood. Christianity adopted the same symbolism; red represented Christ or saints in their purification or martyrdom. The colour green, meantime, signified wisdom, while white showed a person reborn as a Christian. Thus, in a famous 15th-century icon from the city of Novgorod, *Saint George and the Dragon*, red-dressed George sports a green cape, and rides a pure-white stallion. In many icons, Christ and the angels appear in a blaze of red, and the mother of Christ can be identified by her long red veil. In an often-reproduced icon from Yaroslavl, the Archangel Michael wears a brilliant red cloak. However, the fires of Hell that burn sinners are also red, like those in an icon from Pskov.

E A red background for major figures in icons became the norm in representations of mortal beings, partly to add vibrancy to skin tones, and one fine example of this is a portrait of Nikolai Gogol, the writer, from the early 1840s. When wealthy aristocrats wished to be remembered for posterity, they were often depicted in dashing red velvet coats, emulating the cloaks of saints, as in the portraits of Jakob Turgenev in 1696, or of Admiral Ivan Talyzin in the mid-1760s. Portraits of women in Russian art are rare, but the Princess Yekaterina Golitsyna, painted in the early 1800s, wears a fabulous red shawl.

Common people do not appear frequently in Russian fine art until the 19th century, when their peasant costumes are often white with red embroidery, and their elaborate headdresses and scarves are red. The women in the 1915 painting, *Visiting*, by Abram Arkhipov seem aflame with life: their dresses are red; their cheeks are red; and, a jug of vermillion lingonberry cordial glows on the table beside them.

Russian avant-garde painters of the early 20th century are famous beyond Russia as some of the greatest abstract artists. Principal among these are Nathan Altman, Natalia Goncharova, Wassily Kandinsky, and Kazimir Malevich, who painted the ground-breaking *White on white* as well as *Red Square*, which is all the more compelling because it isn't quite square. Malevich used primary colours, with red prominent, in much of his mature work. Kuzma Petrov-Vodkin is hailed as a genius at home, but less well-known abroad; his style is often surreal, and his palette is restricted to the many hues of red, contrasting with green or blue. The head in his 1915 *Head of a youth* is entirely red, while his 1925 painting, *Fantasy*, shows a man in blue, on a larger-than-life all-red horse, with a blue town in blue mountains behind.

F Part of the enthusiasm for red in the early 20th century was due to the rise of the political movement, communism. Red had first been used as a symbol of revolution in France in the late 18th century. The Russian army from 1918-45 called itself the Red Army to continue this revolutionary tradition, and the flag of the Soviet Union was the Red Flag.

Soviet poster artists and book illustrators also used swathes of red. Some Social Realist painters have been discredited for their political associations, but their art was potent, and a viewer cannot help but be moved by Nikolai Rutkovsky's 1934 *Stalin at Kirov's coffin*. Likewise, Alexander Gerasimov's 1942 *Hymn to October* or Dmitry Zhilinsky's 1965 *Gymnasts of the USSR* stand on their own as memorable paintings, both of which include plenty of red.

G In English, red has many negative connotations – red for debt, a red card for football fouls, or a red-light district – but in Russian, red is beautiful, vivacious, spiritual, and revolutionary. And Russian art contains countless examples of its power.

Questions 7-12

Complete the table below.

Choose **ONE WORD OR A NUMBER** *from the passage for each answer.*

Write your answers in boxes 7-12 on your answer sheet.

Russian Applied Arts	
Household goods:	Red wooden objects, toys, figurines, & embroidered (**7**)...............
Garments:	Red coats, dresses, headdresses, shawls & scarves
Russian Fine Arts	
Painting: Icon	• Red, white & gold = main colours • (**8**)...............-century Novgorod icon of St George in red • Christ, saints, angels & mother of Christ in red • Fires of Hell = red
Portrait	• 1840s Gogol painted with red (**9**)..............., like figures in icons • 1696 Turgenev & mid-1760s Talyzin in red coats, like saints' cloaks • 1800s Princess Golitsyna in red shawl • 1915 *Visiting* = peasant women & lots of red
Abstract	• Painters famous worldwide: Altman, Goncharova & Kandinsky • Malevich's *White on white* & *Red Square* = impressive
Surrealist	• Petrov-Vodkin famous in Russia • 1915 *Head of a* (**10**)............... = head all red • 1925 *Fantasy* = blue man on huge red horse
Social (**11**).........	• Lots of red in: Rutkovsky's 1934 *Stalin at Kirov's coffin* • Gerasimov's 1942 *Hymn to October* • Zhilinsky's (**12**).............. *Gymnasts of the USSR*

Question 13

Choose **TWO** *letters: A-E.*

Write the correct letters in box 13 on your answer sheet.

The list below includes associations Russians make with the colour red.

Which **TWO** are mentioned by the writer of the passage?

    A   danger

    B   wealth

    C   intelligence

    D   faith

    E   energy

PASSAGE 2

*Spend about 20 minutes on **Questions 14-27**, based on Passage 2 below.*

Lepidoptera

Myths and Misnomers

A buttercup is a small, bright yellow flower; a butternut is a yellow-fleshed squash; and, there is also a butter bean. The origin of the word 'butterfly' may be similar to these plants – a creature with wings the colour of butter – but a more fanciful notion is that 'flutterby' was misspelt by an early English scribe since a butterfly's method of flight is to flutter by. Etymologists may not concur, but entomologists agree with each other that butterflies belong to the order of Lepidoptera, which includes moths, and that 'lepidoptera' accurately describes the insects since 'lepis' means 'scale' and 'pteron' means 'wing' in Greek.

Until recently, butterflies were prized for their evanescence – people believed that adults lived for a single day; it is now known this is untrue, and some, like monarch butterflies, live for up to nine months.

Butterflies versus Moths

Butterflies and moths have some similarities: as adults, both have four membranous wings covered in minute scales, attached to a short thorax and a longer abdomen with three pairs of legs. They have moderately large heads, long antennae, and compound eyes; tiny palps for smell; and, a curling proboscis for sucking nectar. Otherwise their size, colouration, and lifecycles are the same.

Fewer than one percent of all insects are butterflies, but they hold a special place in the popular imagination as being beautiful and benign. Views of moths, however, are less kind since some live indoors and feast on cloth; others damage crops; and, most commit suicide, being nocturnal and drawn to artificial light. There are other differences between butterflies and moths; for example, when resting, the former fold their wings vertically above their bodies, while the latter lay theirs flat. Significantly, butterfly antennae thicken slightly towards their tips, whereas moth antennae end in something that looks like a V-shaped TV aerial.

The Monarch Butterfly

Originating in North America, the black-orange-and-white monarch butterfly lives as far away as Australia and New Zealand, and for many children it represents a lesson in metamorphosis, which can even be viewed in one's living room if a pupa is brought indoors.

It is easy to identify the four stages of a monarch's lifecycle – egg, larva, pupa, and adult – but there are really seven. This is because, unlike vertebrates, insects do not have an internal skeleton, but a tough outer covering called an exoskeleton. This is often shell-like and sometimes indigestible by predators. Muscles are hinged to its inside. As the insect grows, however, the constraining exoskeleton must be moulted, and a monarch butterfly undergoes seven moults, including four as a larva.

Temperature dramatically affects butterfly growth: in warm weather, a monarch may go through its seven moults in just over a month. Time spent inside the egg, for instance, may last three to four days in 25° Celsius, but in 18°, the whole process may take closer to eight weeks, with time inside the egg eight to twelve days. Naturally, longer development means lower populations due to increased predation.

A reliable food supply influences survival, and the female monarch butterfly is able to sniff out one particular plant its young can feed off – milkweed or swan plant. There are a few other plants larvae can eat, but they will resort to these only if the milkweed is exhausted and alternatives are very close by. Moreover, a female butterfly may be conscious of the size of the milkweed on which she lays her eggs since she spaces them, but another butterfly may deposit on the same plant, lessening everyone's chance of survival.

While many other butterflies are close to extinction due to pollution or dwindling habitat, the global numbers of monarchs have decreased in the past two decades, but less dramatically.

Monarch larvae absorb toxins from milkweed that render them poisonous to most avian predators who attack them. Insect predators, like aphids, flies, and wasps, seem unaffected by the poison, and are therefore common. A recent disturbing occurrence is the death of monarch eggs and larvae from bacterial infection.

Another reason for population decline is reduced wintering conditions. Like many birds, monarch butterflies migrate to warmer climates in winter, often flying extremely long distances, for example, from Canada to southern California or northern Mexico, or from southern Australia to the tropical north. They also spend some time in semi-hibernation in dense colonies deep in forests. In isolated New Zealand, monarchs do not migrate, instead finding particular trees on which to congregate. In some parts of California, wintering sites are protected, but in Mexico, much of the forest is being logged, and the insects are in grave danger.

Milkweed is native to southern Africa and North America, but it is easy to grow in suburban gardens. Its swan-shaped seedpods contain fluffy seeds used in the 19th century to stuff mattresses, pillows, and lifejackets. After milkweed had hitched a lift on sailing ships around the Pacific, the American butterflies followed with Hawaii seeing their permanent arrival in 1840, Samoa in 1867, Australia in 1870, and New Zealand in 1873. As butterfly numbers decline sharply in the Americas, it may be these Pacific outposts that save the monarch.

Questions 14-17

Do the following statements agree with the information given in Reading Passage 2?

In boxes 14-17 on your answer sheet, write:

> **TRUE**　　　*if the statement agrees with the information.*
>
> **FALSE**　　*if the statement contradicts the information.*
>
> **NOT GIVEN**　*if there is no information on this.*

14　One theory is that the word 'butterfly' means an insect the colour of butter.

15　Another theory is that a 'butterfly' was a mistake for a 'flutterby'.

16　The Greeks had a special reverence for butterflies.

17　The relative longevity of butterflies has been understood for some time.

Questions 18-21

Classify the things on the following page that relate to:

> **A**　butterflies only.
>
> **B**　moths only.
>
> **C**　both butterflies and moths.

Write the correct letter, A, B, or C, in boxes 18-21 on your answer sheet.

18   They have complex eyes.

19   Humans view them negatively.

20   They fold their wings upright.

21   They have more pronounced antennae.

Questions 22-27

Complete the summary below using the numbers or words, A-I, below.

Write the correct letter, A-I, in boxes 22-27 on your answer sheet.

A	bacteria	B	California	C	Canada
D	four	E	Mexico	F	milkweed
G	North America	H	the Pacific	I	seven

The Monarch Butterfly

Monarch butterflies can live for up to nine months. Indigenous to (**22**)……………….., they are now found throughout the Pacific as well.

Since all insects have brittle exoskeletons, they must shed these regularly while growing. In the life of a monarch butterfly, there are (**23**)………………. moults.

Several factors affect butterfly populations. Low temperatures mean animals take longer to develop, increasing the risk of predation. A steady supply of a specific plant called (**24**)……………….. is necessary; and a small number of eggs laid per plant. Birds do attack monarch butterflies, but as larvae and adults contain toxins, such attacks are infrequent. Insects, unaffected by poison, and (**25**)……………….. pose a greater threat.

The gravest danger to monarch butterflies is the reduction of their wintering grounds, by deforestation, especially in (**26**)……………….. .

Monarchs do not migrate long distances within New Zealand, but they gather in large colonies on certain trees. It is possible that the isolation of this country and some other islands in (**27**)……………….. will save monarchs.

PASSAGE 3

*Spend about 20 minutes on **Questions 28-40**, based on Passage 3 below.*

● ●

HOW FAIR IS FAIR TRADE?

The fair-trade movement began in Europe in earnest in the post-war period, but only in the last 25 years has it grown to include producers and consumers in over 60 countries.

In the 1950s and 60s, many people in the developed world felt passionately about the enormous disparities between developed and developing countries, and they believed the system of international trade shut out African, Asian, and South American producers who could not compete with multi-national companies or who came from states that, for political reasons, were not trading with the West. The catchphrase 'Trade Not Aid' was used by church groups and trade unions – early supporters of fair trade – who also considered that international aid was either a pittance or a covert form of subjugation. These days, much fair trade does include aid: developed-world volunteers offer their services, and there is free training for producers and their workers.

Tea, coffee, cocoa, cotton, flowers, handicrafts, and gold are all major fair-trade items, with coffee being the most recognisable, found on supermarket shelves and at café chains throughout the developed world.

Although around two million farmers and workers produce fair-trade items, this is a tiny number in relation to total global trade. Still, fair-trade advocates maintain that the system has positively impacted upon many more people worldwide, while the critics claim that if those two million returned to the mainstream trading system, they would receive higher prices for their goods or labour.

Fair trade is supposed to be trade that is fair to producers. Its basic tenet is that developed-world consumers will pay slightly more for end products in the knowledge that developing-world producers have been equitably remunerated, and that the products have been made in decent circumstances. Additionally, the fair-trade system differs from that of the open market because there is a minimum price paid for goods, which may be higher than that of the open market. Secondly, a small premium, earmarked for community development, is added in good years; for example, coffee co-operatives in South America frequently receive an additional 25c per kilogram. Lastly, purchasers of fair-trade products may assist with crop pre-financing or with training of producers and workers, which could take the form of improving product quality, using environmentally friendly fertilisers, or raising literacy. Research has shown that non-fair-trade farmers copy some fair-trade farming practices, and, occasionally, encourage social progress. In exchange for ethical purchase and other assistance, fair-trade producers agree not to use child or slave labour, to adhere to the United Nations Charter on Human Rights, to provide safe workplaces, and to protect the environment despite these not being legally binding in their own countries. However, few non-fair-trade farmers have adopted these practices, viewing them as little more than rich-world conceits.

So that consumers know which products are made under fair-trade conditions, goods are labelled, and, these days, a single European and American umbrella organisation supervises labelling, standardisation, and inspection.

While fair trade is increasing, the system is far from perfect. First and foremost, there are expenses involved in becoming a fair-trade-certified producer, meaning the desperately poor rarely participate, so the very farmers fair-trade advocates originally hoped to support are excluded. Secondly, because conforming to the standards of fair-trade certification is costly, some producers deliberately mislabel their goods. The fair-trade monitoring process is patchy, and unfortunately, around 12% of fair-trade-labelled produce is nothing of the kind. Next, a crop may genuinely be produced under fair-trade conditions, but due to a lack of demand cannot be sold as fair trade, so goes onto the open market, where prices are mostly lower. It is estimated that only between 18-37% of fair-trade output is

LISTENING
READING
WRITING
SPEAKING

PASSAGE 1   PASSAGE 2   PASSAGE 3

actually sold as fair trade. Sadly, there is little reliable research on the real relationship between costs incurred and revenue for fair-trade farmers, although empirical evidence suggests that many never realise a profit. Partly, reporting from producers is inadequate, and ways of determining profit may not include credit, harvesting, transport, or processing. Sometimes, the price paid to fair-trade producers is lower than that of the open market, so while a crop may be sold, elsewhere it could have earnt more, or where there are profits, they are often taken by the corporate firms that buy the goods and sell them on to retailers.

There are problems with the developed-world part of the equation too. People who volunteer to work for fair-trade concerns may do so believing they are assisting farmers and communities, whereas their labour serves to enrich middlemen and retailers. Companies involved in West African cocoa production have been criticised for this. In the developed world, the right to use a fair-trade logo is also expensive for packers and retailers, and sometimes a substantial amount of the money received from sale is ploughed back into marketing. In richer parts of the developed world, notably in London, packers and retailers charge high prices for fair-trade products. Consumers imagine they are paying so much because more money is returned to producers, when profit-taking by retailers or packers is a more likely scenario. One UK café chain is known to have passed on 1.6% of the extra 18% it charged for fair-trade coffee to producers. However, this happens with other items at the supermarket or café, so perhaps consumers are naïve to believe fair-traders behave otherwise. In addition, there are struggling farmers in rich countries, too, so some critics think fair-trade associations should certify them. Other critics find the entire fair-trade system flawed – nothing more than a colossal marketing scam – and they would rather assist the genuinely poor in more transparent ways, but this criticism may be overblown since fair trade has endured for and been praised in the developing world itself.

● ●

Questions 28-32

Answer the questions below.

*Choose **NO MORE THAN THREE WORDS** from the passage for each answer.*

Write your answers in boxes 28-32 on your answer sheet.

28   What was an early slogan about addressing the imbalance between the developed and developing worlds?

   ....

29   What is probably the most well-known fair-trade commodity?

   ....

30   According to the writer, in terms of total global trade, what do fair-trade producers represent?

   ....

31   How do its supporters think fair trade has affected many people?

   ....

32   What do its critics think fair-trade producers would get if they went back to mainstream trade?

   ....

Questions 33-36

*Complete each sentence with the correct ending, **A-H**, below.*

*Write the correct letter, **A-H**, in boxes 33-36 on your answer sheet.*

33 Consumers of fair-trade products are happy

34 The fair-trade system may include

35 Some fair-trade practices

36 Fair-trade producers must adopt international employment standards

A	loans or training for producers and employees.
B	although they may not be obliged to do so in their own country.
C	for the various social benefits fair trade brings.
D	to pay more for what they see as ethical products.
E	has influenced non-fair-trade producers.
F	because these are United Nations obligations.
G	too much corruption.
H	have been adopted by non-fair-trade producers.

Questions 37-40

Do the following statements agree with the claims of the writer in Reading Passage 3?

In boxes 37-40 on your answer sheet, write:

YES	*if the statement agrees with the claims of the writer.*
NO	*if the statement contradicts the claims of the writer.*
NOT GIVEN	*if it is impossible to say what the writer thinks about this.*

37 The fair-trade system assists farmers who are extremely poor.

38 Some produce labelled as fair-trade is in fact not.

39 UK supermarkets and cafés should not charge such high prices for fair-trade items.

40 Fair trade is mainly a marketing ploy and not a valid way of helping the poor.

LISTENING
READING
WRITING
SPEAKING

TASK 1   TASK 2

LISTENING
READING
WRITING
SPEAKING

| TASK 1 | TASK 2 |

Writing

The Writing test lasts for 60 minutes.

Task 1

Spend about 20 minutes on this task.

> **The table below gives information about two atolls: Bassas da India, and Ile Europa.**
>
> **Write a summary of the information. Select and report the main features, and make comparisons where necessary.**

Write at least 150 words.

Atolls[1]	Bassas da India	Ile Europa
Location	385 km W of Madagascar & 110 km NW of Ile Europa	Madagascar Channel (Between Mozambique in East Africa & Madagascar)
Size		
Diameter	c[2] 12 km (kilometre)	c 6 km
Coastline	35.2 km	22.2 km
Lagoon	Area: 34,000 ha (hectare) Depth: c 15 m (metre)	Area: c 900 ha Depth: c 1 m
Status		
Part of French Southern & Antarctic Lands since 1897; claimed by Madagascar		
Population		
Former	None	French farmers: 1860-1920
Current		A few short-term French military, weather station, & scientific personnel
Other		
Shipwrecks	More than 100	c 30
Land forms & use	Mostly lagoon – 10 very small rocky islands & 100 m of sand exposed at all times (some land exposed for 6 hours around low tide); nature reserve	Island & lagoons; highest point 11 m; nature reserve
Plants	None on land	Dry forest, grass, scrub; large area of mangroves; introduced hemp & sisal
Animals	Sharks & tropical fish; 0 introduced animals	Tropical fish; nesting birds, green sea turtles & other reptiles; introduced goats & rats

---

[1]An atoll consists of a ring-shaped coral reef around a lagoon. It is the visible part of an extinct undersea volcano that has been built up by marine organisms.

[2]c = *circa* or 'about'

Task 2

Spend about 40 minutes on this task.

Write about the following topic:

> **Some people believe positive thinking has benefits, while others consider it has drawbacks.**
>
> **Discuss both these views, and give your own opinion.**

Provide reasons for your answer, including relevant examples from your own knowledge or experience.

Write at least 250 words.

Speaking

PART 1

How might you answer the following questions?

1   Could you tell me what you're doing at the moment: are you working or studying?

2   What are you studying?

3   What do you like most about your studies?

4   What do you remember about your first day at school / college / university?

5   Now, let's talk about taking driving lessons. Do you drive?

6   How difficult was it for you to get a driver's licence?

7   Do you think there should be an upper age limit on drivers? Why? / Why not?

8   Let's move on to talk about the theatre. How often do you go to the theatre?

9   Why do some people prefer to go to the theatre than to the cinema?

10   What would be the thrills and challenges of being a theatre director?

PART 2

How might you speak about the following topic for two minutes?

I'd like you to tell me about a very good piece of advice someone gave you. * Who was the person? * What was the advice? * Did you take the advice? And, how do you feel about the experience now?

PART 3

1   First of all, advice about one's private life.

When are some occasions it's great to get advice from family members, and when might advice from friends be more useful?

Should school or university teachers advise their students about their private lives?

What qualities does a person need to give sound advice?

2   Now, let's consider advice about careers.

Who gives advice about careers in your country?

Do you think it is better to choose a career on one's own, or to take advice from others about the choice?

Answers

LISTENING

Section 1: **1.** Aarav; **2.** Life; **3.** 50 / fifty; **4.** C; **5.** D; **6.** space; **7.** play; **8.** hidden costs; **9.** holidays; **10.** well informed. Section 2: **11.** A; **12.** B; **13.** B; **14.** C; **15.** B; **16.** shower; **17.** share; **18.** functional and/& beautiful; **19.** 400/four hundred; **20.** time. Section 3: **21.** A; **22.** B; **23.** A; **24.** C; **25.** C; **26.** A; **27.** Personnel; **28.** Supporting documents; **29.** Structure; **30.** Requirements. Section 4: **31.** literary fiction; **32.** different; **33.** classic; **34.** unchallenged // intact; **35.** C; **36.** A; **37.** C; **38.** B; **39.** C; **40.** A.

The highlighted text below is evidence for the answers above.

Narrator	Recording 19. Practice Listening Test 4. Section 1. Children's day care. You will hear a man and a woman talking about day care for their children. Read the example.
Angela	Hi Sanjit? How are you?
Sanjit	Pretty well, Angela. Tom won't be here for another ten minutes. Shall we have coffee while we're waiting?
Angela	Why not?
Narrator	The answer is 'coffee'. On this occasion only, the first part of the conversation is played twice. Before you listen again, you have 30 seconds to read questions 1 to 5.
Angela	Hi Sanjit? How are you?
Sanjit	Pretty well, Angela. Tom won't be here for another ten minutes. Shall we have coffee while we're waiting?
Angela	Why not? How's your family?
Sanjit	Not too bad, except my son, (1) Aarav, had a cold last week, and then my wife, Navreet, caught it.
Angela	Oh dear. My daughter, Zoe, had a temperature this morning, and I wasn't sure whether to send her to day care, but my husband's away, in Toronto, and I can't take any more time off myself.
Sanjit	I guess kids get all kinds of things at day care.
Angela	I don't know. They also build up resistance there. By the way, I'm sending out invitations for Zoe's birthday party. How do you spell (1) Aarav?
Sanjit	(1) Double ARAV.
Angela	Thanks. I've never heard the name before. What does it mean?
Sanjit	'Peaceful' or 'wise'. It's popular in India because the film stars Twinkle Khanna and Akshay Kumar called their son Aarav. What does Zoe mean?
Angela	It's the Greek form of Eve, which was my mother's name. It means (2) 'life'.
Sanjit	Nice. Navreet and I have put Aarav's name down at a day care centre in East Lindsay, but we've heard a few odd things about it, so we're looking elsewhere. What's Zoe's day care like?
Angela	Pretty good. My son went there for two years, and *he* survived.
Sanjit	If you don't mind my asking, what does it cost?
Angela	It varies. If you provide things yourself, like diapers and snacks, it's reasonable, around $30 a day; but, if the centre provides everything, it starts to add up, and can go as high as (3) 50.
Sanjit	I see.
Angela	Also, there are quite a few (8) hidden costs.
Sanjit	Such as?

162

Angela	Well, the parents are, kind of, competitive. If a child has a birthday, mum or dad is expected to bring a snack for the whole room – (4-5) the day care's divided into rooms, by age. Right now, Zoe's in Penguins. Sometimes, I think parents spend a lot of time and money on those birthday snacks.
Sanjit	Once Navreet's back at work, she may well be too busy.
Angela	Absolutely. (4-5) Also, if you set a pick-up time, but get there 15 minutes late, the centre fines you $5, and five more dollars for every quarter-hour thereafter.
Sanjit	That's a bit steep, especially if you were just caught in traffic.
Narrator	Before you listen to the rest of the conversation, you have 30 seconds to read questions 6 to 10.
Angela	So, tell me about the centre in East Lindsay.
Sanjit	At first, I was impressed: it's spotless throughout, and the staff seems caring and responsible. I like the fact there's a decent amount of (6) space, especially outdoors. However, I'm worried that the children aren't explicitly taught anything – all they do is (7) play. Sure, Aarav's only one, but, in an eight-hour day, there's a lot he can learn.
Angela	At Zoe's day care, there is some structure to the week and some tuition. In (4-5) Penguins, Monday is alphabet day, and Wednesday is numbers. In (4-5) Tigers, Monday's computer day, and Wednesday's music.
Sanjit	Computer day?
Angela	Yeah. Parents have to provide tablets for their children when they turn two – another of the (8) hidden costs I was telling you about.
Sanjit	Right.
Angela	But, there's one good thing at Zoe's day care: you're not charged if your child's off sick for a day. And, as long as you give notice, you can take your child out for (9) holidays, which, again, you don't pay for. Many centres will only allow a one-month fee-free break in a year.
Sanjit	What's the hygiene like?
Angela	Good enough. The kids do get things in their hair, which is a bit embarrassing, but supermarkets stock shampoo, and parents are contacted as soon as there's an outbreak.
Sanjit	(10) Would you say the centre kept parents well informed?
Angela	Yes, I would. There you go: a reminder about Zoe's birthday. Her snack can't contain peanuts because a boy in Penguins has an allergy.
Narrator	You now have 30 seconds to check your answers. That is the end of Section 1.
Narrator	Recording 20. Section 2. A very small house. You will hear a woman being interviewed on the radio about living in a very small house. Before you listen, you have 30 seconds to read questions 11 to 15.
Simon	Welcome to today's show, coming to you from the home of Charlotte Williams. Good morning, Charlotte.
Charlotte	Morning Simon.
Simon	Thanks for letting us into your home, which, I believe, has been inundated with guests recently.
Charlotte	Yes, I held my birthday party here.
Simon	Surely that was a squeeze, given (11) your whole house is eight square metres, about the size of my kitchen.
Charlotte	The party was in the garden.
Simon	I understand there's been an upsurge in interest in the tiny-house movement.
Charlotte	That's right. Even Oprah has interviewed some of its devotees. (12) We're no longer the weirdos at the end of the street.
Simon	(12) But you were for some time, weren't you?
Charlotte	(12) Yes, I was. I'm sorry to say, I've had unpleasant text messages, rubbish strewn across my lawn, and rats put into my water tanks.

Simon	Goodness!
Charlotte	(13) But, y'know, when I was a kid, people used to smoke in doctors' waiting rooms and on airplanes. Once, on a flight to LA, I practically choked. My mother said crossly, 'Settle down; it's only smoke.' Now, of course, no one smokes on airplanes, and my mother is the first person to tell anyone off who lights up in a surgery.
Simon	So, your mother's one of your fans?
Charlotte	I wouldn't say that exactly. Anyway, she lives in France. In my opinion, in the developed world, we all consume too much. (14) I mean, In 1945, the average house in this city for a five-to-seven-person family was 111 square metres; two generations later, it's twice that size, while the family has only 3.5-to-four people.
Simon	I note you say 'in the developed world'. Perhaps an immigrant might still think you're weird. After all, isn't the American dream to think big?
Charlotte	Yes, one criticism levelled at me is that my lifestyle is anti-American. It's true that, while working in Mozambique and (15) Vietnam, I was inspired by my neighbours who used few resources.
Narrator	Before you listen to the rest of the conversation, you have 30 seconds to read questions 16 to 20.
Charlotte	In Mozambique, people use far less water and electricity than here. That's when I started to live without a fridge or a (16) shower, like the locals. I washed in a basin of water, which I still do.
Simon	I don't think I could live without a shower!
Charlotte	In Vietnam, many of my neighbours didn't have a kitchen, but cooked and ate outside. This meant there was life in the streets. Here, my kitchen consists of two elements and that basin. And, as you know, my party was outside. Also, in my part of Ho Chi Minh City, children generally slept in one bedroom. Indeed, children do (17) share more when they're in small spaces, and they're less likely to acquire all the junky toys that fill up many American homes.
Simon	But you live alone, Charlotte, and the climate here is rather different.
Charlotte	Sure. My son's grown up, and my partner lives in Chicago although he visits often. The climate is cold here, but my heating bill is low because this is a small space. I do still need quilts and winter clothes, which I store under my bed. However, I own two coats while my sister's got ten.
Simon	If you don't mind my saying so, Charlotte, isn't (11) eight square metres rather cramped? Haven't you had to give up all kinds of things?
Charlotte	Firstly, I have a great view of trees from my bed, so I feel part of nature – of the great expanse of nature. When I lived in a larger house, all I could see were other large houses. Honestly, I haven't given up anything. Every single item I now own has to be (18) functional *and* beautiful. I don't keep anything out of guilt, because it was a present, or I paid a lot for it. I had 4,000 possessions before moving here; now I've got (19) 400.
Simon	What other savings have you made?
Charlotte	I didn't pay much for this property, so I'm mortgage-free, which means I can work part-time. Without a doubt, the greatest saving I've made is of (20) time. I clean my house for one hour a week; in the past, I was a slave to chores and maintenance. Most people think I live in a tiny house out of poverty or fanaticism when really it's through choice. I'm just getting on with life.
Narrator	You now have 30 seconds to check your answers. That is the end of Section 2.
Narrator	Recording 21. Section 3. A business assignment. You will hear two students discussing an assignment they are doing on Business Plans. Before you listen, you have 30 seconds to read questions 21 to 26.
Natasha	I don't know Luca – 800 words don't seem like many to me.
Luca	Except I've only written (21) 450.
Natasha	Why don't you talk through what you've got, and I can suggest where you might add some in?
Luca	I can show you my essay, if you like, on my computer.
Natasha	Telling me about it may be better; it'll help you clarify what you have, and you'll probably notice what's missing as you speak. So, what *is* a Business Plan?
Luca	Something that projects ahead for at least three years.

Natasha	Something?
Luca	Well, in essence, it's…um…
Natasha	(22) An analysis of the current situation a business finds itself in, *and* a projection of its growth.
Luca	Right.
Natasha	And what else?
Luca	Basically, I suppose…
Natasha	What about the standards a Business Plan creates?
Luca	Oh, yeah. The plan creates standards. And it discusses viability.
Natasha	Indeed. (23) Who does it provide a tool for?
Luca	(23) Investors. I mean, potential investors. Let me turn on my computer to type that in. 'It discusses… viability… and provides… a sales tool for (23) potential… investors.'
Natasha	Good. Now, what about the five steps involved in creating the plan?
Luca	Five? I wrote down three in the lecture. One, carry out a situational analysis; two, understand the operating environment; and, three, define business objectives. Were there any others?
Natasha	I'm sure there were five, but I've forgotten them, myself, now.
Luca	Oh, I remember. Something about formulating strategies.
Natasha	Yes. Formulate strategies to follow.
Luca	And five?
Natasha	(24) Design controls to measure success. Though I've no idea what those controls might be.
Luca	(24) Me neither. I don't have any real-world experience for this course. I'm doing it because my cousin told me it was easy.
Natasha	Anyway, the last thing to note in the essay is that there's not just *one* business plan – (25) a company usually composes separate plans for all sections of the master plan. That means another Marketing Plan, another Production Plan etc.
Luca	(26) I'd no idea there was so much planning. How do businesses have any time to actually work?
Narrator	Before you listen to the rest of the conversation, you have 30 seconds to read questions 27 to 30.
Natasha	Let's look at the short answers, now. My friend who took this course last year said the final exam contained the short answers from this assignment and the next one.
Luca	Then, I'd better learn them off by heart.
Natasha	So, without reading from your computer screen, what *are* the five functions a business can be divided into?
Luca	You mean, MP3F?
Natasha	Yes.
Luca	M for Marketing. The three Ps for Purchasing, Production, and … what's the last one?
Natasha	(27) Personnel.
Luca	Right, (27) Personnel. And F for Finance.
Natasha	Good. I see you've remembered that the Business Profile and Appendices open and close the plan, but I think your definition of 'appendices' is a bit vague.
Luca	What's wrong with 'End notes'?
Natasha	Certainly, appendices are found at the end of a plan, but the phrase (28) 'supporting documents' might describe them more clearly.
Luca	OK. I'll write that down. (28) 'Sup-por-ting do-cu-ments.'
Natasha	The key here is that there's support for every section of the plan because an investor wants to see a strong case presented for your business, to know you're not just making assertions.
Luca	Right.

Natasha	The first few components of your Business Profile look fine. Business Name … Location … Ownership (29) Structure.
Luca	And Business Activity is easy enough to describe.
Natasha	True. But I'm afraid your Market Entry Strategy and Future Objectives look a little thin.
Luca	The thing is, Natasha, I don't understand what a Market Entry Strategy is. And Future Objectives seem equally nebulous.
Natasha	I know what you mean. I see you've mentioned Legal (30) Requirements in the Business Profile.
Luca	Don't you remember, the lecturer said that in today's environment of tight regulation, without this section in the plan, the whole business could end up being an expensive failure?
Natasha	Oh help. I forgot about Legal (30) Requirements in my profile! Thanks for reminding me. I'm sorry, Luca, I'll have to go. Let's meet again after the tutorial.
Narrator	You now have 30 seconds to check your answers. That is the end of Section 3.
Narrator:	Recording 22. Section 4. The benefits of literature. You will hear a lecture on the benefits of reading literature. Before you listen, you have 45 seconds to read questions 31 to 40.
Lecturer:	Last week, my sixteen-year-old neighbour asked me to look over her essay on the value of reading. I read the text, and was impressed by her elegant prose. But there was one glaring omission. Most of her essay was about how we read or why we read. In my opinion, how or why is far less important than *what* we read.

No one today would deny that reading improves *cognitive* intelligence: I bet the top three students here are also the three biggest readers. However, a growing number of experts attribute (31) literary fiction to a reader's enhanced capacity for emotional as well as cognitive intelligence.

But what are emotional intelligence and literary fiction? Actually, 'emotional intelligence' is a phrase popularised by the media; academics, like me, prefer the term 'Theory of Mind' or TOM.

TOM is the ability to attribute mental states – beliefs, intentions, desires, pretence, and knowledge – to oneself and others; and, to understand that others have states (32) *different* from one's own. Notable deficits in TOM occur in people with schizophrenia, attention deficit and autism spectrum disorders, or with neurotoxicity, due to drug or alcohol abuse.

What is literary fiction? Well, it's writing considered as (33) classic – winning widespread acclaim, translated into many languages, and enduring over time. Think: Jane Austen, Anton Chekhov, or F. Scott Fitzgerald, and people like Alaa al Aswany, Paulo Cuelho, or Alice Munro.

The vast majority of books, however, are not literary: they're non-fiction or popular fiction. Non-fiction deals with facts, and popular fiction with formulaic stories. True, in pop fiction, readers go on an emotional journey, often in exotic settings, but, while events may be dramatic, the external and internal lives of characters are predictable. This means readers' expectations remain (34) unchallenged; their view of the world is (34) intact.

By contrast, literary fiction focuses on the psychological states of characters and on their complex interpersonal relationships. Some writers adopt a technique called 'stream of consciousness' in which they minutely describe what is occurring in a character's head; others only allude to a character's state of mind. In the first instance, readers may be exposed to ways of perceiving the world quite different from their own. In the second, their need to interpret intentions or motivations expands their emotional problem-solving capacity. So, despite being set in the real, often humdrum, world, literary works defy expectations by challenging prejudices and undermining stereotypes.

Five experiments by the New York academics (35) David Kidd and Emanuele Castano have confirmed this. They invited hundreds of online participants to read extracts from non-fiction, popular fiction, or literary fiction; or, not to read anything at all. On cognitive and emotional tests, Kidd and Castano demonstrated that readers of (31) literary fiction performed better compared to readers of other genres or those who did not read.

(36) It's conceivable that including literary fiction in the daily routine of prisons, as well as in schools and universities, would bear fruit. It is already known that those in the correctional system who receive credits towards liberal arts college degrees survive better on release. Medicating children with autism or ADHD has been fashionable, but having them read literature may improve their conditions.

There are some lesser benefits to reading literary fiction. Firstly, it encourages discipline and connectedness. Discipline because the language or style may be complex, and a length of time is needed to finish it. Connectedness because readers identify strongly with great characters. (37) Think about a generation of children who read the seven Harry Potter books, devoting around 40 hours to them. An equivalent amount of time spent watching a

TV series would not generate an equivalent emotional response. Secondly, neuroscientists, in 2013, discovered enhanced neural activity in subjects who read fine literature daily. Those who read just before falling asleep were more likely to awaken soothed and focused, unlike TV viewers.

So, why aren't schools, universities, and prisons insisting on more literary fiction? Why aren't sales of Nobel-prizewinners soaring? Some say, life is too demanding. (38) Common Sense Media, a San Francisco, based non-profit organisation, produced a report called 'Why aren't teens reading?' It showed that, currently, 27% of seventeen-year-olds read for pleasure almost every day, whereas, in 1984, 31% did. Thirty years ago, nine percent of seventeen-year-olds said they seldom or never read for pleasure. By 2014, those figures had tripled to 27%. (39) Many respondents attribute this change to needing time for other life skills, but (40) it is my argument that, as complexity increases, the young become more adept at dealing with it when they read literary fiction.

So, did I suggest my neighbour redraft her essay? No. I gave her a copy of *The Little Prince*, a French classic from 1943, and asked her to pass it on to a friend when she'd finished.

Narrator: That is the end of the Listening test.
You now have ten minutes to transfer your answers to your answer sheet.

READING: <u>Passage 1:</u> **1.** iv; **2.** i; **3.** v; **4.** ix; **5.** vii; **6.** ii; **7.** cloths; **8.** 15th / Fifteenth; **9.** background; **10.** youth; **11.** Realism; **12.** 1965; **13.** D&E / E&D. <u>Passage 2:</u> **14.** T/True; **15.** T/True; **16.** NG/Not Given; **17.** F/False; **18.** C; **19.** B; **20.** A; **21.** B; **22.** G; **23.** I; **24.** F; **25.** A; **26.** E; **27.** H. <u>Passage 3:</u> **28.** 'Trade Not Aid' (*Quotation marks optional*); **29.** Coffee; **30.** A tiny number (*Must include 'A'*); **31.** Positively; **32.** Higher prices; **33.** D; **34.** A; **35.** H; **36.** B; **37.** N/No; **38.** Y/Yes; **39.** NG/Not Given; **40.** N/No.

> The highlighted text below is evidence for the answers above.
>
> If there is a question where 'Not given' is the answer, no evidence can be found, so there is no highlighted text.

Red in Russian art

A In Old Slavonic, a language that precedes Russian, 'red' has a similar root to the words 'good' and 'beautiful'. Indeed, until the 20th century, *Krasnaya Ploshchad*, or Red Square, in central Moscow, was understood by locals as 'Beautiful Square'. For Russians, red has great symbolic meaning, being associated with goodness, beauty, warmth, (12-13) vitality, jubilation, (12-13) faith, love, salvation, and power.

B (1) Because red is a long-wave colour at the end of the spectrum, its effect on a viewer is striking: it appears closer than colours with shorter waves, like green, and it also intensifies colours placed alongside it, which accounts for the popularity of red and green combinations in Russian painting.

C (2) Russians love red. In the applied arts, it predominates: bowls, boxes, trays, wooden spoons, and distaffs for spinning all feature red, as do children's toys, decorative figurines, Easter eggs, embroidered (7) cloths, and garments. In the fine arts, red, white, and gold form the basis of much icon painting.

D (3) In pre-Christian times, red symbolised blood. Christianity adopted the same symbolism; red represented Christ or saints in their purification or martyrdom. The colour green, meantime, signified wisdom, while white showed a person reborn as a Christian. Thus, in a famous (8) 15th-century icon from the city of Novgorod, *Saint George and the Dragon*, red-dressed George sports a green cape, and rides a pure-white stallion. In many icons, Christ and the angels appear in a blaze of red, and the mother of Christ can be identified by her long red veil. In an often-reproduced icon from Yaroslavl, the Archangel Michael wears a brilliant red cloak. However, the fires of Hell that burn sinners are also red, like those in an icon from Pskov.

E (4) A red (9) background for major figures in icons became the norm in representations of mortal beings, partly to add vibrancy to skin tones, and one fine example of this is a portrait of Nikolai Gogol, the writer, from the early 1840s. (4) When wealthy aristocrats wished to be remembered for posterity, they were often depicted in dashing red velvet coats, emulating the cloaks of saints, as in the portraits of Jakob Turgenev in 1696, or of Admiral Ivan Talyzin in the mid-1760s. Portraits of women in Russian art are rare, but the Princess Yekaterina Golitsyna, painted in the early 1800s, wears a fabulous red shawl.

Common people do not appear frequently in Russian fine art until the 19th century, when their peasant costumes are often white with red embroidery, and their elaborate headdresses and scarves are red. (4) The women in the 1915 painting, *Visiting*, by Abram Arkhipov seem aflame with life: their dresses are red; their cheeks are red; and, a jug of vermillion lingonberry cordial glows on the table beside them.

Russian avant-garde painters of the early 20th century are famous beyond Russia as some of the greatest abstract artists. Principal among these are Nathan Altman, Natalia Goncharova, Wassily Kandinsky, and Kazimir Malevich, who painted the ground-breaking *White on white* as well as *Red Square*, which is all the more compelling because it isn't quite square. Malevich used primary colours, with red prominent, in much of his mature work. Kuzma Petrov-Vodkin is hailed as a genius at home, but less well-known abroad; his style is often surreal, and his palette is restricted to the many hues of red, contrasting with green or blue. The head in his 1915 *Head of a* (10) *youth* is entirely red, while his 1925 painting, *Fantasy*, shows a man in blue, on a larger-than-life all-red horse, with a blue town in blue mountains behind.

F (5) Part of the enthusiasm for red in the early 20th century was due to the rise of the political movement, communism. Red had first been used as a symbol of revolution in France in the late 18th century. The Russian army from 1918-45 called itself the Red Army to continue this revolutionary tradition, (5) and the flag of the Soviet Union was the Red Flag.

Soviet poster artists and book illustrators also used swathes of red. (5) Some Social (11) Realist painters have been discredited for their political associations, but their art was potent, and a viewer cannot help but be moved by Nikolai Rutkovsky's 1934 *Stalin at Kirov's coffin*. Likewise, Alexander Gerasimov's 1942 *Hymn to October* or Dmitry Zhilinsky's (12) 1965 *Gymnasts of the USSR* stand on their own as memorable paintings, both of which include plenty of red.

G (6) In English, red has many negative connotations – red for debt, a red card for football fouls, or a red-light district – but in Russian, red is beautiful, (12-13) vivacious, spiritual, and revolutionary. And Russian art contains countless examples of its power.

Lepidoptera

Myths and Misnomers

A buttercup is a small, bright yellow flower; a butternut is a yellow-fleshed squash; and, there is also a butter bean. (14) The origin of the word 'butterfly' may be similar to these plants – a creature with wings the colour of butter – (15) but a more fanciful notion is that 'flutterby' was misspelt by an early English scribe since a butterfly's method of flight is to flutter by. Etymologists may not concur, but entomologists agree with each other that butterflies belong to the order of Lepidoptera, which includes moths, and that 'lepidoptera' accurately describes the insects since 'lepis' means 'scale' and 'pteron' means 'wing' in Greek.

(17) Until recently, butterflies were prized for their evanescence – people believed that adults lived for a single day; it is now known this is untrue, and some, like monarch butterflies, live for up to nine months.

Butterflies versus Moths

(18) Butterflies and moths have some similarities: as adults, both have four membranous wings covered in minute scales, attached to a short thorax and a longer abdomen with three pairs of legs. (18) They have moderately large heads, long antennae, and (18) compound eyes; tiny palps for smell; and, a curling proboscis for sucking nectar. Otherwise their size, colouration, and life-cycles are the same.

Fewer than 1% of all insects are butterflies, but they hold a special place in the popular imagination as being beautiful and benign. (19) Views of moths, however, are less kind since some live indoors and feast on cloth; others damage crops; and, most commit suicide, being nocturnal and drawn to artificial light. (20) There are other differences between butterflies and moths; for example, when resting, the former fold their wings vertically above their bodies, while the latter lay theirs flat. Significantly, butterfly antennae thicken slightly towards their tips, whereas (21) moth antennae end in something that looks like a V-shaped TV aerial.

The Monarch Butterfly

Originating in (22) North America, the black-orange-and-white monarch butterfly lives as far away as Australia and New Zealand, and for many children it represents a lesson in metamorphosis, which can even be viewed in one's living room if a pupa is brought indoors.

It is easy to identify the four stages of a monarch's lifecycle – egg, larva, pupa, and adult – but there are really seven. This is because, unlike vertebrates, insects do not have an internal skeleton, but a tough outer covering called an exoskeleton. This is often shell-like and sometimes indigestible by predators. Muscles are hinged to its inside. As the insect grows, however, the constraining exoskeleton must be moulted, and a monarch butterfly undergoes (23) seven moults, including four as a larva.

Temperature dramatically affects butterfly growth: in warm weather, a monarch may go through its seven moults in just over a month. Time spent inside the egg, for instance, may last three to four days in 25° Celsius, but in 18°, the whole process may take closer to eight weeks, with time inside the egg eight to twelve days. Naturally, longer development means lower populations due to increased predation.

A reliable food supply influences survival, and the female monarch butterfly is able to sniff out one particular plant its young can feed off – (24) milkweed or swan plant. There are a few other plants larvae can eat, but they will resort to these only if the milkweed is exhausted and alternatives are very close by. Moreover, a female butterfly may be conscious of the size of the milkweed on which she lays her eggs since she spaces them, but another butterfly may deposit on the same plant, lessening everyone's chance of survival.

While many other butterflies are close to extinction due to pollution or dwindling habitat, the global numbers of monarchs have decreased in the past two decades, but less dramatically.

Monarch larvae absorb toxins from milkweed that render them poisonous to most avian predators who attack them. Insect predators, like aphids, flies, and wasps, seem unaffected by the poison, and are therefore common. A recent disturbing occurrence is the death of monarch eggs and larvae from (25) bacterial infection.

Another reason for population decline is reduced wintering conditions. Like many birds, monarch butterflies migrate to warmer climates in winter, often flying extremely long distances, for example, from Canada to southern California or northern Mexico, or from southern Australia to the tropical north. They also spend some time in semi-hibernation in dense colonies deep in forests. In isolated New Zealand, monarchs do not migrate, instead finding particular trees on which to congregate. In some parts of California, wintering sites are protected, but in (26) Mexico, much of the forest is being logged, and the insects are in grave danger.

Milkweed is native to southern Africa and North America, but it is easy to grow in suburban gardens. Its swan-shaped seedpods contain fluffy seeds used in the 19th century to stuff mattresses, pillows, and lifejackets. After milkweed had hitched a lift on sailing ships around the Pacific, the American butterflies followed with Hawaii seeing their permanent arrival in 1840, Samoa in 1867, Australia in 1870, and New Zealand in 1873. As butterfly numbers decline sharply in the Americas, it may be (27) these Pacific outposts that save the monarch.

How fair is fair trade?

The fair-trade movement began in Europe in earnest in the post-war period, but only in the last 25 years has it grown to include producers and consumers in over 60 countries.

In the 1950s and 60s, many people in the developed world felt passionately about the enormous disparities between developed and developing countries, and they believed the system of international trade shut out African, Asian, and South American producers who could not compete with multi-national companies or who came from states that, for political reasons, were not trading with the West. The catchphrase (28) 'Trade Not Aid' was used by church groups and trade unions – early supporters of fair trade – who also considered that international aid was either a pittance or a covert form of subjugation. These days, much fair trade does include aid: developed-world volunteers offer their services, and there is free training for producers and their workers.

Tea, coffee, cocoa, cotton, flowers, handicrafts, and gold are all major fair-trade items, with (29) coffee being the most recognisable, found on supermarket shelves and at café chains throughout the developed world.

Although around two million farmers and workers produce fair-trade items, this is (30) a tiny number in relation to total global trade. Still, fair-trade advocates maintain that the system has (31) positively impacted upon many more people worldwide, while the critics claim that if those two million returned to the mainstream trading system, they would receive (32) higher prices for their goods or labour.

Fair trade is supposed to be trade that is fair to producers. (33) Its basic tenet is that developed-world consumers will pay slightly more for end products in the knowledge that developing-world producers have been equitably remunerated, and that the products have been made in decent circumstances. Additionally, the fair-trade system differs from that of the open market because there is a minimum price paid for goods, which may be higher than that of the open market. Secondly, a small premium, earmarked for community development, is added in good years; for example, coffee co-operatives in South America frequently receive an additional 25c per kilogram. (34) Lastly, purchasers of fair-trade products may assist with crop pre-financing or with training of producers and workers, which could take the form of improving product quality, using environmentally friendly fertilisers, or raising literacy. (35) Research has shown that non-fair-trade farmers copy some fair-trade farming practices, and, occasionally, encourage social progress. In exchange for ethical purchase and other assistance, (36) fair-trade producers agree not to use child or slave labour, to adhere to the United Nations Charter on Human Rights, to provide safe workplaces, and to protect the environment (36) despite these not being legally binding in their own countries. However, few non-fair-trade farmers have adopted these practices, viewing them as little more than rich-world conceits.

So that consumers know which products are made under fair-trade conditions, goods are labelled, and, these days, a single European and American umbrella organisation supervises labelling, standardisation, and inspection.

While fair trade is increasing, the system is far from perfect. First and foremost, (37) there are expenses involved in becoming a fair-trade-certified producer, meaning the desperately poor rarely participate, (37) so the very farmers fair-trade advocates originally hoped to support are excluded. Secondly, because conforming to the standards of fair-trade certification is costly, (38) some producers deliberately mislabel their goods. The fair-trade monitoring process is patchy, (38) and unfortunately, around 12% of fair-trade-labelled produce is nothing of the kind. Next, a crop may genuinely be produced under fair-trade conditions, but due to a lack of demand cannot be sold as fair trade, so goes onto the open market, where prices are mostly lower. It is estimated that only between 18-37% of fair-trade output is actually sold as fair trade. Sadly, there is little reliable research on the real relationship between costs incurred and revenue for fair-trade farmers, although empirical evidence suggests that many never realise a profit. Partly, reporting from producers is inadequate, and ways of determining profit may not include credit, harvesting, transport, or processing. Sometimes, the price paid to fair-trade producers is lower than that of the open market, so while a crop may be sold, elsewhere it could have earnt more, or where there are profits, they are often taken by the corporate firms that buy the goods and sell them on to retailers.

There are problems with the developed-world part of the equation too. People who volunteer to work for fair-trade concerns may do so believing they are assisting farmers and communities, whereas their labour serves to enrich middlemen and retailers. Companies involved in West African cocoa production have been criticised for this. In the developed world, the right to use a fair-trade logo is also expensive for packers and retailers, and sometimes a substantial amount of the money received from sale is ploughed back into marketing. In richer parts of the developed world, notably in London, packers and retailers charge high prices for fair-trade products. (39) Consumers imagine they are paying so much because more money is returned to producers, when profit-taking by retailers or packers is a more likely scenario. One UK café chain is known to have passed on 1.6% of the extra 18% it charged for fair-trade coffee to producers. However, this happens with other items at the supermarket or café, so perhaps consumers are naïve to believe fair-traders behave otherwise. In addition, there are struggling farmers in rich countries, too, so some critics think fair-trade associations should certify them. (40) Other critics find the entire fair-trade system flawed – nothing more than a colossal marketing scam – and they would rather assist the genuinely poor in more transparent ways, but this criticism may be overblown since fair trade has endured for and been praised in the developing world itself.

WRITING: Task 1

The atolls Bassas da India and Ile Europa lie between Mozambique and Madagascar. They are relatively small: Bassas da India is around 12 kilometres in diameter, with a coastline of 35.2 km; Ile Europa is six kilometres in diameter, with a 22.2 km coastline. Both have been part of the French Southern and Antarctic Lands since 1897 although they are also claimed by Madagascar. Both have been the cause of numerous shipwrecks. Since Bassas da India, a coral formation, is almost all submerged at high tide, it presents a considerable danger to navigation.

Otherwise, the atolls are rather different. Bassas da India is uninhabited as it is mainly lagoon. The reef is uncovered for only six hours each day, around low tide, and the rocky islets permanently above sea level have no vegetation. Ile Europe has a lagoon covering approximately one third of its area. Vegetation includes forest, grass, scrub, and extensive mangroves. Famous for its nesting sites for many bird species and green turtles, introduced goats, rats, sisal and hemp, may pose a threat. Ile Europe was farmed by the French between 1860 and 1920, but currently has no permanent civilian population; instead, it is used by the military, by meteorologists, and other scientists. (205 words)

Task 2

The concept of positive thinking has been around for many years. Some people believe that if we focus our minds positively, then everything will be all right; that, by being optimistic we will have happy, carefree existences, be healthier, and live longer.

Thinking positively inspires us to endure in adversity, gives us a sense of wellbeing, and reduces anxieties. If we tell ourselves we 'can do it', then any negative feelings of not being able to do something will disappear.

By assuring ourselves we can achieve, then, we become more motivated and take the initiative. Say, for example, you have just been offered a promotion at work whereby you need to learn more skills, assume more responsibility, and supervise a much larger staff. If you have negative thoughts about your ability to cope, then you may refuse the promotion. However, if you are more optimistic and tell yourself it is just a matter of easing into the job, learning along the way as others have done before you, you will accept the challenge. Naturally, you will be better off financially in your new position. Positive thinking, then, is what is in the mind.

However, I think that people who are always optimistic without considering possible pitfalls are living in a dream world, avoiding realistically assessing issues and problems. I think our lives are governed more by how we feel and act rather than by just thinking positively about every issue. We need to feel positive about an issue before making a decision to act, not just think everything will be all right, without weighing the pros and cons. Thus positive thinking can have its drawbacks.

An overly optimistic person will not always face facts, and is not prepared to deal with life's crises. Just thinking rich won't make anyone rich; not accepting that a relative or friend is dying won't make him or her well again; a hurricane heading our way won't stop in its path. There are times when we have to prepare for the worst – financially, socially, and environmentally – and act accordingly. Although positive thinking is a useful attitude to have and has many benefits, we must also weigh up the negatives, looking at any opposing implications, so that we have a balanced view of life. (378 words)

TEST 5

Listening

Firstly, tear out the Test 5 Listening / Reading Answer Sheet at the back of this book.

The Listening test lasts for about 20 minutes.

Write your answers on the pages below as you listen. After Section 4 has finished, you have ten minutes to transfer your answers to your Listening Answer Sheet. You will need to time yourself for this transfer.

After checking your answers on pp 190-194, go to page 9 for the raw-score conversion table.

 PLAY RECORDING #23.

SECTION 1   Questions 1-10

JOINING UP

Questions 1-4

Choose the correct letter, A, B, or C.

Example The tour takes

    A   5-10 minutes.

    B   10-20 minutes.

    C   20-30 minutes. √

1   The visitors found out about the facility from

    A   an online review.

    B   a new sign on the street.

    C   a personal recommendation.

2   According to the guide, people stop going to a pool or gym because

    A   it becomes too expensive.

    B   they lack motivation.

    C   they run out of time.

3   The temperature, in Celsius, of the main pool is

    A   25°

    B   27°

    C   31°

4   Louise apologises to Terry because she thought he was

    A   unable to swim.

    B   Charlie's father.

    C   from another country.

LISTENING   SECTION 1   SECTION 2   SECTION 3   SECTION 4
READING
WRITING
SPEAKING

Questions 5-10

Complete the table below.

Write **NO MORE THAN TWO WORDS OR A NUMBER** *for each answer.*

Member	Membership Type	Activity or Class	Days	Time	Other information
Wei Wei	Weekly	Water Polo	Tuesdays & Thursdays	(5)..........AM-1:00 PM	Her son will need (8)............... .
		(6) Stroke	(7)	7:30-8:30 AM	
Terry	(9)...............	Weight Training	Mondays	6:30-8:00 PM	He would like to trial (10) a ....

Play Audio **PLAY RECORDING #24.**

SECTION 2   Questions 11-20

WHARF REDEVELOPMENT

Questions 11-16

Classify the following plans that Cato and Brown or the local council

    A   wants included.

    B   is considering.

    C   has rejected.

Write the correct letter, **A**, **B**, *or* **C**, *on your answer sheet.*

11   Another floor

12   A jetty for water taxis

13   A long canopy

14   A long bus shelter

15   The corridor

16   New posts and walkways

LISTENING
READING
WRITING
SPEAKING

| SECTION 1 | SECTION 2 | SECTION 3 | SECTION 4 |

Questions 17-20

Label the plan.

Write **ONE WORD ONLY** *for each answer.*

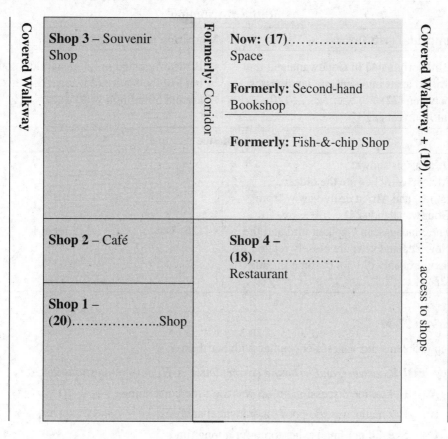

 PLAY RECORDING #25.

SECTION 3   Questions 21-30

POST-GRADUATE RESEARCH

Question 21

Choose the correct letter, A, B, or C.

21   How did Marcus feel about working in a laboratory in South Africa?

    A   He absolutely loved it.

    B   He mostly enjoyed it.

    C   He didn't really like it.

LISTENING   SECTION 1   SECTION 2   SECTION 3   SECTION 4
READING
WRITING
SPEAKING

Questions 22-26

Complete the table below.

*Write **NO MORE THAN TWO WORDS OR A NUMBER** for each answer.*

Ratite distribution	
Continental drift theory	**Migration theory**
• Birds originated in Gondwanaland that drifted apart into separate landmasses between (**22**)..................-120 million years ago.	• Birds originated in Laurasia, flew south, but lost the ability (**23**)................... around 50 million years ago.
Evidence	
DNA analysis shows: • African ostriches are the oldest ratites, and Africa drifted away from Gondwanaland (**24**)................... . • The Madagascan elephant bird and the New Zealand kiwi are closely related, so they probably did not become flightless (**25**)................... .	• (**26**) The...................record

Questions 27-30

Which problems did Vanessa encounter with her thesis?

*Choose **FOUR** answers, and write the correct letter, **A-H**, next to questions 27-30.*

    A   Her online discussion group was too time-consuming.

    B   Her maths was too poor for statistical analysis.

    C   She did not finalise her topic for a long time.

    D   She was not allowed to interview some patients.

    E   She had to work in a hospital while studying.

    F   She was unfamiliar with regression analysis.

    G   Her sample was too small for quantitative analysis.

    H   Results from her survey were all rather similar.

PLAY RECORDING #26.

SECTION 4   Questions 31-40

EARTH'S COUSIN

Questions 31-33

Answer the questions below.
*Write **NO MORE THAN THREE WORDS** for each answer.*

31   In contrast to previous ones, what is the focus of the Kepler Mission?

....

32   What is the area called between a star and its planet where humans could live?

....

33   For which development is Johannes Kepler most renowned?

....

Questions 34-36

*Choose the correct letter, **A**, **B**, or **C**.*

34   What does the Kepler photometer record?

    A   Light emitted from stars in one area of the galaxy

    B   The age of thousands of distant planets

    C   The distance between Cygnus and Lyrae and Earth

35   What level of sensitivity does the photometer have?

    A   A moderate level

    B   A high level

    C   An extremely high level

36   Why do scientists measure light from behind a new planet?

    A   To determine the composition of its atmosphere

    B   To discover whether liquid water could exist there

    C   To test the laws of physics and chemistry

Questions 37-40

Complete the notes below.

Write **NO MORE THAN TWO WORDS AND A NUMBER** *for each answer.*

Kepler 62e & 62f
• Discovered 2013
• Initially thought to be similar to Earth
• Later found to have greater (**37**)....................& weaker gravity
Kepler 186f
• Discovered 2014
• 14,000 km diameter = (**38**)...................wider than Earth
• ? Rocky surface + iron, ice, & liquid H_2O
• ? Distance from Kepler 186 may mean surface water frozen, or thicker atmosphere may mean enough (**39**)....................
• Distance from Earth = (**40**)..................., currently around 8-12 million years' travel time

Reading

Firstly, turn over the Test 5 Listening Answer Sheet you used earlier to write your Reading answers on the back.

The Reading test lasts exactly 60 minutes.

Certainly, make any marks on the pages below, but transfer your answers to the answer sheet <u>as you read</u> since there is no extra time at the end to do so.

After checking your answers on pp 194-197, go to page 9 for the raw-score conversion table.

PASSAGE 1

*Spend about 20 minutes on **Questions 1-13**, based on Passage 1 below.*

THE PLIGHT OF RICE

Rice is a tall grass with a drooping panicle that contains numerous edible grains, and has been cultivated in China for more than 6,000 years. A staple throughout Asia and large parts of Africa, it is now grown in flooded paddy fields from sea level to high mountains and harvested three times a year. According to the Food and Health Organisation of the United Nations, around four billion people currently receive a fifth of their calories from rice.

Recently, Japan, South Korea, and Taiwan have slightly reduced rice consumption due to the adoption of more western diets, but almost all other countries have raised their consumption due to population increase. Yet, since 1984, there have been diminishing rice yields around the world.

From the 1950s to the early 1960s, rice production was also suffering: India was on the brink of famine, and China was already experiencing one. In the late 1950s, Norman Borlaug, an American plant pathologist, began advising Punjab State in northwestern India to grow a new semi-dwarf variety of wheat. This was so successful that, in 1962, a semi-dwarf variety of rice, called IR8, developed by the Philippine International Rice Research Institute (IRRI), was planted throughout Southeast Asia and India. This semi-dwarf variety heralded the Green Revolution, which saved the lives of millions of people by almost doubling rice yields: from 1.9 metric tons per hectare in 1950-64, to 3.5 metric tons in 1985-98.

IR8 survived because, as a semi-dwarf, it only grows to a moderate height, and it does not thin out, keel over, and drown like traditional varieties. Furthermore, its short thick stem is able to absorb chemical fertilisers, but, as stem growth is limited, the plant expends energy on producing a large panicle of heavy seeds, ensuring a greater crop.

However, even with a massive increase in rice production, semi-dwarf varieties managed to keep up with population growth for only ten years. In Africa, where rice consumption is rising by 20% annually, and where one third of the population now depends on the cereal, this is disturbing. At the current rate, within the next 20 years, rice will surpass maize as the major source of calories on that continent. Meantime, even in ideal circumstances, paddies worldwide are not producing what they once did, for reasons largely unknown to science. An average 0.8% fall in yields has been noted in rich rice-growing regions; in less ideal ones, flood, drought and salinity have meant yields have fallen drastically, sometimes up to 40%.

The sequencing of the rice genome took place in 2005, after which the IRRI developed genetically modified flood-resistant varieties of rice, called Sub 1, which produce up to four times more edible grain than non-modified strains. In 2010, a handful of farmers worldwide were planting IRRI Sub 1 rice; now, over five million are doing so. Currently, drought- and salt-resistant varieties are being trialled since most rice is grown in the great river basins of the Brahmaputra, the Irrawaddy, and the Mekong that are all drying up or becoming far saltier.

With global warming, many rice-growing regions are hotter than 20 years ago. Nearly all varieties of rice, including IR8, flower in the afternoon, but the anthers – little sacs that contain male pollen – wither and die in soaring temperatures. IRRI scientists have identified one variety of rice, known as Odisha, that flowers in the early morning, and they are in the process of genetically modifying IR8 so it contains Odisha-flowering genes, although it may be some time before this is released.

While there is a clear need for more rice, many states and countries seem less keen to influence agricultural policy directly than they were in the past. Some believe rice demand will dip in wealthier places, as occurred in Japan, South Korea, and Taiwan; others consider it more prudent to devote resources to tackling obesity or to limiting intensive farming that is environmentally destructive.

Some experts say where there is state intervention it should take the form of reducing subsidies to rice farmers to stimulate production; others propose that small land holdings should be consolidated into more economically viable ones. There is no denying that land reform is pressing, but many governments shy away from it, fearing losses at the ballot box, all the while knowing that rural populations are heading for the city in droves anyway. And, as they do so, cities expand, eating up fertile land for food production.

One can only hope that the IRRI and other research institutions will spearhead half a dozen mini green revolutions, independently of uncommitted states.

Questions 1-5

Do the following statements agree with the information given in Reading Passage 1?

In boxes 1-5 on your answer sheet, write:

>*TRUE*   *if the statement agrees with the information.*
>*FALSE*   *if the statement contradicts the information.*
>*NOT GIVEN* *if there is no information on this.*

1   Rice is only grown at a low elevation.

2   Rice has been cultivated in Africa for 3,000 years.

3   Since 1984, rice yields have decreased due to infestations of pests.

4   Norman Borlaug believed Punjabi farmers should grow semi-dwarf rice.

5   The Green Revolution increased rice yields by around 100%.

Questions 6-11

Complete the notes below.

*Choose **ONE WORD AND / OR A NUMBER** from the passage for each answer.*

Write your answers in boxes 6-11 on your answer sheet.

Traditional varieties of rice	• Grow tall and (**6**)................, leading to collapse
IR8 variety	• Absorbs fertiliser in its short (**7**)................... • With a large panicle of heavy seeds, it produces a bigger (**8**)...................
Sub 1 varieties	• Are flood-resistant • Produce up to (**9**).................. times the amount of grain than non-modified varieties • Now grown by over (**10**).................. farmers
Odisha variety	• Flowers in the early (**11**).................., so its anthers remain intact and pollination can occur

Questions 12-13

*Choose the correct letter, **A**, **B**, **C**, or **D**.*

Write the correct letter in boxes 12-13 on your answer sheet.

12   States are more interested in......than stimulating rice production.

    A   increasing wheat production

    B   reducing farm subsidies

    C   confronting obesity

    D   consolidating land holdings

13   ......disappearing as urbanisation speeds up.

    A   Intensive farming is

    B   Fertile land is

    C   Clean water is

    D   Agricultural institutes are

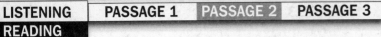

PASSAGE 2

*Spend about 20 minutes on **Questions 14-26**, based on Passage 2 below.*

A New Perspective on Bacteria

A Microbes are organisms too small to be seen by the naked eye, including bacteria, blue-green algae, yeasts, fungi, viruses, and viroids.

A large, diverse group, almost all bacteria are between one and ten μ[1] (larger ones reach 0.5 mm). Generally single-celled, with a distinctive cellular structure lacking a true nucleus, most bacterial genetic information is carried on a DNA loop in the cytoplasm[2] with the membrane possessing some nuclear properties.

There are three main kinds of bacteria – spherical, rod-like, and spiral – known by their Latin names of coccus, bacillus, and spirillum. Bacteria occur alone, in pairs, clusters, chains, or more complex configurations. Some live where oxygen is present; others, where it is absent.

The relationship between bacteria and their hosts is symbiotic, benefitting both organisms, or the hosts may be destroyed by parasitic or disease-causing bacteria.

B In general, humans view bacteria suspiciously, yet it is now thought they partly owe their existence to microbes living long, long ago.

During photosynthesis, plants produce oxygen that humans need to fuel blood cells. Most geologists believe the early atmosphere on Earth contained very little oxygen until around 2½ billion years ago, when microbes bloomed. Ancestral forms of cyanobacteria, for example, evolved into chloroplasts – the cells that carry out photosynthesis. Once plants inhabited the oceans, oxygen levels rose dramatically, so complex life forms could eventually be sustained.

The air humans breathe today is oxygen-rich, and the majority of airborne microbes are harmless, but the air does contain industrial pollutants, allergens, and infectious microbes or pathogens that cause illness.

C The fact is that scientists barely understand microbes. Bacteria have been proven to exist only in the past 350 years; viruses were discovered just over 100 years ago, but in the past three decades, the ubiquity of microbes has been established with bacteria found kilometres below the Earth's crust and in the upper atmosphere. Surprisingly, they survive in dry deserts and the frozen reaches of Antarctica; they dwell in rain and snow clouds, as well as inside every living creature.

Air samples taken in 2006 from two cities in Texas contained at least 1,800 distinct species of bacteria, making the air as rich as the soil. These species originated both in Texas and as far away as western China. It now seems that the number of microbe species far exceeds the number of stars.

D Inside every human being there are trillions of bacteria with their weight estimated at 1.36 kg in an average adult, or about as heavy as the brain. Although tiny, 90% of cells in a human are bacterial. With around eight million genes, these bacteria outnumber genes in human cells by 300 times.

The large intestine contains the most bacteria – almost 34,000 species – but the crook of the elbow harbours over 2,000 species. Many bacteria are helpful: digesting food; aiding the immune system; creating moisturiser; and, manufacturing vitamins. Some have highly specialised functions, like *Bacteroides thetaiotaomicron*, which breaks down plant starch, so an infant can make the transition from mother's milk to a more varied diet.

[1] A micron = 10^{-6} m
[2] Material inside a cell

Test 5 181

LISTENING
READING
WRITING
SPEAKING

PASSAGE 1 | PASSAGE 2 | PASSAGE 3

Undeniably, some bacteria are life-threatening. One, known as golden staph, *Staphylococcus aureus*, plagues hospitals, where it infects instruments and devours human tissue until patients die from toxic shock. Worse, it is still resistant to antibiotics.

E Antibiotics themselves are bacteria. In 1928, Alexander Fleming discovered that a mould in his laboratory produced a chemical he named penicillin. In 1951, William Bouw collected soil from the jungles of Borneo that eventually became vancomycin. Pharmaceutical companies still hunt for beneficial bacteria, but Michael Fischbach from University of California believes that the human body itself is a ready supply.

F Scientific ignorance about bacteria is largely due to an inability to cultivate many of them in a laboratory, but recent DNA sequencing has meant populations can be analysed by computer program without having to grow them.

Fischbach and his team have created and trained a computer program to identify gene clusters in microbial DNA sequences that might produce useful molecules. Having collected microbial DNA from 242 healthy human volunteers, the scientists sequenced the genomes of 2,340 different species of microbes, most of which were completely new discoveries.

In searching the gene clusters, Fischbach et al found 3,118 common ones that could be used in pharmaceuticals, for example, a gene cluster from the bacterium *Lactobacillus gasseri*, successfully reared in the lab, produced a molecule they named lactocillin. Later, they discovered the structure of this was very similar to an antibiotic, LFF571, undergoing clinical trials by a major pharmaceutical company. To date, lactocillin has killed harmful bacteria, so it may also be a reliable antibiotic.

G Naturally, the path to patenting medicine is strewn with failures, but, since bacteria have been living inside humans for millions of years, they are probably safe to reintroduce in new combinations and in large amounts.

Undoubtedly, the fight against pathogens, like golden staph, must continue, but as scientists learn more about microbes, respect and excitement for them grows, and their positive applications become ever more probable.

Questions 14-18

Passage 2 has seven sections, **A-G**.

Which section contains the following information?

Write the correct letter, A-G, in boxes 14-18 on your answer sheet.

NB: Any section can be chosen more than once.

14 examples of bacteria as patented medicine

15 a description of bacteria

16 gene cluster detection and culture

17 humans are teeming with bacteria

18 Fischbach's hypothesis

Questions 19-22

*Choose the correct letter, **A**, **B**, **C**, or **D**.*

Write the correct letter in boxes 19-22 on your answer sheet.

19   What do almost all bacteria share?

    A   Their simple configurations

    B   Their cellular organisation

    C   Their survival without oxygen

    D   Their parasitic nature

20   From the suffix '-bacillus', what shape would you expect the bacterium *Paenibacillus* to be?

    A   spherical

    B   rod-like

    C   spiral

    D   amorphous

21   Why were ancient bacteria invaluable to humans?

    A   They contributed to higher levels of oxygen.

    B   They reduced widespread industrial pollution.

    C   They protected humans from intestinal ailments.

    D   They provided scientists with antibiotics.

22   How prevalent are microbes?

    A   Not at all

    B   Somewhat

    C   Very

    D   Extremely

Questions 23-26

Answer the questions below.

*Choose **NO MORE THAN THREE WORDS OR A NUMBER** from the passage for each answer.*

Write your answers in boxes 23-26 on your answer sheet.

23   Which organ does the total weight of bacteria in a human body equal?

    ....

24   Roughly how many bacterial species live in a human's large intestine?

    ....

25   In Fischbach's view, where might useful bacteria come from in the future?

    ....

26   What do some scientists now feel towards microbes?

    ....

Test 5 183

LISTENING
READING
WRITING
SPEAKING

PASSAGE 1   PASSAGE 2   PASSAGE 3

PASSAGE 3

Spend about 20 minutes on **Questions 27-40**, *based on Passage 3 below.*

• •

In the last century, Vikings have been perceived in numerous different ways – vilified as conquerors and romanticised as adventurers. How Vikings have been employed in nation-building is a topic of some interest.

In English, Vikings are also known as Norse or Norsemen. Their language greatly influenced English, with the nouns, 'Hell', 'husband', 'law', and 'window', and the verbs, 'blunder', 'snub', 'take', and 'want', all coming from Old Norse. However, the origins of the word 'Viking', itself, are obscure: it may mean 'a Scandinavian pirate', or it may refer to 'an inlet', or a place called Vik, in modern-day Norway, from where the pirates came. These various names – Vikings, Norse, or Norsemen, and doubts about the very word 'Viking' suggest historical confusion.

Loosely speaking, the Viking Age endured from the late eighth to the mid-eleventh centuries. Vikings sailed to England in AD 793 to storm coastal monasteries, and subsequently large swathes of England fell under Viking rule – indeed several Viking kings sat on the English throne. It is generally agreed that the Battle of Hastings, in 1066, when the Norman French invaded, marks the end of the English Viking Age, but the Irish Viking age ended earlier, while Viking colonies in Iceland and Greenland did not dissolve until around AD 1500.

How much territory Vikings controlled is also in dispute – Scandinavia and Western Europe certainly, but their reach east and south is uncertain. They plundered and settled down the Volga and Dnieper rivers, and traded with modern-day Istanbul, but the archaeological record has yet to verify that Vikings raided as far away as Northwest Africa, as some writers claim.

The issue of control and extent is complex because many Vikings did not return to Scandinavia after raiding but assimilated into local populations, often becoming Christian. To some degree, the Viking Age is defined by religion. Initially, Vikings were polytheists, believing in many gods, but by the end of the age, they had permanently accepted a new monotheistic religious system – Christianity.

This transition from so-called pagan plunderers to civilised Christians is significant, and is the view promulgated throughout much of recent history. In the UK, in the 1970s for example, school children were taught that until the Vikings accepted Christianity they were nasty heathens who rampaged throughout Britain. By contrast, today's children can visit museums where Vikings are celebrated as merchants, pastoralists, and artists with a unique worldview as well as conquerors.

What are some other interpretations of Vikings? In the nineteenth century, historians in Denmark, Norway, and Sweden constructed their own Viking ages for nationalistic reasons. At that time, all three countries were in crisis. Denmark had been beaten in a war, and ceded territory to what is now Germany. Norway had become independent from Sweden in 1905, but was economically vulnerable, so Norwegians sought to create a separate identity for themselves in the past *as well as* the present. The Norwegian historian, Gustav Storm, was adamant it was *his* forebears and not the Swedes' or Danes' who had colonised Iceland, Greenland, and Vinland, in what is now Canada. Sweden, meanwhile, had relinquished Norway to the Norwegians and Finland to the Russians; thus, in the late nineteenth century, Sweden was keen to boost its image with rich archaeological finds to show the glory of *its* Viking past.

In addition to augmenting nationalism, nineteenth-century thinkers were influenced by an Englishman, Herbert Spencer, who described peoples and cultures in evolutionary terms similar to those of Charles Darwin. Spencer coined the phrase 'survival of the fittest', which includes the notion that, over time, there is not only technological but also moral progress. Therefore, Viking heathens' adoption of Christianity was considered an advantageous move. These days, historians do not compare

LISTENING
READING
WRITING
SPEAKING

PASSAGE 1   PASSAGE 2   PASSAGE 3

cultures in the same way, especially since, in this case, the archaeological record seems to show that heathen Vikings and Christian Europeans were equally brutal.

Views of Vikings change according not only to forces affecting historians at the time of their research, but also according to the materials they read. Since much knowledge of Vikings comes from literature composed up to 300 years after the events they chronicle, some Danish historians call these sources 'mere legends'.

Vikings did have a written language carved on large stones, but as few of these survive today, the most reliable contemporary sources on Vikings come from writers from other cultures, like the ninth-century Persian geographer, Ibn Khordadbeh.

In the last four decades, there have been wildly varying interpretations of the Viking influence in Russia. Most non-Russian scholars believe the Vikings created a kingdom in western Russia and modern-day Ukraine led by a man called Rurik. After AD 862, Rurik's descendants continued to rule. There is considerable evidence of this colonisation: in Sweden, carved stones, still standing, describe the conquerors' journeys; both Russian and Ukrainian have loan words from Old Norse; and, Scandinavian first names, like Igor and Olga, are still popular. However, during the Soviet period, there was an emphasis on the Slavic origins of most Russians. (Appearing in the historical record around the sixth century AD, the Slavs are thought to have originated in Eastern Europe.) This Slavic identity was promoted to contrast with that of the neighbouring Viking Swedes, who were enemies during the Cold War.

These days, many Russians consider themselves hybrids. Indeed recent genetic studies support a Norse-colonisation theory: western Russian DNA is consistent with that of the inhabitants of a region north of Stockholm in Sweden.

The tools available to modern historians are many and varied, and their findings may seem less open to debate. There are linguistics, numismatics, dendrochronology, archaeozoology, palaeobotany, ice crystallography, climate and DNA analysis to add to the translation of runes and the raising of mighty warships. Despite these, historians remain children of their times.

• •

Questions 27-31

Complete the notes below.

Write **NO MORE THAN TWO WORDS OR A NUMBER** *for each answer.*

Write your answers in boxes 27-31 on your answer sheet.

Origins:	• Word 'Viking' is (**27**)....................
	• Vikings came from Scandinavia.
Dates of the Viking Age	• In Britain: AD (**28**)....................-1066
	• Length varies elsewhere
Territorial extent:	• In doubt – but most of Europe
	• Possibly raided as far away as (**29**)....................
End of the Viking Age:	• Vikings had assimilated into (**30**)...................., & adopted a new (**31**)....................system.

Questions 32-39

Look at the following statements and the list of times and places below.

*Match each statement with the correct place or time: **A-H**.*

*Write the correct letter, **A-H**, in boxes 32-39 on your answer sheet.*

32   A geographer documents Viking culture as it happens.

33   A philosopher classifies cultures hierarchically.

34   Historians assert that Viking history is based more on legends than facts.

35   Young people learn about Viking cultural and economic activities.

36   People see themselves as unrelated to Vikings.

37   An historian claims Viking colonists to modern-day Canada came from his land.

38   Viking conquests are exaggerated to bolster the country's ego after territorial loss.

39   DNA tests show locals are closely related to Swedes.

List of times & places
A   In the UK today
B   In 19th-century Norway
C   In 19th-century Sweden
D   In 19th-century England
E   In Denmark today
F   In 9th-century Persia
G   In mid-20th century Soviet Union
H   In Russia today

Question 40

Which might be a suitable title for passage 3?

*Choose the correct letter, **A-E**.*

Write the correct letter in box 40 on your answer sheet.

    A   A brief history of Vikings

    B   Recent Viking discoveries

    C   A modern fascination with Vikings

    D   Interpretations of Viking history

    E   Viking history and nationalism

LISTENING
READING
WRITING
SPEAKING

TASK 1   TASK 2

Writing

The Writing test lasts for 60 minutes.

Task 1

Spend about 20 minutes on this task.

> **The table below shows the number of babies born to New Zealand women over time.**
>
> **Write a summary of the information. Select and report the main features, and make comparisons where necessary.**

Write at least 150 words.

Number of babies per 1,000 women in New Zealand

	Under 15 years of age	15-19	20-24	25-29	30-34	35-39	40-44	45+
2013	0.1	22.0	66.7	100.7	114.0	70.8	15.0	0.9
2008	0.3	32.8	78.1	112.1	125.9	72.0	13.9	0.7
2003	0.2	25.9	68.6	107.7	112.4	58.7	12.1	0.6
1998	0.2	29.2	75.3	110.6	107.1	48.1	8.5	0.4

Task 2

Spend about 40 minutes on this task.

Write about the following topic:

> **In most countries, there is an age at which people are permitted to drive but no age limit for drivers.**
>
> **Some experts have proposed that drivers be aged between 20 to 70.**
>
> **Why have they proposed this?**
>
> **What are the drawbacks of this proposal?**

Provide reasons for your answer, including relevant examples from your own knowledge or experience.

Write at least 250 words.

LISTENING
READING
WRITING
SPEAKING

PART 1   PART 2   PART 3

Speaking

PART 1

How might you answer the following questions?

1   Could you tell me about the area you're living in now?

2   Would you say it was a good place to bring up children? Why? / Why not?

3   Is there anything famous about your area?

4   Now, let's talk about street markets. Do you ever shop at street markets?

5   What is the benefit of shopping at street markets?

6   Have you ever been to a night market? What was special about it?

7   Do you think there will be more street markets in your city in the future or fewer?

8   Let's move on to talk about meeting people. How easy is it in your city to meet new people?

9   How do you feel about meeting people online?

10 Do you agree or disagree: it's easier to meet people as one gets older.

PART 2

How might you speak about the following topic for two minutes?

> **I'd like you to tell me about a piece of equipment of yours that recently stopped working.**
>
> * What was the equipment?
> * What happened to it?
> * What did you do with the equipment?
>
> And, how do you feel about the experience now?

PART 3

1   First of all, equipment in daily life.

 What are some really useful pieces of equipment, and what are some that are less useful?

 Do you agree or disagree: so much equipment makes people lazy?

2   Now, let's consider inventions.

 To what extent are human beings more inventive now than they were in the past?

 How important are inventors to a country's economy?

 How can inventors be encouraged?

Answers

LISTENING

Section 1: **1.** C; **2.** B; **3.** B; **4.** B; **5.** 12 / 12:00 / twelve; **6.** Correction; **7.** Saturdays (*must have an 's' at the end*); **8.** wheelchair access // a ramp (*must include 'a'*); **9.** Annual; **10.** personal trainer. Section 2: **11.** C; **12.** C; **13.** B; **14.** C; **15.** C; **16.** A; **17.** Public; **18.** Thai; **19.** external; **20.** Bicycle. Section 3: **21.** A; **22.** 200; **23.** to fly; **24.** first; **25.** independently; **26.** fossil; **27-30.** ACDG (*in any order*). Section 4: **31.** Smaller planets; **32.** (A) habitable zone; **33.** (The) scientific method; **34.** C; **35.** C; **36.** A; **37.** mass; **38.** 10%/ten percent/per cent; **39.** insulation; **40.** 500 / five hundred light-years/light years.

The highlighted text below is evidence for the answers above.

Narrator	Recording 23. Practice Listening Test 5. Section 1. Joining up. You will hear a woman showing two people around a pool and gym. Read the example.
Louise	Good evening. I'm Louise, and I'll be showing you the complex.
Wei Wei	Nice to meet you, Louise. I'm Wei wei.
Terry	And I'm Terry.
Louise	The tour takes 20 to 30 minutes. Do you have time?
Wei Wei & Terry	Sure. No problem.
Narrator	The answer is 'C'. On this occasion only, the first part of the conversation is played twice. Before you listen again, you have 30 seconds to read questions 1 to 4.
Louise	Good evening. I'm Louise, and I'll be showing you the complex.
Wei Wei	Nice to meet you, Louise. I'm Wei wei.
Terry	And I'm Terry.
Louise	The tour takes 20 to 30 minutes. Do you have time?
Wei Wei & Terry	Sure. No problem.
Louise	(1) We always like to ask people who come here for the first time how they found out about us.
Wei Wei	We work on Albert Street, not far away.
Louise	So, you saw our new sign?
Terry	I must say I love the blue dolphin, but, in fact, I didn't notice it until this evening.
Louise	Did you read about us online? We've had some great reviews.
Wei Wei & Terry	No, I didn't. I'm afraid not.
Louise	So?
Wei Wei	(1) A woman at work comes here, and she loves it. She swims every lunchtime. I'm hoping to join her.
Louise	In winter, midday classes are popular. Or were you thinking of swimming by yourself?
Wei Wei	I'm not sure. Taking a class could be more motivating than doing laps on my own.
Louise	True. (2) The number one reason people stop going to a pool or a gym is not the cost, nor even the time, but a lack of enthusiasm. They just run out of steam.
Terry	Speaking of steam, you've got a sauna here, haven't you?
Louise	Yes, we have. It's a great place to relax. (3) But, let's have a look at the main pool, first. Recently renovated, this eight-lane 25-metre pool is heated to 27° Celsius.
Wei Wei	Sounds nice.

Louise	The Children's Pool, next door, is even warmer at 31.
Terry	Charlie might like that, Wei wei.
Louise	(4) Does your son, Charlie, swim, Terry?
Terry	Actually, Charlie's not my son.
Louise	Oh, I'm terribly sorry.
Terry	It's a common mistake. We're from the same country, and we work for the same company, but we're not a couple.
Narrator	Before you listen to the rest of the conversation, you have 30 seconds to read questions 5 to 10.
Louise	Well, I've shown you everything.
Terry	It certainly is impressive. I think I could easily hang out and work out here.
Louise	So, let's talk about membership.
Wei Wei	I think I'll start with a Weekly Membership. I'm all too conscious of my limitations, and you're right about people giving up. I've done that before!
	I'd like to sign up for the Water Polo class, between (5) twelve and one, and for the Stroke (6) Correction class.
Louise	I teach Stroke (6) Correction on (7) Saturdays. You may find it's a struggle at first, but within a few lessons, your speed will really increase. Most swimmers have no idea that the way they use their arms affects their performance.
Wei Wei	Do you also work on swimmers' legs? Mine are very weak.
Louise	That's for another class, called Kick Correction. What about classes for Charlie?
Wei Wei	Charlie's in a wheelchair at the moment. He's just had an operation. I see you've got (8) wheelchair access through the parking lot and (8) a ramp into the Children's Pool. He'll need both of those. Maybe once Charlie's comfortable in the water, we'll think about classes.
Louise	I do hope so. What about you, Terry?
Terry	I think I'll go for an (9) Annual Membership. I'm moving into an apartment just two blocks away this weekend. First up, I'd like to take the Monday-night Weight Training class in the gym. And, I noticed your offer of a (10) personal trainer for a one-month trial. Once my (10) personal trainer has developed a programme for me, I'm sure I'll take some more classes.
Narrator	You now have 30 seconds to check your answers. That is the end of Section 1.
Narrator	Recording 24. Section 2. Wharf redevelopment. You will hear a man talking about plans to redevelop a wharf. Before you listen, you have 30 seconds to read questions 11 to 16.
Speaker	Good afternoon, ladies and gentleman. Thanks for coming to this forum about the redevelopment of Queen's Wharf. I hope you've got some tea or coffee, and you've put your phones on silent.
	Right. Essentially, we're now dealing with the final phase of the project. If you've looked at the plans, you'll've noticed that a couple of changes have been made to the previous ones – the most noticeable being the removal of accommodation. You may recall that the original developer went bankrupt; when Cato and Brown took the project over, they scaled things down. As a result, there are no apartments on the second floor of the wharf – in fact, (11) there won't be a second floor at all. I'm sure a fair few of you will applaud this decision since you thought you'd lose your harbour views.
	(12) What else has been scrapped? Oh yes, the fourth jetty for water taxis. It seems the contract with Fletcher's Taxis has been amended so vessels can dock at any of the three jetties as long as no ferry is within five minutes of arrival.
	(13) Depending on your feedback, there are some other features of the plan that Cato and Brown may yet dispense with. For instance, the canopy extension was highly controversial in the first consultation; and, since the canopy doesn't go on until the very end, (13) its size is yet to be determined. It has to cover the existing structure, but whether it goes out over the bus shelter is another matter. (14) The length of the bus shelter has also been reviewed. As many members of the public pointed out, there are only two buses that connect to this wharf, so (14) a long shelter isn't necessary. Years ago, there was no shelter at all; people used to wait inside the wharf building. However, the owners of the commercial space complained: bus passengers rarely bought anything more than a newspaper or a chocolate bar, and there were instances of shoplifting. The owners also got tired of children who rode their bicycles and skateboards up and down the corridor, even though it was forbidden, (15) so this is one reason why the corridor is absent from the latest plan.

Let's move on to (16) what's set in stone, so to speak – (16) things that the council insists upon. Cato and Brown are adding a third jetty for the new ferry service to Green Island. With a permanent community on the island, it's profitable to run a ferry. The council hopes the wharf will generate much of its own income, so this third jetty is not up for discussion. Likewise, (16) renovation has to be done to parts of the wharf that no longer meet safety standards, like the weathered or rotten posts and planks; and, the wooden eastern walkway will be almost entirely replaced.

Narrator	Before you listen to the rest of the talk, you have 30 seconds to read questions 17 to 20.

Now I'd like to spend a few minutes outlining the redesign of the space inside the wharf building.

Firstly, public comment was made during the initial planning phase, so the only input we're asking for now relates to the (17) public space where there used to be a bookshop and a food outlet. Probably toilets will go there, along with seats, vending machines, plants, and sculptures. We're hoping local artists will submit ideas for artworks, and that the plants will be native.

As you can see from the plan, the size of the internal space remains the same, but the corridor will be subsumed into the floor space of the (17) public area and the (18) Thai restaurant in Shop 4. Access to the shops will be (19) external only, via the eastern and western walkways. I think the (20) bicycle shop, next to the café, made a submission against (19) external access, (15) requesting the corridor be retained, but this was rejected.

OK. Let's have another drink while we discuss parking at the wharf…

Narrator	You now have 30 seconds to check your answers. That is the end of Section 2.

Narrator	Recording 25. Section 3. Post-graduate research. You will hear two students talking about their post-graduate research. Before you listen, you have 30 seconds to read questions 21 to 25.
Vanessa	Hey, Marcus, how are you?
Marcus	I'm really well.
Vanessa	I thought you were in South Africa.
Marcus	I was until a month ago. I came back to do a PhD.
Vanessa	D'you know what you're getting into? I'm writing a Master's thesis, and it's driving me crazy.
Marcus	Oh dear.
Vanessa	I heard you had an amazing job in a national park. Why would you give that up?
Marcus	(21) It's true, I started out working in a national park, looking after ostriches, and it did seem like my dream job. But, almost by accident, I got involved in taking DNA samples from the birds. I ended up analysing the samples, myself, in a lab in Cape Town. (21) It was incredible – working in the lab. Suddenly, I realised I had greater ambitions than being a park ranger.
Vanessa	Well, well. What was the DNA for?
Marcus	You see, ostriches are part of a group of flightless birds called ratites, and there's a mystery in ornithology about how they spread around the globe when they can't fly.
Vanessa	That is weird.
Marcus	There's one hypothesis that they originated in Gondwanaland – a supercontinent that moved apart from Pangaea between (22) 200 and 120 million years ago.
Vanessa	Didn't Gondwanaland separate into Australia, Africa, and South America?
Marcus	That's right. Plus Antarctica and India. The theory is that ratites stayed on the drifting landmasses, which would account for their present distribution. In the opposing hypothesis, borne out in the (26) fossil record, ratites originated in the northern supercontinent, called Laurasia. Then, they flew south, but lost the ability (23) to fly around 50 million years ago.
Vanessa	Which theory do you favour?
Marcus	I'm keen on the Gondwanaland one because DNA analysis shows ostriches are the oldest of the ratites, and, according to geologists, Africa broke away from Gondwanaland (24) first. Also, DNA analysis of the extinct elephant bird of Madagascar and the kiwi of New Zealand suggests they're close relatives, so it's unlikely they became flightless (25) independently.

Vanessa	But isn't the (26) fossil record more reliable?
Marcus	Not really. It's open to interpretation.
Narrator	Before you listen to the rest of the conversation, you have 30 seconds to read questions 27 to 30.
Marcus	How's your research going?
Vanessa	Not so well, I'm afraid.
Marcus	I presume you're doing a Master's in Public Health. (27-30) What's the topic of your thesis?
Vanessa	Well, that was my first problem. It's changed about 20 times. Currently, I'm looking at fathers' visiting habits in neonatal wards.
Marcus	Remind me how old neonatal babies are.
Vanessa	Up to four weeks.
Marcus	And what's the aim of your research?
Vanessa	I'd like to propose a change to hospital policy. I think limited access by fathers to their newborns would improve the health of infants and their mothers, especially in intensive care.
Marcus	Whoa! That's a radical idea. Letting the family be part of the birth process has been standard practice in hospitals for 40 years.
Vanessa	And because of that I chose a quantitative research methodology.
Marcus	You'll have to tell me what *that* is again as well.
Vanessa	Quantitative research collects data that can be explained numerically. It's used to determine general trends.
Marcus	Uh huh.
Vanessa	(27-30) But, my next obstacle was that I couldn't get a large enough sample of paternal behaviour to analyse it quantitatively.
Marcus	Why not?
Vanessa	(27-30) Four of the hospitals I approached refused me access to their patients. I did get permission from two others, where I used to work, but the results of my survey were so scattered I couldn't model anything.
Marcus	So, what did you do?
Vanessa	I opted for a qualitative approach. I gave up large data collection, and did in-depth interviews with a handful of fathers. At the same time, (27-30) I set up an online discussion group for fathers.
Marcus	How did that go?
Vanessa	(27-30) Frankly, it was too slow to be useful. I've got to finish my thesis by the end of the year, and (27-30) managing the website took too much time.
Marcus	Have you considered regression analysis? That is, determining the strength of the relationship between variables. It's used for things like trying to prove that video games lead to more violence among young viewers.
Vanessa	Yes, I have. In fact, I've changed supervisors, and my new one has guided me towards regression analysis, so at last I'm making progress.
Narrator	You now have 30 seconds to check your answers. That is the end of Section 3.
Narrator	Recording 26. Section 4. Earth's cousin. You will hear a lecture on searching for planets similar to Earth. Before you listen, you have 45 seconds to read questions 31 to 40.
Lecturer	For hundreds of years, people have wondered whether other planets could sustain human life. Twentieth-century space missions cast doubt over colonisation of our own solar system, but there's plenty of hope beyond. Distant bodies orbiting far-away stars are known as exoplanets. Since 1996, thousands of exoplanets have been found, most of which are massive hot balls of gas, like Jupiter. However, a new US mission is focusing on (31) smaller planets, one half to twice the size of Earth. These must also be close enough to their star to be in a (32) habitable zone. Today, I'd like to discuss NASA's Kepler Mission, which began in 2009 and is ongoing. But first, who was Kepler? Well, Johannes Kepler lived from 1571 to 1630 mostly in what is now Germany. He was a physicist, astronomer, and optician. He was the first person to explain planetary motion correctly, and,

more importantly, he developed a way of working in which he sought to prove that theories must be universal, verifiable, and precise. This is known as (33) the scientific method.

I do think it is fitting that a tiny spacecraft is named after a giant of astronomy.

NASA's Kepler satellite is small and relatively simple. Other telescopes, like Hubble, provide exciting data, (34) but Kepler surveys just one area of the galaxy – the constellations Cygnus and Lyrae – and records events over several years. It has already identified around 1,000 new planets, and provided data on another 3,000 potential planets.

Kepler is powered by a solar array. Its largest instrument is a photometer – (35) a sensor that measures the light emitted by more than 100,000 stars. The photometer is so sensitive it can detect a drop in brightness when a planet moves, or transits, in front of a star, of one part in 10,000. This is like recording the decreased brightness of a car headlight when a small insect flies across it.

When a planet transits, NASA's computers graph the curving light from the star. Regular, repeated dips in the curve could indicate a new planet. A smaller dip, (36) when a planet passes *behind* its star, creates reflections. Scientists can draw conclusions about the planet's atmosphere from these reflections, because, as Kepler knew, the laws of physics and chemistry are universal – even way out in space. For example, light is absorbed by different atoms at different wavelengths, so a light signature provides data on a planet's atmosphere. Hydrogen, carbon, oxygen, sodium, and other elements have been identified in new planets. However, the proportion of their composition is uncertain, making the detection of water difficult.

But back to the Kepler data, and some recent candidates for human habitation.

In 2013, a star named Kepler 62 was found with two planets in its (32) habitable zone. At first, these were considered similar to Earth, but on further analysis, each planet's (37) mass was found to be several times greater than that of Earth. Their gravity might be strong enough to pull in helium and hydrogen gas, but this makes them similar to Neptune rather than Earth.

The following year, a star called Kepler 186 came under scrutiny. Its fifth planet, known as Kepler 186f, seemed a more likely candidate. With a diameter of 14,000 kilometres, it is roughly (38) ten percent wider than Earth. It orbits close enough to Kepler 186 for it to be temperate, allowing water to flow at the surface.

Smaller than the planets orbiting Kepler 62, Kepler 186f is more likely to have similar gravity to Earth's and a rocky surface, perhaps containing iron, ice, and liquid water. At the outer edge of the habitable zone, its surface may freeze, as it receives one sixth of the light from *its* star that Earth does from the Sun. On the other hand, with a greater mass, Kepler 186f may have a thicker atmosphere, providing sufficient (39) insulation. This has led astronomers to dub Kepler 186f 'Earth's cousin', not its twin.

But I can hear you thinking, OK, there are planets out there that sound Earth-like, but can we reach them? Currently: No. In the near to medium-term future? Afraid not.

The only known man-made object to have left the solar system is the unmanned Voyager 1 probe. This happened in late 2013, and it had taken 37 years to travel from Earth. Voyager travels at around 61,000 kilometers per hour. Kepler 186f is about (40) 500 light years away. At Voyager's current speed, it'd take 17,400 years to travel a *single* light year, or 8.7 million years for the journey from Earth to Kepler 186f. The Space Shuttle, the only speedy manned spacecraft, is far slower than Voyager, with speeds of just 45,000 kilometres per hour, meaning a twelve-million-year journey!

Meantime, the Hubble Telescope is investigating a suitable planet called GJ124b, at a distance of 40 light years away. But whether a planet is 40 or (40) 500 light years away is immaterial.

Humans have always reached for the stars. Kepler the man, and Kepler the spacecraft have raised the possibility of human habitation; only our transport remains primitive.

Narrator	That is the end of the Listening test. You now have ten minutes to transfer your answers to your answer sheet.

READING: Passage 1: **1.** F/False; **2.** NG/Not Given; **3.** NG/Not Given; **4.** F/False; **5.** T/True; **6.** thin; **7.** stem; **8.** crop (*'yield' is incorrect as it does not appear in the singular in the passage*); **9.** 4/four; **10.** 5/five million; **11.** morning; **12.** C; **13.** B. Passage 2: **14.** E; **15.** A; **16.** F; **17.** D; **18.** E; **19.** B; **20.** B; **21.** A; **22.** D; **23.** The brain; **24.** 34,000/Thirty-four thousand; **25.** The human body // Human beings; **26.** Respect and excitement // Excitement and respect. Passage 3: **27.** obscure; **28.** 793; **29.** Northwest Africa; **30.** local populations; **31.** religious; **32.** F; **33.** D; **34.** E; **35.** A; **36.** G; **37.** B; **38.** C; **39.** H; **40.** D.

The highlighted text below is evidence for the answers above.

If there is a question where 'Not given' is the answer, no evidence can be found, so there is no highlighted text.

The plight of rice

Rice is a tall grass with a drooping panicle that contains numerous edible grains, and has been cultivated in China for more than 6,000 years. A staple throughout Asia and large parts of Africa, it is now (1) grown in flooded paddy fields from sea level to high mountains and harvested three times a year. According to the Food and Health Organisation of the United Nations, around four billion people currently receive a fifth of their calories from rice.

Recently, Japan, South Korea, and Taiwan have slightly reduced rice consumption due to the adoption of more western diets, but almost all other countries have raised their consumption due to population increase. Yet, since 1984, there have been diminishing rice yields around the world.

From the 1950s to the early 1960s, rice production was also suffering: India was on the brink of famine, and China was already experiencing one. In the late 1950s, (4) Norman Borlaug, an American plant pathologist, began advising Punjab State in northwestern India to grow a new semi-dwarf variety of wheat. This was so successful that, in 1962, a semi-dwarf variety of rice, called IR8, developed by the Philippine International Rice Research Institute (IRRI), was planted throughout Southeast Asia and India. This semi-dwarf variety heralded (5) the Green Revolution, which saved the lives of millions of people by almost doubling rice yields: from 1.9 metric tons per hectare in 1950-64, to 3.5 metric tons in 1985-98.

IR8 survived because, as a semi-dwarf, it only grows to a moderate height, and it does not (6) thin out, keel over, and drown like traditional varieties. Furthermore, its short thick (7) stem is able to absorb chemical fertilisers, but, as stem growth is limited, the plant expends energy on producing a large panicle of heavy seeds, ensuring a greater (8) crop.

However, even with a massive increase in rice production, semi-dwarf varieties managed to keep up with population growth for only ten years. In Africa, where rice consumption is rising by 20% annually, and where one third of the population now depends on the cereal, this is disturbing. At the current rate, within the next 20 years, rice will surpass maize as the major source of calories on that continent. Meantime, even in ideal circumstances, paddies worldwide are not producing what they once did, for reasons largely unknown to science. An average 0.8% fall in yields has been noted in rich rice-growing regions; in less ideal ones, flood, drought and salinity have meant yields have fallen drastically, sometimes up to 40%.

The sequencing of the rice genome took place in 2005, after which the IRRI developed genetically modified flood-resistant varieties of rice, called Sub 1, which produce up to (9) four times the amount of edible grain from non-modified strains. In 2010, a handful of farmers worldwide were planting IRRI Sub 1 rice; now, over (10) five million are doing so. Currently, drought- and salt-resistent varieties are being trialled since most rice is grown in the great river basins of the Brahmaputra, the Irawaddy, and the Mekong that are all drying up or becoming far saltier.

With global warming, many rice-growing regions are hotter than 20 years ago. Nearly all varieties of rice, including IR8, flower in the afternoon, but the anthers – little sacs that contain male pollen – wither and die in soaring temperatures. IRRI scientists have identified one variety of rice, known as Odisha, that flowers in the early (11) morning, and they are in the process of genetically modifying IR8 so it contains Odisha-flowering genes, although it may be some time before this is released.

While there is a clear need for more rice, many states and countries seem less keen to influence agricultural policy directly than they were in the past. Some believe rice demand will dip in wealthier places, as occurred in Japan, South Korea, and Taiwan; (12) others consider it more prudent to devote resources to tackling obesity or to limiting intensive farming that is environmentally destructive.

Some experts say where there is state intervention it should take the form of reducing subsidies to rice farmers to stimulate production; others propose that small land holdings should be consolidated into more economically viable ones. There is no denying that land reform is pressing, but many governments shy away from it, fearing losses at the ballot box, all the while knowing that rural populations are heading for the city in droves anyway. (13) And, as they do so, cities expand, eating up fertile land for food production.

One can only hope that the IRRI and other research institutions will spearhead half a dozen mini green revolutions, independently of uncommitted states.

A new perspective on bacteria

A Microbes are organisms too small to be seen by the naked eye, including bacteria, blue-green algae, yeasts, fungi, viruses, and viroids.

(15) A large, diverse group, almost all bacteria are between one and ten μ^3 (larger ones reach 0.5 mm). (19) Generally single-celled, with a distinctive cellular structure lacking a true nucleus, most bacterial genetic information is carried on a DNA loop in the cytoplasm[4] with the membrane possessing some nuclear properties.

(15) There are three main kinds of bacteria – spherical, (20) rod-like, and spiral – known by their Latin names of coccus, (20) bacillus, and spirillum. Bacteria occur alone, in pairs, clusters, chains, or more complex configurations. Some live where oxygen is present; others, where it is absent.

The relationship between bacteria and their hosts is symbiotic, benefitting both organisms, or the hosts may be destroyed by parasitic or disease-causing bacteria.

---

[3]A micron = 10^{-6} m
[4]Material inside a cell

B In general, humans view bacteria suspiciously, yet it is now thought they partly owe their existence to microbes living long, long ago.

During photosynthesis, plants produce oxygen that humans need to fuel blood cells. Most geologists believe the early atmosphere on (21) Earth contained very little oxygen until around 2½ billion years ago, when microbes bloomed. Ancestral forms of cyanobacteria, for example, evolved into chloroplasts – the cells that carry out photosynthesis. Once plants inhabited the oceans, oxygen levels rose dramatically, so complex life forms could eventually be sustained.

The air humans breathe today is oxygen-rich, and the majority of airborne microbes are harmless, but the air does contain industrial pollutants, allergens, and infectious microbes or pathogens that cause illness.

C The fact is that scientists barely understand microbes. Bacteria have been proven to exist only in the past 350 years; viruses were discovered just over 100 years ago, but in the past three decades, the ubiquity of microbes has been established with bacteria found kilometres below the Earth's crust and in the upper atmosphere. Surprisingly, they survive in dry deserts and the frozen reaches of Antarctica; they dwell in rain and snow clouds, as well as inside every living creature.

Air samples taken in 2006 from two cities in Texas contained at least 1,800 distinct species of bacteria, making the air as rich as the soil. These species originated both in Texas and as far away as western China. (22) It now seems that the number of microbe species far exceeds the number of stars.

D (17) Inside every human being there are trillions of bacteria with their weight estimated at 1.36 kg in an average adult, or about as heavy as (23) the brain. Although tiny, 90% of cells in a human are bacterial. With around eight million genes, these bacteria outnumber genes in human cells by 300 times.

The large intestine contains the most bacteria – almost (24) 34,000 species – but the crook of the elbow harbours over 2,000 species. Many bacteria are helpful: digesting food; aiding the immune system; creating moisturiser; and, manufacturing vitamins. Some have highly specialised functions, like *Bacteroides thetaiotaomicron*, which breaks down plant starch, so an infant can make the transition from mother's milk to a more varied diet.

Undeniably, some bacteria are life-threatening. One, known as golden staph, *Staphylococcus aureus*, plagues hospitals, where it infects instruments and devours human tissue until patients die from toxic shock. Worse, it is still resistant to antibiotics.

E Antibiotics themselves are bacteria. (14) In 1928, Alexander Fleming discovered that a mould in his laboratory produced a chemical he named penicillin. In 1951, William Bouw collected soil from the jungles of Borneo that eventually became vancomycin. Pharmaceutical companies still hunt for beneficial bacteria, but (18) Michael Fischbach from University of California believes that (25) the human body itself is a ready supply.

F Scientific ignorance about bacteria is largely due to an inability to cultivate many of them in a laboratory, but recent DNA sequencing has meant populations can be analysed by computer program without having to grow them.

Fischbach and his team have created and trained a computer program to identify gene clusters in microbial DNA sequences that might produce useful molecules. Having collected microbial DNA from 242 healthy human volunteers, the scientists sequenced the genomes of 2,340 different species of microbes, most of which were completely new discoveries.

In searching the gene clusters, (16) Fischbach et al found 3,118 common ones that could be used in pharmaceuticals, for example, a gene cluster from the bacterium *Lactobacillus gasseri*, successfully reared in the lab, produced a molecule they named lactocillin. Later, they discovered the structure of this was very similar to an antibiotic, LFF571, undergoing clinical trials by a major pharmaceutical company. To date, lactocillin has killed harmful bacteria, so it may also be a reliable antibiotic.

G Naturally, the path to patenting medicine is strewn with failures, but, since bacteria have been living inside humans for millions of years, they are probably safe to reintroduce in new combinations and in large amounts.

Undoubtedly, the fight against pathogens, like golden staph, must continue, but as scientists learn more about microbes, (26) respect and excitement for them grows, and their positive applications become ever more probable.

In the last century, Vikings have been perceived in numerous different ways – vilified as conquerors and romanticised as adventurers. How Vikings have been employed in nation-building is a topic of some interest.

In English, Vikings are also known as Norse or Norsemen. Their language greatly influenced English, with the nouns, 'Hell', 'husband', 'law', and 'window', and the verbs, 'blunder', 'snub', 'take', and 'want', all coming from Old Norse. However, the origins of the word 'Viking', itself, are (27) obscure: it may mean 'a Scandinavian pirate', or it may refer to 'an inlet', or a place called Vik, in modern-day Norway, from where the pirates came. These various names – Vikings, Norse, or Norsemen, and doubts about the very word 'Viking' suggest historical confusion.

Loosely speaking, the Viking Age endured from the late eighth to the mid-eleventh centuries. Vikings sailed to England in (28) AD 793 to storm coastal monasteries, and subsequently large swathes of England fell under Viking rule – indeed several Viking kings sat on the English throne. It is generally agreed that the Battle of Hastings, in 1066, when the Norman French invaded, marks the end of the English Viking Age, but the Irish Viking age ended earlier, while Viking colonies in Iceland and Greenland did not dissolve until around AD 1500.

How much territory Vikings controlled is also in dispute – Scandinavia and Western Europe certainly, but their reach east and south is uncertain. They plundered and settled down the Volga and Dnieper rivers, and traded with modern-day Istanbul, but the archaeological record has yet to verify that Vikings raided as far away as (29) Northwest Africa, as some writers claim.

The issue of control and extent is complex because many Vikings did not return to Scandinavia after raiding but assimilated into (30) local populations, often becoming Christian. To some degree, the Viking Age is defined by religion. Initially, Vikings were polytheists, believing in many gods, but by the end of the age, they had permanently accepted a new monotheistic (31) religious system – Christianity.

This transition from so-called pagan plunderers to civilised Christians is significant, and is the view promulgated throughout much of recent history. In the UK, in the 1970s for example, school children were taught that until the Vikings accepted Christianity they were nasty heathens who rampaged throughout Britain. (35) By contrast, today's children can visit museums where Vikings are celebrated as merchants, pastoralists, and artists with a unique worldview as well as conquerors.

What are some other interpretations of Vikings? In the nineteenth century, historians in Denmark, Norway, and Sweden constructed their own Viking ages for nationalistic reasons. At that time, all three countries were in crisis. Denmark had been beaten in a war, and ceded territory to what is now Germany. Norway had become independent from Sweden in 1905, but was economically vulnerable, so Norwegians sought to create a separate identity for themselves in the past *as well as* the present, (37) thus the Norwegian historian, Gustav Storm, was adamant it was *his* forebears and not the Swedes' or Danes' who had colonised Iceland, Greenland, and Vinland, in what is now Canada. (38) Sweden, meanwhile, had relinquished Norway to the Norwegians and Finland to the Russians; thus, in the late nineteenth century, Sweden was keen to boost its image with rich archaeological finds to show the glory of *its* Viking past.

In addition to augmenting nationalism, (33) nineteenth-century thinkers were influenced by an Englishman, Herbert Spencer, who described peoples and cultures in evolutionary terms similar to those of Charles Darwin. Spencer coined the phrase 'survival of the fittest', which includes the notion that, over time, there is not only technological but also moral progress. Therefore, Viking heathens' adoption of Christianity was considered an advantageous move. These days, historians do not compare cultures in the same way, especially since, in this case, the archaeological record seems to show that heathen Vikings and Christian Europeans were equally brutal.

Views of Vikings change according not only to forces affecting historians at the time of their research, but also according to the materials they read. (34) Since much knowledge of Vikings comes from literature composed up to 300 years after the events they chronicle, some Danish historians call these sources 'mere legends'.

Vikings did have a written language carved on large stones, but as few of these survive today, (32) the most reliable contemporary sources on Vikings come from writers from other cultures, like the ninth-century Persian geographer, Ibn Khordadbeh.

In the last four decades, there have been wildly varying interpretations of the Viking influence in Russia. Most non-Russian scholars believe the Vikings created a kingdom in western Russia and modern-day Ukraine led by a man called Rurik. After AD 862, Rurik's descendants continued to rule. There is considerable evidence of this colonisation: in Sweden, carved stones, still standing, describe the conquerors' journeys; both Russian and Ukrainian have loan words from Old Norse; and, Scandinavian first names, like Igor and Olga, are still popular. (36) However, during the Soviet period, there was an emphasis on the Slavic origins of most Russians. (Appearing in the historical record around the sixth century AD, the Slavs are thought to have originated in Eastern Europe.) This Slavic identity was promoted to contrast with that of the neighbouring Viking Swedes, who were enemies during the Cold War.

These days, many Russians consider themselves hybrids. (39) Indeed recent genetic studies support a Norse-colonisation theory: western Russian DNA is consistent with that of the inhabitants of a region north of Stockholm in Sweden.

(40) The tools available to modern historians are many and varied, and their findings may seem less open to debate. There are linguistics, numismatics, dendrochronology, archaeozoology, palaeobotany, ice crystallography, climate and DNA analysis to add to the translation of runes and the raising of mighty warships. Despite these, historians remain children of their times.

LISTENING	SECTION 1	SECTION 2	SECTION 3	SECTION 4
READING				
WRITING				
SPEAKING				

TEST 6

Listening

Firstly, tear out the Test 6 Listening / Reading Answer Sheet at the back of this book.

The Listening test lasts for about 20 minutes.

Write your answers on the pages below as you listen. After Section 4 has finished, you have ten minutes to transfer your answers to your Listening Answer Sheet. You will need to time yourself for this transfer.

After checking your answers on pp 220-224, go to page 9 for the raw-score conversion table.

PLAY RECORDING #27.

SECTION 1   Questions 1-10

NEW JOBS

Questions 1-5

Complete the sentences below.

*Write **NO MORE THAN TWO WORDS** for each answer.*

Example James has not seen Annie lately due to spending *long hours* at work.

1   James enjoys the…………………….of his work.

2   Annie does not enjoy all the…………………....for her work.

3   Annie's job involves………………..…….., and offering advice to land managers or owners who wish to make changes.

4   Annie works in the council's…………………..……division.

5   Annie outlines her clients' legal obligations, and proposes the……………..…of their land.

Questions 6-7

*Choose **TWO** letters, A-E.*

Which **TWO** of the following are likely to cause the farmer difficulties in her development application?

    A   New accommodation

    B   A new road

    C   Olive trees

    D   A volcano

    E   A wetland

Questions 8-10

Answer the questions below.

*Write **NO MORE THAN TWO WORDS OR A NUMBER** for each answer.*

8   For whom does Annie think carefully controlled land use is valuable?

………………..………………..

9   When did a tram service cease in James and Annie's town?

………………..………………..

10   What did James study at university?

………………..………………..

PLAY RECORDING #28.

SECTION 2   Questions 11-20

HOW TO MAKE A GUITAR

Questions 11-14

Classify the following things that:

    A   Hamish the musician did or does.

    B   Juliette the interviewer did or does.

    C   Ray Rogers the music show host did or does.

*Write the correct letter, **A**, **B**, or **C**, on your answer sheet.*

11   He / She went to rock concerts as a teenager.

12   He / She cried on the radio.

13   He / She was very nervous about performing in public.

14   He / She thinks work adversely affected his / her private life.

Questions 15-18

Complete the table below.

Write **NO MORE THAN THREE WORDS** *for each answer.*

Part of the process of making an acoustic guitar	
1. Sourcing the wood:	The back of a good guitar is made from rosewood. Cedar is used for the top, but mahogany is used for the neck as it can endure changes in (**15**)……………. and humidity.
2. Book matching **3. Shaping** **4. Creating a sound hole**	
5. Strutting:	Braces are glued onto the top and back to improve (**16**)…………… and reflect sound waves.
6. Creating the sides:	Wet wooden strips are placed into a curved mould.
7. Preparing the neck:	The neck is carved from a single piece of wood, and a metal rod is driven up it for (**17**)……………
8. Clamping:	The back, sides, top, and neck are glued and clamped together (**18**)…………..

Questions 19-20

Choose the correct letter, **A**, **B**, *or* **C**.

19   Why does Hamish enjoy making guitars?

    A   Because he also likes to play them

    B   Because he enjoys careful woodwork

    C   Because his mental health has benefitted

20   How is the name of Hamish's old band spelt?

    A   Sound Wall

    B   Sound Whole

    C   Sound Hole

Play
Audio   **PLAY RECORDING #29.**

SECTION 3   Questions 21-30

VERTICAL GARDENING

Questions 21-25

Complete the table below.

*Write **NO MORE THAN TWO WORDS** for each answer.*

A presentation on vertical gardening	
Part II Marina's work	• (21)................two domestic vertical gardens
Part III David's work	• Reviewing material on (22)................works in Europe
Parts I & IV Both students' work	• Describing the movement's history and explaining its (23)................ • Noting Patrick Blanc's inspiration by (24)................ • Evaluating vertical gardening. (Does it provide visual relief to cities, or is it too costly with constant (25)................, polluting fertiliser, and unrecyclable parts?)

Questions 26-28

Label the diagram below on the following page.

*Choose **THREE** answers from the box, and write the correct answer, **A-E**, next to questions 26-28.*

A	Wooden batten
B	PVC panel
C	Mosquito repellant
D	Matting
E	Supporting wall

Cross section of a domestic vertical garden

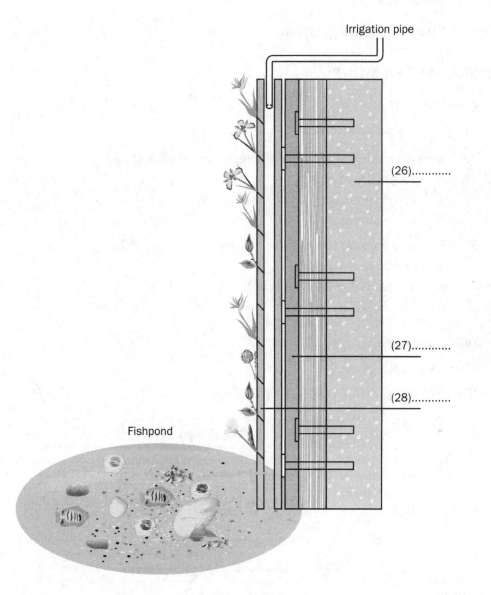

Questions 29-30

*Choose the correct letter, **A**, **B**, or **C**.*

29   Overall, how does Marina feel about vertical gardening?

    A   Rather skeptical

    B   Keen with reservations

    C   Enthusiastic

30   To whom does David think vertical gardening will mostly appeal?

    A   Big businesses rather than individuals

    B   The developing world

    C   People all over the world

PLAY RECORDING #30.

SECTION 4   Questions 31-40

SELF-FULFILMENT

Questions 31-32

Choose the correct letter, A, B, or C.

31   What is a concern of a growing number of the speaker's clients?

   A   Financial hardship

   B   Future uncertainty

   C   Vague discontent

32   Why did the female client stop her sessions with the psychologist?

   A   She did not have time.

   B   The psychologist did not help.

   C   The reasons are unclear.

Questions 33-40

Complete the table below.

Write **NO MORE THAN THREE WORDS** for each answer.

Is self-fulfilment right?	
Writers / Philosophers / Others who symbolise (33)...............rather than self-fulfilment:	• Dietrich Bonhoeffer; Emmanuel Kant; Martin Luther King; Nelson Mandela • People in (34)..............., ghost towns, & parts of the developing world • The speaker's (35)..............
King's 3 dimensions: Length + Breadth + Height	
Height	• Height = especially hard for (36)...............to accept • For King, Height = God • For non-religious people, Height = Something (37)............... than oneself / An abstract idea, like equality or (38)...............
Conclusion	
The speaker questions the do-what-you-love principle as it may degrade menial (39)............... . True self-fulfilment is sometimes doing disagreeable things for the sake of (40)............... .	

Reading

Firstly, turn over the Test 6 Listening Answer Sheet you used earlier to write your Reading answers on the back.

The Reading test lasts exactly 60 minutes.

Certainly, make any marks on the pages below, but transfer your answers to the answer sheet <u>as you read</u> since there is no extra time at the end to do so.

After checking your answers on pp 224-227, go to page 9 for the raw-score conversion table.

PASSAGE 1

*Spend about 20 minutes on **Questions 1-13**, based on Passage 1 below.*

‖‖‖

With rapid urbanisation, more people now live in cities than in the countryside, and this number is set to rise. For all the benefits cities bestow, they are expensive places. In some years, Tokyo records the highest cost of living; in others, Moscow. In 2014, for expatriates, Luanda, the capital of Angola, received the dubious accolade; and, for Angolans themselves, it had also suddenly become pricey with real estate going through the roof, so to speak, and food being prohibitive – even locally sourced mangoes were $5 a kilo.

What can urbanites do to reduce the financial burden of paying for food? Diet? Grow their own? Beg for subsidies? Some economists have proposed that they buy contracts giving rights to a food stream in perpetuity, for example, a kilogram of beef would be delivered weekly from the date the contract started until the end of the owner's life. In essence, this is what house purchase is – indefinite security of a single commodity. As is the case with buying a house, a loan from a financial institution might be necessary for the beef contract, even if it were merely for Australian blade steak and not Japanese Wagu. The contract could also be sold at the current market price if its owner moved out of delivery range or renounced beef.

In order to maintain or increase the value of their investment, it is likely some owners would support national and international policies to limit food production – a sound idea in a world where 40% of food goes to waste.

But let's imagine, in this system, a consumer purchased a 25-year contract for beef, which, over time, doubled in value. Naturally, at sale, the owner would make a tidy profit. Conversely, if mad cow disease erupted, and no one dared eat beef, then the vendor would suffer. If the owner had bought ten beef contracts, he or she might even go bankrupt in this scenario.

Let's also imagine that people bought contracts on items they had no intention of consuming: that the health-conscious purchased, yet eschewed, saturated-fat meat; that shrewd amoral vegetarians speculated in beef, as they already buy share portfolios in which multinational agri-business is represented, or they deposit money into banks that do just that on their behalf.

It is quite plausible that this speculative behaviour could lead to the overheating of the food-stream market. The state may intervene, attempting to cool things down, or it may tolerate such activity. Indeed, a government that proposed a capital gains tax or high death duties on food-stream contracts

LISTENING
READING
WRITING
SPEAKING

PASSAGE 1   PASSAGE 2   PASSAGE 3

might be voted out in favour of another that believed in laissez-faire.* Besides which, an investment contract may be a way to realise wealth when there are few other possibilities either because the stock market is highly volatile, or much of the local economy generates little revenue, as is the case in Angola and many developing countries. Indeed, food-stream speculation could become a middle class prerogative, indulged in by legislative members themselves.

I hope by now, you've realised this essay is a spoof. Yet, the fantastic food-stream market is reminiscent of the global housing market, where home ownership and property speculation have become the privilege of a few at great expense to the many, who either cannot participate, or sign their lives away to banks. You may also have realised that when I bring this topic up at a dinner party, for instance, I am usually shouted down, despite what I believe to be its inherent logic, because my friends consider a house as more tangible than a steak, and their identities are bound up with vague but powerful notions of property rights and independence.

I do concede that home-ownership offers security (not having to move, being connected to one particular neighbourhood) and creativity (being able to modify and decorate as you please), but I would prefer people rent rather than buy in an effort to lower property prices, and to encourage investment in other sectors of the economy. Economists Moretti and Chang-Tai Hsieh of the University of Chicago have estimated that US output between 1999 and 2009 was 13% lower than it could have been because high housing costs forced so many people to move. Income locked up in housing could otherwise have been spent on local businesses, like restaurants or gyms, and job creation would likely have ensued.

So, next time you toss a steak on the barbecue, ponder whether we should treat food in the same way we treat housing, or whether we should treat housing as we do food.

Questions 1-7

Complete the notes below.

*Choose **NO MORE THAN TWO WORDS** from the passage.*

Write your answer in boxes 1-7 on your answer sheet.

A food-stream contract
• Would guarantee access to one kind of food stream (**1**)................
• Due to its expense, a bank (**2**)...............might be needed to buy one
• Could be bought and sold at the current (**3**)...............
• When sold, could result in a decent (**4**)...............or a considerable loss
• Could be purchased on food a person did not plan on (**5**)...............
• May be one of the few legitimate ways to make money when the stock market is very (**6**)...............or other parts of the economy perform poorly
• Would probably be a privilege of the (**7**)...............and members of parliament

---

*French for 'allow to do'. An economic doctrine advocating that commerce should be free of state controls of any kind.

LISTENING
READING
WRITING
SPEAKING

PASSAGE 1   PASSAGE 2   PASSAGE 3

Questions 8-12

Do the statements below agree with the information given in Passage 1?

In boxes 8-12 on your answer sheet, write:

> **TRUE**   *if the statement agrees with the information.*
> **FALSE**   *if the statement contradicts the information.*
> **NOT GIVEN** *if there is no information on this.*

8   The writer makes an analogy between the current housing and food markets.

9   The writer rents his or her own home.

10   The writer's friends share his or her ideas on the property market.

11   The writer thinks people like to own their homes because they can customise them.

12   Because Americans spent so much on housing, other parts of the economy suffered.

Question 13

What would be a suitable title for Passage 1?

*Choose the correct letter, **A**, **B**, **C**, **D**, or **E**.*

Write the correct letter in box 13 on your answer sheet.

> **A**   How to make homes affordable
> **B**   Buying a house is a bad investment
> **C**   Rethinking the housing market
> **D**   A new model for buying and selling food
> **E**   The madness of house and food prices

PASSAGE 2

Spend about 20 minutes on **Questions 14-26**, *based on Passage 2 below.*

- -

Egypt's beautiful game

<u>A</u> It is estimated that over a billion people watched the 2014 World Cup – the biggest TV event in human history – and that football is a trillion-dollar industry.

The fact that a handful of countries dominate the World Cup does not lessen interest in the competition or the sport by people in the remotest of regions. Take the largely inaccessible Omo Valley of southern Ethiopia, where shepherds with few possessions sport Arsenal or AC Milan T-shirts, and where women who may not know of the existence of the UK wear pendants with Wayne Rooney's face on them. In Qiqihar, in northern China, middle-school children choose 'English' names for themselves, like David Beckham or Ronaldo, while in the Sinai, where temperatures soar and there are no other signs of life outdoors, adolescent boys dribble, kick, header, and feint with homemade footballs, dreaming of lifting themselves from abject poverty by playing for a famous team.

Although football generally stimulates the economy, many places grind to a halt when a big match is on – indeed the inhabitants of Cairo quip that the best time to drive across town to shop is during a final between Al Ahly and Zamalek.

<u>B</u> As a codified game, football is a modern phenomenon, but the fifth-century-BC Greek historian, Herodotus, noted that young Egyptian males played with a ball made from straw-filled goatskin. The 1882 occupation of Egypt by the British saw the introduction of the game prescribed by the English Football Association in 1863, and almost immediately, football became the national sport and gripped the Egyptian psyche.

<u>C</u> Psychologists propose that football appeals to fans for two main reasons: firstly, however vicariously, they participate in a triumphal world greater than their own, especially important when their lives seem mundane or troublesome; secondly, by attaching themselves to one club, they experience a powerful sense of belonging.

In the past 50 years, Egypt's population has risen exponentially while its quality of life – but for a fortunate few – has deteriorated markedly. Injustice, corruption, and tyranny have borne down upon the average Egyptian, who, for 90 minutes once or twice a week, forgets his woes in a football match. Fans also believe that on the field, there are still some rules, though that is not to say there is no corruption or lawlessness within football: referees are not always fair, and fans, themselves, behave fanatically and dangerously.

<u>D</u> In Egypt's case, a fan's loyalty to a club is interwoven with class and political allegiances. Al Ahly, for example, founded in 1907, boasted a famous anti-British revolutionary as one of its honorary presidents, and in 1956, the beloved Gamal Abdel Nasser was honorary club president as well as President of the Republic of Egypt. In some ways, Al Ahly remains the people's club, whereas Zamalek, by contrast, established in 1911, allowed foreigners to play for it, and was associated with affluent Egyptians allied to Kings Fuad and Farouk. In fact, the club was named Farouk in the 1950s.

<u>E</u> In more recent times, Hosni Mubarak, president until 2011, was accused of using football as a way to divert the masses from the parlous state of the nation, or coerce them into outbursts against teams from other African nations, like Algeria. He, himself, seldom missed a game played by the national team, and his appearance brought on a media frenzy along with patriotic songs and the chanting of slogans. Two of his sons – fabulously wealthy playboys – were frequently photographed socialising with football stars. On the financial side, club owners and managers contributed funds to Mubarak's campaigns. It is rumoured that, even in disgrace, he is supported by football stars and billionaires.

F Egypt has been in turmoil for the last decade. During the 2011 revolution, when Mubarak was deposed, a group of Ahly fans known as the Ultras took an active role in demonstrations in Cairo's Tahrir Square. In February 2012, during a football match in Port Said, the Ultras were attacked: 74 people died in the brawl. The Ultras claim they were assaulted by both fans from the opposing team and members of the security forces as punishment for their role in Tahrir Square. Other examples of apparently unprovoked violence may signal that even football no longer serves as a fantasy for the frustrated masses. In any case, it is as thorny a game off the field as it is on.

G It seems the beautiful game in Egypt may need a radical facelift. Egypt's poor showing in the 2014 World Cup – it failed to qualify whereas its rival Algeria did – meant that more Egyptians have started following European teams. Match violence and unprecedented social upheaval had already reduced support. Still, as every fan knows, when life is sweeter in Egypt again, there will be magical moments to savour at local stadiums too.

Questions 14-19

Reading Passage 2 has seven sections, **A-G**.

Which section contains the following information?

*Write the correct letter, **A-G**, in boxes 14-19 on your answer sheet.*

14   a comparison of football clubs

15   a hope for the future

16   a brief history of Egyptian football

17   a description of the manipulation of football for political ends

18   hypotheses on the allure of football for spectators

19   examples of the global reach of football

Questions 20-24

Do the following statements agree with the claims of the writer in Reading Passage 2?

In boxes 20-24 on your answer sheet, write:

> **YES**   *if the statement agrees with the claims of the writer*
>
> **NO**   *if the statement contradicts the claims of the writer*
>
> **NOT GIVEN** *if it is impossible to say what the writer thinks about this*

20   Egyptian football players are represented in South American teams.

21   FIFA estimates that Egypt's football economy is worth $2 billion a year.

22   European football stars have great importance in rural Africa.

23   While their own lives may be chaotic, some Egyptians like the rule-bound nature of a football game.

24   The Mubarak family involvement with football was largely sporting.

Questions 25-26

Choose the correct letter, A, B, C, or D.

Write the correct letter in boxes 25-26 on your answer sheet.

25   According to the writer, what has caused the violence at Egyptian football matches?

    A   Alcohol consumed by fans

    B   Police assaulting fans

    C   The very poor standard of play

    D   A number of complex issues

26   What does the writer think will happen to Egyptian football teams?

    A   They should qualify for the World Cup.

    B   They will thrill their fans again.

    C   They may continue to suffer losses.

    D   They should limit their political affiliations.

Test 6 211

LISTENING
READING
WRITING
SPEAKING

| PASSAGE 1 | PASSAGE 2 | PASSAGE 3 |

PASSAGE 3

*Spend about 20 minutes on **Questions 27-40**, based on Passage 3 below.*

• •

CARBON CAPTURE AND STORAGE

High coal dependence

Renewable energy is much discussed, but coal still plays the greatest role in the generation of electricity, with recent figures from the International Energy Agency showing that China relies on it for 79% of its power, Australia for 78%, and the US for 45%. Germany has less reliance at 41%, which is also the global average. Furthermore, many countries have large, easily accessible deposits of coal, and numerous highly skilled miners, chemists, and engineers. Meanwhile, 70% of the world's steel production requires coal, and plastic and rayon are usually coal derivatives.

Currently, coal-fired power plants feed voracious appetites, but they produce carbon dioxide (CO_2) in staggering amounts. Urbanites may grumble about an average monthly electricity bill of $113, yet they steadfastly ignore the fact that they are not billed for the 6-7 million metric tons of CO_2 their local plant belches out, which contribute to the 44% of global CO_2 levels from fossil-fuel emissions. Yet, as skies fill with smog and temperatures soar, people crave clean air *and* cheap power.

The Intergovernmental Panel on Climate Change that advises the United Nations has testified that the threshold of serious harm to the Earth's temperature is a mere 2° Celsius above current levels, so it is essential to reduce carbon emissions by 80% over the next 30 years, even as demand for energy will rise by 50%, and one proposal for this is the adoption of carbon capture and storage (CCS).

Underground carbon storage

Currently, CO_2 storage, or sequestration as it is known, is practised by the oil and gas industry, where CO_2 is pumped into oil fields to maintain pressure and ease extraction – one metric ton dissolves out about three barrels, or separated from natural gas and pumped out of exhausted coal fields or other deep seams. The CO_2 remains underground or is channelled into disused sandstone reservoirs. However, the sale of oil and natural gas is profitable, so the $17-per-ton sequestration cost is easily borne. There is also a plan for the injection of CO_2 into saline aquifers, 1,000 metres beneath the seabed, to prevent its release into the atmosphere.

Carbon capture

While CO_2 storage has been accomplished, its capture from power plants remains largely hypothetical, although CCS plants throughout Western Europe and North America are on the drawing board.

There are three main forms of CCS: pre-combustion, post-combustion, and oxy-firing. In a 2012 paper from the US Congressional Budget Office (CBO), post-combustion capture was viewed most favourably since existing power plants can be retro-fitted with it, whereas pre-combustion and oxy-firing mean the construction of entirely new plants. However, pre-combustion and oxy-firing remove more CO_2 than post-combustion, and generate more electricity.

Post-combustion capture means CO_2 is separated from gas after coal is burnt but before electricity is generated, while in oxy-firing, coal is combusted in pure oxygen. In pre-combustion, as in an Integrated Gasification Combined Cycle system (IGCC), oxygen, coal, and water are burnt together to produce a synthetic gas called Syngas – mainly hydrogen – which drives two sets of turbines, firstly gas-driven ones, then, as the cooling Syngas travels through water, steam-driven ones. Emissions from this process contain around ten percent of the CO_2 that burning coal produces.

LISTENING   PASSAGE 1   PASSAGE 2   PASSAGE 3
READING
WRITING
SPEAKING

The pros and cons of CCS

Several countries are keen to scale up CCS as it may reduce carbon emissions quickly, and powerful lobby groups for CCS exist among professionals in mining and engineering. Foundries and refineries that produce steel and emit carbon may also benefit, and the oil and gas industry is interested because power-plant equipment consumes their products. In addition, recent clean energy acts in many countries mandate that a percentage of electricity be generated by renewables or by more energy-efficient systems, like CCS.

As with desalination, where powerful lobbies wield influence, states sometimes find it easier to engage in large projects involving a few players rather than change behaviours on a more scattered household scale. Furthermore, replacing coal with zero-emission photovoltaic (PV) cells to produce solar energy would require covering an area nearly 20,720 square kilometres, roughly twice the size of Lebanon or half of Denmark.

Still, there are many reservations about CCS. Principally, it is enormously expensive: conservative estimates put the electricity it generates at more than five times the current retail price. As consumers are unlikely to want to bear this price hike, massive state subsidies would be necessary for CCS to work.

The capital outlay of purchasing equipment for retro-fitting existing power plants is high enough, but the energy needed to capture CO_2 means one third more coal must be burnt; and building new CCS plants is at least 75% more expensive than retro-fitting.

Some CCS technology is untried, for example, the Syngas-driven turbines in an IGCC system have not been used on an industrial scale. Post capture, CO_2 must be compressed into a supercritical liquid for transport and storage, which is also costly. The Qatar Carbonates and Carbon Storage Research Centre predicts 700 million barrels per day of this liquid would be produced if CCS were adopted modestly. It is worth noting that current oil production is around 85 million barrels per day, so CCS would produce *eleven times* more waste for burial than oil that was simultaneously being extracted.

Sequestration has been used successfully, but there are limited coal and oil fields where optimal conditions exist. In rock that is too brittle, earthquakes could release the CO_2. Moreover, proposals to store CO_2 in saline aquifers are just that – proposals: sequestration has never been attempted in aquifers.

Most problematic of all, CCS reduces carbon emissions but does not end them, rendering it a medium-term solution.

Alternatives

There are at least four reasonably-priced alternatives to CCS. Firstly, conventional pulverised coal power plants are undergoing redesign so more electricity can be produced from less coal. Before coal is phased out – as ultimately it will have to be – these plants could be more cost-effective. Secondly, hybrid plants using natural gas and coal could be built. Thirdly, natural gas could be used on its own. Lastly, solar power is fast gaining credibility.

In all this, an agreed measure of cost for electricity generation must be used. This is called a levelized cost of energy (LCOE) – an average cost of producing electricity over the lifetime of a power plant, including construction, financing, and operation, although pollution is not counted. In 2012, the CBO demonstrated that a new CCS plant had an LCOE of about $0.09-0.15 per kilowatt-hour (kWh), but according to the US Energy Information Administration, the LCOE from a conventional natural gas power plant without CCS is $0.0686/kWh, making it the cheapest way to produce clean energy.

Solar power costs are falling rapidly. In 2013, the Los Angeles Department of Water and Power reported that energy via a purchase agreement from a large solar plant was $0.095/kWh, and

LISTENING
READING
WRITING
SPEAKING

PASSAGE 1   PASSAGE 2   PASSAGE 3

Greentech Media, a company that reviews environmental projects, found a 2014 New Mexico solar project that generates power for \$0.0849/kWh.

Still, while so much coal and so many coal-fired plants exist, decommissioning them all may not be realistic. Whatever happens, the conundrum of cheap power *and* clean air may remain unsolved for some time.

• •

Questions 27-28

*Choose the correct letter, **A, B, C**, or **D**.*

Write the correct letter in boxes 27-28 on your answer sheet.

27   What is the global average for electricity generated from coal?

   A   41%

   B   44%

   C   49%

   D   70%

28   What does the average American pay each month for CO_2 produced by a local power plant?

   A   \$17

   B   \$80

   C   \$113

   D   Nothing

Questions 29-34

Label the diagrams on the following page.

*Write the correct letter, **A-H**, in boxes 29-34 on your answer sheet.*

A	CO_2	B	Coal	C	Natural gas	D	Oil
E	Saline aquifer	F	Steam-driven turbines	G	Syngas	H	Syngas-driven turbines

LISTENING | PASSAGE 1 | PASSAGE 2 | PASSAGE 3
READING
WRITING
SPEAKING

Carbon dioxide sequestration

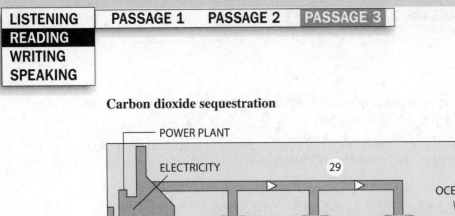

An IGCC system

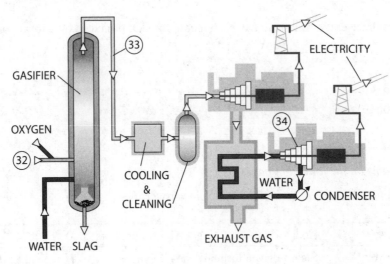

Questions 35-40

Complete the table below.

*Choose **NO MORE THAN THREE WORDS AND/OR A NUMBER** from the passage for each answer.*

Write your answers in boxes 35-40 on your answer sheet.

Advantages of CCS	Disadvantages of CCS
Sequestration is already used in the oil and gas sector. CCS may cut (**35**)……………….. in a short time. (**36**)……………….in labour, industry, and states already support CCS. Alternatives, like (**37**)……………….energy, take up vast amounts of space.	The construction of new and the conversion of existing power plants, and the liquifaction and transport of CO_2 are very costly. While sequestration is possible, the scale would be enormous. Therefore, CCS would need (**38**)……………….. . Some CCS technology is (**39**)……………….. . Gas-driven turbines for IGCC have not been used on an industrial scale. Shallow underground storage may be limited; deep ocean storage is currently impossible. Geologists fear leaks in quake-prone regions. Natural gas and solar PVs are cheaper. LCOE estimates for CCS = \$0.09-15/kWh; for natural gas = (**40**)………………..; and, for solar PV = \$0.0849/kWh.

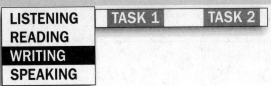

Writing

The Writing test lasts for 60 minutes.

Task 1

Spend about 20 minutes on this task.

> The drawings below show the process of desertification.
>
> Write a summary of the information. Select and report the main features, and make comparisons where necessary.

Write at least 150 words.

DESERTIFICATION

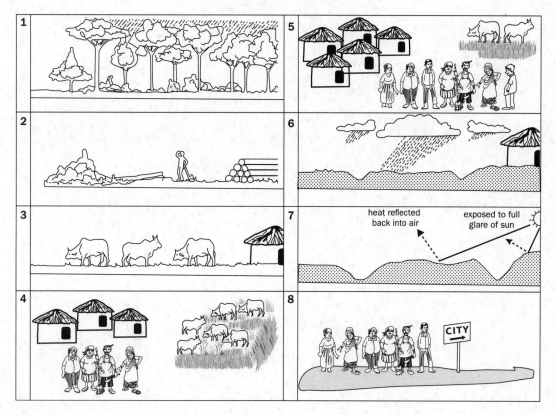

Task 2

Spend about 40 minutes on this task.
Write about the following topic:

> Historians and archaeologists now believe that, over time and around the world, the amount of violence in which people are killed has been going down.
>
> Why do you think this is the case?
>
> What can be done to make sure violence stays low?

Provide reasons for your answer, including relevant examples from your own knowledge or experience.
Write at least 250 words.

LISTENING
READING
WRITING
SPEAKING

PART 1   PART 2   PART 3

Speaking

PART 1

How might you answer the following questions?

1   Could you tell me what you're doing at the moment: are you working or studying?

2   What are you studying? Why did you choose that subject?

3   How much practical knowledge do you learn in your course, and how much theoretical?

4   Now, let's talk about sport. Have you ever played a team sport? What was it like? / Why not?

5   Do you think men or women enjoy individual sports more? Why?

6   Many people no longer watch sport because they think it has become too commercial. What do you think?

7   Let's move on to talk about animals. What animal represents your country? Do you think it is a suitable animal?

8   What might having a pet teach children?

9   In some countries, people who own dogs have to pay an annual licence fee. Do you think this should be a lot of money?

10   Many wild animals are rapidly becoming endangered or extinct. What are your views on this?

PART 2

How might you speak about the following topic for two minutes?

> **I'd like you to tell me about a law in your country that you think is very good.**
>
> * What is the law?
> * Why was it introduced?
> * What effect has it had?
>
> And, do other people also think the law is good?

PART 3

1   First of all, people who work with the law.

   Could you compare being a police officer with being a lawyer?

   Why might it be difficult these days to be a lawyer?

2   Now, let's consider international law.

   What are the benefits of international law?

   Are there any international laws or bodies, like the United Nations, that you think are not useful? Why?

   What are some future laws or conventions that might be created?

Answers

Section 1: **1.** location; **2.** travel(l)ing; **3.** surveying; **4.** Ecological Assessment; **5.** best use; **6-7.** BE (*in either order*); **8.** Future generations; **9.** 1956; **10.** Psychology. Section 2: **11.** B; **12.** C; **13.** A; **14.** A; **15.** temperature; **16.** tone; **17.** reinforcement; **18.** for several days; **19.** C; **20.** B. Section 3: **21.** Designing; **22.** large-scale / large scale; **23.** growth; **24.** tropical rainforests; **25.** watering; **26.** E; **27.** B; **28.** D; **29.** A; **30.** B. Section 4: **31.** C; **32.** C; **33.** self-sacrifice / self sacrifice; **34.** rural areas; **35.** mother; **36.** the young (*must include 'the'*); **37.** greater; **38.** justice; **39.** work; **40.** others.

The highlighted text below is evidence for the answers above.

Narrator	Recording 27. Practice Listening Test 6. Section 1. New jobs. You will hear two recent graduates talking about their jobs. Read the example.
James	Hello Annie. Haven't seen you for ages.
Annie	Hi James. You're right. I've been working really long hours.
Narrator	The answer is 'long hours'. On this occasion only, the first part of the conversation is played twice. Before you listen again, you have 30 seconds to read questions 1 to 5.
James	Hello Annie. Haven't seen you for ages.
Annie	Hi James. You're right. I've been working really long hours.
James	How's your job going?
Annie	Pretty well. And yours?
James	I'll have to admit, it's not what I expected, but at least I've got a job. Plenty of people who graduated with me are still looking.
Annie	You're working in the city archives, aren't you?
James	Yes, near Central Library. It's a terrific (1) location.
Annie	Lucky you. The one thing I don't like about my job is all the (2) travelling. I'd no idea how big the region was until I had to catch so many buses, trains, and taxis.
James	Why don't you drive?
Annie	I haven't saved up enough for a car.
James	Too bad. I'm sure you've told me before, but what exactly is your job?
Annie	I'm a biodiversity advisor for the council.
James	What does that involve?
Annie	A lot of (3) surveying. There are four divisions in our team: (4) Ecological Assessment; Native Species Management; Ecosystem Restoration; and... I've forgotten the last one. Anyway, I'm in (4) Ecological Assessment.
James	What kind of land do you survey?
Annie	All kinds.
James	And who do you advise?
Annie	Anyone who manages or owns property – public or private. When a person wants to make changes, we run through his or her legal obligations, and suggest the (5) best use of the land, while protecting or restoring ecosystems.
James	Ecology was your major at university, wasn't it?
Annie	Yes, but the real world is rather more complex than the one we described in our assignments.
Narrator	Before you listen to the rest of the conversation, you have 30 seconds to read questions 6 to 10.
James	What are you working on at the moment?
Annie	A development application. A farmer wants to reduce her reliance on sheep by planting olives. She'd also like to build some tourist accommodation, plus some walking tracks, and a road.

James	That's quite a lot of work.
Annie	It is. Moreover, there's a deep volcanic crater on her property as well as a large wetland, home to a rare bird.
James	So, what should she do?
Annie	The tourist accommodation will be relatively straightforward as long as it's on high ground. With the track into the crater, where there are unusual rock formations and steam, she'll need to consider health and safety regulations, but they shouldn't be too hard. (6 or 7) It's the wetland that presents a challenge. I doubt she'll be able to drain it. (6 or 7) At some expense, she might be able to build a road around it, but it's more likely she'll have to forgo new access to the olive grove.
James	I'd no idea development applications were so detailed.
Annie	Well, this process means a carefully controlled use of land, for which I believe future generations will be grateful.
James	(8) Future generations… Working at the archives, I'm completed immersed in the lives of *past* generations.
Annie	I bet.
James	Although the technology's up-to-date – we've got amazing scanners.
Annie	Really?
James	I spent all last week scanning tram tickets and timetables from 1902 to (9) 1956.
Annie	Why?
James	The archives keep all kinds of documents. 1902 was when the electric tram service began here, and (9) 1956 was when buses took over completely.
Annie	But didn't you major in (10) Psychology?
James	Yes, I did. The archives are about as far away from that as you could imagine. Although, working with so many different staff and the public means I do have to *apply* some (10) psychology from time to time.
Narrator	You now have 30 seconds to check your answers. That is the end of Section 1.
Narrator	Recording 28. Section 2. How to make a guitar. You will hear a man being interviewed on the radio about his work as a musician and a guitar maker. Before you listen, you have 30 seconds to read questions 11 to 14.
Juliette	Great to have you here today, Hamish. I've been a fan of yours for ages. (11) The very first rock concert I went to, when I was thirteen, your band was playing.
Hamish	Gosh! I'd like to thank this station, too, Juliette. If I remember rightly, Ray Rogers' interest in Sound Whole's second album put us on the map.
Juliette	Good old Ray. Alas, who could forget when Sound Whole broke up, and (12) Ray *wept*, live, on his show!
Hamish	But to set the record straight, Sound Whole isn't getting back together despite rumours on social networks. My performing days are over.
Juliette	Even solo?
Hamish	Especially solo. Frankly, solo gigs were a nightmare. (13) I was so anxious every time I went out onto a stage. Live audiences seriously scare me.
Juliette	Yet you've got such a rapport with them. You look so relaxed in those clips on YouTube.
Hamish	Yeah, well… One thing the social networks did get right is the reason I quit performing.
Juliette	Oh?
Hamish	I was manic when I was on the road with the band – crazy; I'd stay up days on end. Back home, I was horribly depressed; I'd sleep for a week. (14) My life was a mess. My first wife left me, and my second wife left me. I've got three children I hardly know. My son sent me a card, just before Sound Whole split up, in which he'd written he'd seen more of me on TV than in the flesh!
Narrator	Before you listen to the rest of the talk, you have 30 seconds to read questions 15 to 20.
Juliette	So, how long have you been making acoustic guitars, Hamish?

Hamish	Full time for about three years. My sister and I work together. She sources the materials, and does the books; I build the instruments.
Juliette	I checked on the Internet last night, and it's a long process to make a guitar.
Hamish	You bet. There's at least fifteen steps. I won't go into them all now, but sourcing the wood – the first step – is crucial. Cheap guitars use softer wood, which equates with poorer sound quality; but harder wood is scarce these days. For instance, the back of a great guitar, historically, was made from Brazilian rosewood, but the supply is miniscule now. I use East Indian rosewood, which'll also disappear soon. Likewise spruce was once preferred for the top of a guitar, but I use cedar, which is more plentiful.
Juliette	I thought guitars were mainly mahogany.
Hamish	Cheap guitars, yes, but only the necks of good ones. The neck must resist distortion when pulled by the strings, and it mustn't swell or contract with changes in (15) temperature and humidity. Mahogany's perfect for the neck.
Juliette	I like that wavy pattern you get on the tops and backs of guitars. How's that done?
Hamish	That pattern is called book matching. A thickish block of wood, about half the size of the body, is sliced horizontally. The two pieces are laid together, with the grain continuous, before they're glued.
Juliette	Right.
Hamish	The next two steps are to saw the top of the guitar into that sensual shape, and cut out the sound hole.
Juliette	What's inside the guitar to control its vibration and improve its (16) tone?
Hamish	Braces – narrow little bits of wood – glued in an X-pattern. The process is known as strutting. The back also has strutting to reflect sound waves.
Juliette	Interesting. How's the neck made?
Hamish	It's carved from a single piece of mahogany, and a metal rod is driven up into it for (17) reinforcement.
Juliette	How d'you get those lovely curved sides?
Hamish	Strips are cut, sanded, and soaked in water. They're moulded until they're set in that shape. When everything's been glued together – the back, the sides, the top, and the neck – the guitar is put into clamps (18) for several days. There are some other reinforcements too, like endblocks and bindings.
Juliette	I guess precision is the key to much of this work.
Hamish	Absolutely. (19) In fact, guitar-making has improved my mental health because everything's nice and slow, and precise. I'm alone in my workshop, dealing with wood. It has a calming effect.
Juliette	It seems as though you sound whole again?
Hamish	Pu-lease! No more silly puns on the name of our band. I spent 14 years explaining that (20) 'Whole' was spelt with a 'W'.
Narrator	You now have 30 seconds to check your answers. That is the end of Section 2.
Narrator	Recording 29. Section 3. Vertical gardening. You will hear two students discussing a new trend in landscape design called vertical gardening. Before you listen, you have 30 seconds to read questions 21 to 25.
David	Hi Marina, how are you?
Marina	Fine, David, but this assignment's taking longer than I'd hoped.
David	Yes, it's quite detailed.
Marina	(21) Designing two small vertical gardens doesn't seem too hard, but there's so much stuff online about (22) large-scale projects that reads like propaganda.
David	I know what you mean. Vertical gardening is flavour of the month, when all it amounts to is growing plants on surfaces not used in the past.
Marina	(29) Tricky surfaces at that.
David	Yes. Walls do present challenges.
Marina	(29) Vertical gardening is popular in warmer climates, and where there's cash to spare. I can't see people in my country adopting it, or indeed anyone who doesn't own their own home – all that construction effort, then watering your plants five times a day. How ever would you transport your wall if you moved?

David	We should certainly include your concerns at the end of our presentation when we assess whether vertical gardening will become a design fundamental or remain a passing fad.
Marina	OK. How are we going to divide up the presentation? I'm happy to do the second part.
David	Our domestic designs?
Marina	Yes. (29) I'm afraid I can't get interested in the (22) large-scale works, like the wall at the Caixa Forum Museum in Madrid – (29) they seem gratuitous to me.
David	Don't worry, I'll comment on them. However, I do think the vertical garden in the Rue d'Alsace in Paris is amazing. It's like having a vast mossy forest floor stood up on its side amidst all the concrete and tarseal.
Marina	So we just need to work on the first part together – the history of the movement and the reasons for its (23) growth. I read that a French botanist, Patrick Blanc, invented vertical gardening in 2008.
David	And I read that he got the idea from (24) tropical rainforests in Malaysia, where plants grow at any height, and their superficial root systems don't need any soil.
Marina	(29) Still, I don't understand why the movement took off, and companies from Sydney to Tokyo commission him to cover walls with plants, especially when the walls need so much watering.
David	I suppose businesses want to show how green they are.
Narrator	Before you listen to the rest of the conversation, you have 30 seconds to read questions 26 to 30.
David	So how do you build a vertical garden?
Marina	The principle's quite simple. Firstly, you need a wall, either the wall of a building or a boundary wall. This is called (26) a supporting wall. Vertical wooden battens and (27) a PVC panel are secured to it. Currently, Japan is the only country where PVC is recyclable, meaning, (29) elsewhere, vertical gardens are not environmentally friendly inside.
David	What happens after (27) the PVC panel is in place?
Marina	Irrigation piping and two layers of (28) matting are attached. The (28) matting is made from felt or woven plastic that lasts a long time outdoors, but it can't be recycled either.
David	Speaking about recycling, unless it comes off a nearby roof, the great amount of water needed to keep the wall growing seems the biggest drawback to me – especially when (25) watering five times a day, as you mentioned.
Marina	In a (21) tropical rainforest, there's plenty of water, but not so in downtown Paris. Also Parisian water has few nutrients, so (29) the amount of fertiliser for vertical gardens is high – 0.4 grams of macronutrients and 0.2 millilitres of trace elements per litre of water. If a designer can ensure the fertiliser is absorbed by the plants or drains into a fishpond, that's OK, but (29) if it goes into the main water supply – which I bet it does most of the time, it just adds to pollution.
David	Good point. How exactly do the plants grow?
Marina	They sprout from slots cut into (28) the matting.
David	What are your designs?
Marina	One is a mosquito-repellent wall, containing scented plants that drive mosquitoes away. The other is a culinary wall, with herbs, salad plants, and strawberries.
David	Sounds delicious.
Marina	(29) Personally, I'd be happier planting my veggies in pots on the balcony.
David	(30) Perhaps. But I do find the giant vertical gardens in Madrid and Paris inspiring. Once obstacles like the plastic components and frequent irrigation are overcome, vertical gardening will be an aesthetic and environmental achievement. I'm not sure the whole world will take it up, but richer countries could well do so.
Narrator	You now have 30 seconds to check your answers. That is the end of Section 3.
Narrator	Recording 30. Section 4. Self-fulfilment. You will hear a lecture on self-fulfilment. Before you listen, you have 45 seconds to read questions 31 to 40.
Lecturer	As you may know, I've been working as a psychologist since the 1990s. In the past few years, in this city, we've enjoyed unparalleled prosperity. All the same, people come to me with concerns about the future. Or should I say, *their* future. (31) One trend I've noticed is an increase in clients who – at least on paper – lead ideal lives, yet worry that they're not fulfilling themselves, however elusive that might be.

Let me give you an example. A woman in her late twenties came to me a month or so ago. She's an HR manager for a big company; she lives in a nice part of town; and, she's been engaged for nine months. Her last holiday was to Tibet, and she's just resumed sailing. In good health, she appeared not to be suffering from clinical depression. Nevertheless, she felt the world owed her more.

I questioned her about her career choice and life partner – were they really right for her? In both cases, the answer was 'yes'. I asked if she spent time with her family. Indeed – and everyone got along fine. I queried her on her friends – she had some from college and some more from work. I asked if she'd ever done any voluntary work. Again, 'yes' was her reply. After graduation, she'd spent two months at an orphanage in Nepal, before trekking in the Himalayas. In her current life, however, she felt she didn't have time to volunteer, what with work, her fiancé, sailing, and a love of travel – she hopes to go to Argentina if she can inveigle her boss into allowing her an extra week's leave. I asked my client what she thought self-fulfilment might be, but she couldn't put a finger on it. (32) I saw her three times, and suggested she read Nelson Mandela's autobiography, but she didn't keep her fourth appointment.

So, why did I suggest Mandela's book? I could equally have directed her towards the writing of Dietrich Bonhoeffer, Martin Luther King, or a philosopher, like Emmanuel Kant. None of whom seemed aggrieved about missing opportunities for self-fulfilment or trips to Tierra del Fuego; and two of whom gave meaning to their lives through decades of (33) self-sacrifice. That is: they did what they had to do.

As do people who live just a two-hour-drive from here – I mean, those in (34) rural areas or towns that are virtually ghost towns, not to mention the billions in the developing world. If they do get through school, they don't leave declaring: 'Now, I must do what I love doing. Now, I must be fulfilled.'

Even my (35) mother did what she had to do. Originally from Puerto Rico, she brought up her children on her own, while working three jobs. She considered it more important to put us through college than to go herself, even though she was clever enough. Likewise, she nursed her sister with cancer, and cooked meals for elderly neighbours. I'm not saying I was raised by a saint, but, in mature people, the notion of self-fulfilment seldom arises.

Let's return to Martin Luther King, who believed there are three dimensions to our lives: Length; Breadth; and, Height. Length refers to self-love; and Breadth, to the community and care of others. For some of us, especially (36) the young, Height may be difficult to accept or to find. For King, it was unequivocally God, although the transcendent doesn't have to be a religious experience. It could translate roughly as 'being part of something (37) greater than oneself'. It could be an ideal, like equality or (38) justice. The reason Height may be hard for the Me Generation to come to grips with is that it requires a disciplined willingness to submerge one's own desires. In a world of instant gratification, that's a big ask.

In my own work as a psychologist, I've now questioned my years of guiding clients towards the do-what-you-love principle. It may be elitist, denigrating (39) work that is done not from love, like my mother's dawn shift in a bakery, which no amount of free donuts could sweeten. I don't believe gifts come from God, so it's our duty not to squander them, but I am persuaded that focussing one's talents on things outside oneself is more important than constant self-improvement.

Of course, it's wonderful to do what we like, particularly when we're good at it, but, from time to time, we should also do what we hate for the benefit of (40) others. If this is a bitter pill to swallow, relish the bitterness. There, lies your self-fulfilment.

Narrator That is the end of the Listening test.
You now have ten minutes to transfer your answers to your answer sheet.

READING: Passage 1: **1.** in perpetuity (*must include 'in'*); **2.** loan; **3.** market price; **4.** profit; **5.** consuming; **6.** volatile; **7.** middle class; **8.** F/False; **9.** NG/Not given; **10.** F/False; **11.** T/True; **12.** T/True; **13.** C. Passage 2: **14.** D; **15.** G; **16.** B; **17.** E; **18.** C; **19.** A; **20.** NG/Not given; **21.** NG/Not given; **22.** Y/Yes; **23.** Y/Yes; **24.** N/No; **25.** D; **26.** B. Passage 3: **27.** A; **28.** D; **29.** A; **30.** C; **31.** E; **32.** B; **33.** G; **34.** F; **35.** carbon emissions // carbon dioxide/CO_2 emissions; **36.** powerful lobbies/lobby groups; **37.** solar; **38.** massive state subsidies (*must include 'massive'*); **39.** untried; **40.** $0.0686/kWh / $0.0686 per kilowatt-hour.

> *The highlighted text below is evidence for the answers above.*
>
> *If there is a question where 'Not given' is the answer, no evidence can be found, so there is no highlighted text.*

With rapid urbanisation, more people now live in cities than in the countryside, and this number is set to rise. For all the benefits cities bestow, they are expensive places. In some years, Tokyo records the highest cost of living; in others, Moscow. In 2014, for expatriates, Luanda, the capital of Angola, received the dubious accolade; and, for Angolans themselves, it had also suddenly become pricey with real estate going through the roof, so to speak, and food being prohibitive – even locally sourced mangoes were $5 a kilo.

What can urbanites do to reduce the financial burden of paying for food? Diet? Grow their own? Beg for subsidies? Some economists have proposed that they buy contracts giving rights to a food stream (1) in perpetuity, for example, a kilogram of beef would be delivered weekly from the date the contract started until the end of the owner's life. In essence, this is what house purchase is – indefinite security of a single commodity. As is the case with buying a house, a (2) loan from a financial institution might be necessary for the beef contract, even if it were merely for Australian blade steak and not Japanese Wagu. The contract could also be sold at the current (3) market price if its owner moved out of delivery range or renounced beef.

In order to maintain or increase the value of their investment, it is likely some owners would support national and international policies to limit food production – a sound idea in a world where 40% of food goes to waste.

But let's imagine, in this system, a consumer purchased a 25-year contract for beef, which, over time, doubled in value. Naturally, at sale, the owner would make a tidy (4) profit. Conversely, if mad cow disease erupted, and no one dared eat beef, then the vendor would suffer. If the owner had bought ten beef contracts, he or she might even go bankrupt in this scenario.

Let's also imagine that people bought contracts on items they had no intention of (5) consuming: that the health-conscious purchased, yet eschewed, saturated-fat meat; that shrewd amoral vegetarians speculated in beef, as they already buy share portfolios in which multinational agri-business is represented, or they deposit money into banks that do just that on their behalf.

It is quite plausible that this speculative behaviour could lead to the overheating of the food-stream market. The state may intervene, attempting to cool things down, or it may tolerate such activity. Indeed, a government that proposed a capital gains tax or high death duties on food-stream contracts may be voted out in favour of another that believed in laissez-faire.* Besides which, an investment contract may be a way to realise wealth when there are few other possibilities either because the stock market is highly (6) volatile, or much of the local economy generates little revenue, as is the case in Angola and many developing countries. Indeed, food-stream speculation could become a (7) middle class prerogative, indulged in by legislative members themselves.

I hope by now, you've realised this essay is a spoof. (8 & 13) Yet, the fantastic food-stream market is reminiscent of the global housing market, where home ownership and property speculation have become the privilege of a few at great expense to the many, who either cannot participate, or sign their lives away to banks. (10) You may also have realised that when I bring this topic up at a dinner party, for instance, I am usually shouted down, despite what I believe to be its inherent logic, because my friends consider a house as more tangible than a steak, and their identities are bound up with vague but powerful notions of property rights and independence.

(11) I do concede that home-ownership offers security (not having to move, being connected to one particular neighbourhood) and creativity (11) (being able to modify and decorate as you please), but I would prefer people rent rather than buy in an effort to lower property prices, and to encourage investment in other sectors of the economy. (12) Economists Moretti and Chang-Tai Hsieh of the University of Chicago have estimated that US output between 1999 and 2009 was 13% lower than it could have been because high housing costs forced so many people to move. Income locked up in housing could otherwise have been spent on local businesses, like restaurants or gyms, and job creation would likely have ensued.

(13) So, next time you toss a steak on the barbecue, ponder whether we should treat food in the same way we treat housing, or whether we should treat housing as we do food.

Egypt's beautiful game

A It is estimated that over a billion people watched the 2014 World Cup – the biggest TV event in human history – and that football is a trillion-dollar industry.

The fact that a handful of countries dominate the World Cup does not lessen interest in the competition or the sport by people in the remotest of regions. (22) Take the largely inaccessible Omo Valley of southern (19) Ethiopia, where shepherds with few possessions sport Arsenal or AC Milan T-shirts, and where women who may not know of the existence of the UK wear pendants with Wayne Rooney's face on them. In Qiqihar, in northern (19) China, middle-school children choose 'English' names for themselves, like David Beckham or Ronaldo, while in the (19) Sinai, where temperatures soar and there are no other signs of life outdoors; adolescent boys dribble, kick, header, and feint with homemade footballs, dreaming of lifting themselves from abject poverty by playing for a famous team.

Although football generally stimulates the economy, many places grind to a halt when a big match is on – indeed the inhabitants of Cairo quip that the best time to drive across town to shop is during a final between Al Ahly and Zamalek.

B (16) As a codified game, football is a modern phenomenon, but the fifth-century-BC Greek historian, Herodotus, noted that young Egyptian males played with a ball made from straw-filled goatskin. The 1882 occupation of Egypt by the British saw the introduction of the game prescribed by the English Football Association in 1863, and almost immediately, football became the national sport and gripped the Egyptian psyche.

C (18) Psychologists propose that football appeals to fans for two main reasons: firstly, however vicariously, they participate in a triumphal world greater than their own, especially important when their lives seem mundane or troublesome; secondly, by attaching themselves to one club, they experience a powerful sense of belonging.

In the past 50 years, (23) Egypt's population has risen exponentially while its quality of life – but for a fortunate few – has deteriorated markedly. Injustice, corruption, and tyranny have borne down upon the average Egyptian, who, for 90 minutes once or twice a week, forgets his woes in a football match. (23) Fans also believe that on the field, there are still some rules, though that is not to say there is no corruption or lawlessness within football: referees are not always fair, and fans, themselves, behave fanatically and dangerously.

D In Egypt's case, a fan's loyalty to a club is interwoven with class and political allegiances. Al Ahly, for example, founded in 1907, boasted a famous anti-British revolutionary as one of its honorary presidents, and in 1956, the beloved Gamal Abdel Nasser was honorary club president as well as President of the Republic of Egypt. (14) In some ways, Al Ahly remains the people's club, whereas Zamalek, by contrast, established in 1911, allowed foreigners to play for it, and was associated with affluent Egyptians allied to Kings Fuad and Farouk. In fact, the club was named Farouk in the 1950s.

---

*French for 'allow to do'. An economic doctrine advocating that commerce should be free of state controls of any kind.

E (17) In more recent times, Hosni Mubarak, president until 2011, was accused of using football as a way to divert the masses from the parlous state of the nation, or coerce them into outbursts against teams from other African nations, like Algeria. He, himself, seldom missed a game played by the national team, and his appearance brought on a media frenzy along with patriotic songs and the chanting of slogans. (24) Two of his sons – fabulously wealthy playboys – were frequently photographed socialising with football stars. On the financial side, club owners and managers contributed funds to Mubarak's campaigns. It is rumoured that, even in disgrace, he is supported by football stars and billionaires.

F Egypt has been in turmoil for the last decade. During the 2011 revolution, when Mubarak was deposed, a group of Ahly fans known as the Ultras took an active role in demonstrations in Cairo's Tahrir Square. In February 2012, during a football match in Port Said, the Ultras were attacked: 74 people died in the brawl. The Ultras claim they were assaulted by both fans from the opposing team and members of the security forces as punishment for their role in Tahrir Square. Other examples of apparently unprovoked violence may signal that even football no longer serves as a fantasy for the frustrated masses. (25) In any case, it is as thorny a game off the field as it is on.

G It seems the beautiful game in Egypt may need a radical facelift. Egypt's poor showing in the 2014 World Cup – it failed to qualify whereas its rival Algeria did – meant that more Egyptians have started following European teams. Match violence and unprecedented social upheaval had already reduced support. (15 & 26) Still, as every fan knows, when life is sweeter in Egypt again, there will be magical moments to savour at local stadiums too.

Carbon Capture and Storage

High coal dependence

Renewable energy is much discussed, but coal still plays the greatest role in the generation of electricity, with recent figures from the International Energy Agency showing that China relies on it for 79% of its power, Australia for 78%, and the US for 45%. Germany has less reliance at (27) 41%, which is also (27) the global average. Furthermore, many countries have large, easily accessible deposits of coal, and numerous highly skilled miners, chemists, and engineers. Meanwhile, 70% of the world's steel production requires coal, and plastic and rayon are usually coal derivatives.

Currently, coal-fired power plants feed voracious appetites, but they produce carbon dioxide (CO_2) in staggering amounts. Urbanites may grumble about an average monthly electricity bill of $113, yet they steadfastly ignore the fact that (28) they are not billed for the 6-7 million metric tons of CO_2 their local plant belches out, which contribute to the 44% of global CO_2 levels from fossil-fuel emissions. Yet, as skies fill with smog and temperatures soar, people crave clean air *and* cheap power.

The Intergovernmental Panel on Climate Change that advises the United Nations has testified that the threshold of serious harm to the Earth's temperature is a mere 2° Celsius above current levels, so it is essential to reduce carbon emissions by 80% over the next 30 years, even as demand for energy will rise by 50%, and one proposal for this is the adoption of carbon capture and storage (CCS).

Underground carbon storage

Currently, CO_2 storage, or sequestration as it is known, is practised by the oil and gas industry, where (29) CO_2 is pumped into oil fields to maintain pressure and ease extraction – one metric ton dissolves out about three barrels, or separated from (30) natural gas and pumped out of exhausted coal fields or other deep seams. The CO_2 remains underground or is channelled into disused sandstone reservoirs. However, the sale of oil and natural gas is profitable, so the $17-per-ton sequestration cost is easily borne. There is also a plan for the injection of CO_2 into (31) saline aquifers, 1,000 metres beneath the seabed, to prevent its release into the atmosphere.

Carbon capture

While CO_2 storage has been accomplished, its capture from power plants remains largely hypothetical, although CCS plants throughout Western Europe and North America are on the drawing board.

There are three main forms of CCS: pre-combustion, post-combustion, and oxy-firing. In a 2012 paper from the US Congressional Budget Office (CBO), post-combustion capture was viewed most favourably since existing power plants can be retro-fitted with it, whereas pre-combustion and oxy-firing mean the construction of entirely new plants. However, pre-combustion and oxy-firing remove more CO_2 than post-combustion, and generate more electricity.

Post-combustion capture means CO_2 is separated from gas after (32) coal is burnt but before electricity is generated, while in oxy-firing, coal is combusted in pure oxygen. In pre-combustion, as in an Integrated Gasification Combined Cycle system (IGCC), oxygen, coal, and water are burnt together to produce a synthetic gas called (33) Syngas – mainly hydrogen – which drives two sets of turbines, firstly gas-driven ones, then, as the cooling Syngas travels through water, (34) steam-driven ones. Emissions from this process contain around ten percent of the CO_2 that burning coal produces.

The pros and cons of CCS

Several countries are keen to scale up CCS as it may reduce (35) carbon emissions quickly, and (36) powerful lobby groups for CCS exist among professionals in mining and engineering. Foundries and refineries that produce steel and emit carbon may also benefit, and the oil and gas industry is interested because power-plant equipment consumes their products. In addition, recent clean energy acts in many countries mandate that a percentage of electricity be generated by renewables or by more energy-efficient systems, like CCS.

As with desalination, where (36) powerful lobbies wield influence, states sometimes find it easier to engage in large projects involving a few players rather than change behaviours on a more scattered household scale. Furthermore, replacing coal with zero-emission photovoltaic (PV) cells to produce (37) solar energy would require covering an area nearly 20,720 square kilometres, roughly twice the size of Lebanon or half of Denmark.

Still, there are many reservations about CCS. Principally, it is enormously expensive: conservative estimates put the electricity it generates at more than five times the current retail price. As consumers are unlikely to want to bear this price hike, (38) massive state subsidies would be necessary for CCS to work.

The capital outlay of purchasing equipment for retro-fitting existing power plants is high enough, but the energy needed to capture CO_2 means one third more coal must be burnt; and building new CCS plants is at least 75% more expensive than retro-fitting.

Some CCS technology is (39) untried, for example, the Syngas-driven turbines in an IGCC system have not been used on an industrial scale. Post capture, CO_2 must be compressed into a supercritical liquid for transport and storage, which is also costly. The Qatar Carbonates and Carbon Storage Research Centre predicts 700 million barrels per day of this liquid would be produced if CCS were adopted modestly. It is worth noting that current oil production is around 85 million barrels per day, so CCS would produce *eleven times* more waste for burial than oil that was simultaneously being extracted.

Sequestration has been used successfully, but there are limited coal and oil fields where optimal conditions exist. In rock that is too brittle, earthquakes could release the CO_2. Moreover, proposals to store CO_2 in saline aquifers are just that – proposals: sequestration has never been attempted in aquifers.

Most problematic of all, CCS reduces carbon emissions but does not end them, rendering it a medium-term solution.

Alternatives

There are at least four reasonably-priced alternatives to CCS. Firstly, conventional pulverised coal power plants are undergoing redesign so more electricity can be produced from less coal. Before coal is phased out – as ultimately it will have to be – these plants could be more cost-effective. Secondly, hybrid plants using natural gas and coal could be built. Thirdly, natural gas could be used on its own. Lastly, solar power is fast gaining credibility.

In all this, an agreed measure of cost for electricity generation must be used. This is called a levelized cost of energy (LCOE) – an average cost of producing electricity over the lifetime of a power plant, including construction, financing, and operation, although pollution is not counted. In 2012, the CBO demonstrated that a new CCS plant had an LCOE of about $0.09-0.15 per kilowatt-hour (kWh), but according to the US Energy Information Administration, the LCOE from a conventional natural gas power plant without CCS is (40) $0.0686/kWh, making it the cheapest way to produce clean energy.

Solar power costs are falling rapidly. In 2013, the Los Angeles Department of Water and Power reported that energy via a purchase agreement from a large solar plant was $0.095/kWh, and Greentech Media, a company that reviews environmental projects, found a 2014 New Mexico solar project that generates power for $0.0849/kWh.

Still, while so much coal and so many coal-fired plants exist, decommissioning them all may not be realistic. Whatever happens, the conundrum of cheap power *and* clean air may remain unsolved for some time.

Answer Sheets

Test 1 – Listening

1		21	
2		22	
3		23	
4		24	
5		25	
6		26	
7		27	
8		28	
9		29	
10		30	
11		31	
12		32	
13		33	
14		34	
15		35	
16		36	
17		37	
18		38	
19		39	
20		40	

Total ____ / 40

Test 1 – Reading

1		21	
2		22	
3		23	
4		24	
5		25	
6		26	
7		27	
8		28	
9		29	
10		30	
11		31	
12		32	
13		33	
14		34	
15		35	
16		36	
17		37	
18		38	
19		39	
20		40	

Total ____ / 40

Test 2 – Listening

1		21	
2		22	
3		23	
4		24	
5		25	
6		26	
7		27	
8		28	
9		29	
10		30	
11		31	
12		32	
13		33	
14		34	
15		35	
16		36	
17		37	
18		38	
19		39	
20		40	

Total ____ / 40

Test 2 – Reading

1		21	
2		22	
3		23	
4		24	
5		25	
6		26	
7		27	
8		28	
9		29	
10		30	
11		31	
12		32	
13		33	
14		34	
15		35	
16		36	
17		37	
18		38	
19		39	
20		40	

Total ____ / 40

Test 3 – Listening

1		21	
2		22	
3		23	
4		24	
5		25	
6		26	
7		27	
8		28	
9		29	
10		30	
11		31	
12		32	
13		33	
14		34	
15		35	
16		36	
17		37	
18		38	
19		39	
20		40	

Total ____ / 40

Test 3 – Reading

1		21	
2		22	
3		23	
4		24	
5		25	
6		26	
7		27	
8		28	
9		29	
10		30	
11		31	
12		32	
13		33	
14		34	
15		35	
16		36	
17		37	
18		38	
19		39	
20		40	

Total ____ / 40

Test 4 – Listening

1		21	
2		22	
3		23	
4		24	
5		25	
6		26	
7		27	
8		28	
9		29	
10		30	
11		31	
12		32	
13		33	
14		34	
15		35	
16		36	
17		37	
18		38	
19		39	
20		40	

Total ____ / 40

Test 4 – Reading

1		21	
2		22	
3		23	
4		24	
5		25	
6		26	
7		27	
8		28	
9		29	
10		30	
11		31	
12		32	
13		33	
14		34	
15		35	
16		36	
17		37	
18		38	
19		39	
20		40	

Total ____ / 40

Test 5 – Listening

1		21	
2		22	
3		23	
4		24	
5		25	
6		26	
7		27	
8		28	
9		29	
10		30	
11		31	
12		32	
13		33	
14		34	
15		35	
16		36	
17		37	
18		38	
19		39	
20		40	

Total ____ / 40

Test 5 – Reading

1		21	
2		22	
3		23	
4		24	
5		25	
6		26	
7		27	
8		28	
9		29	
10		30	
11		31	
12		32	
13		33	
14		34	
15		35	
16		36	
17		37	
18		38	
19		39	
20		40	

Total ____ / 40

Test 6 – Listening

1		21	
2		22	
3		23	
4		24	
5		25	
6		26	
7		27	
8		28	
9		29	
10		30	
11		31	
12		32	
13		33	
14		34	
15		35	
16		36	
17		37	
18		38	
19		39	
20		40	

Total ____ / 40

Test 6 – Reading

1		21	
2		22	
3		23	
4		24	
5		25	
6		26	
7		27	
8		28	
9		29	
10		30	
11		31	
12		32	
13		33	
14		34	
15		35	
16		36	
17		37	
18		38	
19		39	
20		40	

Total _____ / 40